CW00952432

DISABILITY AND COMMUNITY LIVING POLICIES

This book provides a comprehensive analysis of the roots of institutionalization, deinstitutionalization legislation and policies of the twentieth century, and twenty-first-century efforts to promote community living policies domestically and internationally, particularly through the role of the United Nations Convention on the Rights of Persons with Disabilities (UNCRPD), a landmark treaty adopted on December 13, 2006. Rimmerman shows that deinstitutionalization and community living cannot be examined only in terms of the number of institutions closed, but through substantial change in values, legislation and policies supporting personalization, and social participation of people with disabilities. The book includes a significant exploration of US legislation and important Supreme Court decisions compared with European policies toward community living. Finally, it discusses the importance of Articles 12 and 19 of the convention and demonstrates the case of Israel, which has used the convention as a road map for proposing a new policy on community living.

Arie Rimmerman is the Richard Crossman Professor of Social Welfare and Social Planning, and former Dean of Social Welfare and Health Sciences, and Head of School of Social Work at the University of Haifa, Israel. He is the author of two recent books, *Social Inclusion of People with Disabilities* (2013, Cambridge) and *Family Policy and Disability* (2015, Cambridge). He is the recipient of the Lehman Award (1987), the William Trump Award (1998), the 1999 International Award of the American Association on Mental Retardation (AAMR), and the Burton Blatt Leadership Award (2006).

CAMBRIDGE DISABILITY LAW AND POLICY SERIES

Edited by Peter Blanck and Robin Paul Malloy

The Disability Law and Policy series examines these topics in interdisciplinary and comparative terms. The books in the series reflect the diversity of definitions, causes, and consequences of discrimination against persons with disabilities while illuminating fundamental themes that unite countries in their pursuit of human rights laws and policies to improve the social and economic status of persons with disabilities. The series contains historical, contemporary, and comparative scholarship crucial to identifying individual, organizational, cultural, attitudinal, and legal themes necessary for the advancement of disability law and policy.

The book topics covered in the series also are reflective of the new moral and political commitment by countries throughout the world toward equal opportunity for persons with disabilities in such areas as employment, housing, transportation, rehabilitation, and individual human rights. The series will thus play a significant role in informing policy-makers, researchers, and citizens of issues central to disability rights and disability anti-discrimination policies. The series grounds the future of disability law and policy as a vehicle for ensuring that those living with disabilities participate as equal citizens of the world.

Books in the Series

Ruth Colker, *When Is Separate Unequal? A Disability Perspective,* 2009.

Larry M. Logue and Peter Blanck, *Race, Ethnicity, and Disability: Veterans and Benefits in Post–Civil War America,* 2010.

Lisa Vanhala, *Making Rights a Reality? Disability Rights Activists and Legal Mobilization,* 2010.

Alicia Ouellette, *Bioethics and Disability: Toward a Disability-Conscious Bioethics,* 2011

Eilionóir Flynn, *From Rhetoric to Action: Implementing the UN Convention on the Rights of Persons with Disabilities,* 2011.

Isabel Karpin and Kristin Savell, *Perfecting Pregnancy: Law, Disability, and the Future of Reproduction,* 2012.

Arie Rimmerman, *Social Inclusion of People with Disabilities: National and International Perspectives,* 2012.

Andrew Power, Janet E. Lord, and Allison S. deFranco, *Active Citizenship and Disability: Implementing the Personalisation of Support for Persons with Disabilities,* 2012.

Lisa Schur, Douglas Kruse, and Peter Blanck, *People with Disabilities: Sidelined or Mainstreamed?,* 2013.

Eliza Varney, *Disability and Information Technology: A Comparative Study in Media Regulation,* 2013.

Jerome Bickenbach, Franziska Felder, and Barbara Schmitz, *Disability and the Good Human Life,* 2013.

Robin Paul Malloy, *Land Use Law and Disability: Planning and Zoning for Accessible Communities*, 2014.

Peter Blanck, *eQuality: The Struggle for Web Accessibility by Persons with Cognitive Disabilities*, 2014.

Arie Rimmerman, *Family Policy and Disability*, 2015.

Arstein-Kerslake, *Restoring Voice to People with Cognitive Disabilities: Realizing the Right to Equal Recognition Before the Law*, 2017.

Arie Rimmerman, *Disability and Community Living Policies*, 2017.

Disability and Community Living Policies

ARIE RIMMERMAN

University of Haifa

CAMBRIDGE
UNIVERSITY PRESS

CAMBRIDGE
UNIVERSITY PRESS

University Printing House, Cambridge CB2 8BS, United Kingdom

One Liberty Plaza, 20th Floor, New York, NY 10006, USA

477 Williamstown Road, Port Melbourne, VIC 3207, Australia

4843/24, 2nd Floor, Ansari Road, Daryaganj, Delhi – 110002, India

79 Anson Road, #06–04/06, Singapore 079906

Cambridge University Press is part of the University of Cambridge.

It furthers the University's mission by disseminating knowledge in the pursuit of
education, learning, and research at the highest international levels of excellence.

www.cambridge.org
Information on this title: www.cambridge.org/9781107140714
DOI: 10.1017/9781316493045

© Arie Rimmerman 2017

First published 2017

Printed in the United Kingdom by Clays, St Ives plc.

A catalogue record for this publication is available from the British Library.

ISBN 978-1-107-14071-4 Hardback

For my grandchildren, Yarden and Barak

Contents

Contents

Preface

Institutionalization of people with intellectual and psychiatric disabilities is one of the most extreme forms of exclusion; deinstitutionalization is considered to be the first taste of emancipation that came amidst massive civil rights movements in the United States and across the Atlantic. *Disability and Community Living Policies* is based on my earlier book *Social inclusion of people with disabilities: National and international perspectives.*[1] In the book, I offered a broad conceptual analysis of social inclusion and provided a comprehensive review of social and legal strategies to promote social inclusion and participation at the national and international levels.

The new book reflects my analysis of the roots of institutionalization, the deinstitutionalization legislation and policies of the twentieth century in the United States and Europe, and the twenty-first-century efforts to promote community living policies domestically and internationally, particularly through the impact of the United Nations Convention on the Rights of Persons with Disabilities (UNCRPD), a landmark treaty adopted on December 13, 2006, at the United Nations in New York.[2] The convention establishes international standards regarding the rights and freedoms of people with disabilities and a common basis for greater civic and political participation and self-sufficiency. It reflects core values and principles, such as dignity of the individual, access to justice, the importance of family decision-making, and access to education, independent living, and employment.

One of my early impressions of life in mental institutions was from reading Erving Goffman's book *Asylums.*[3] In it, he described the asylums as "total institutions" and as creating "... [a] basic split between a large managed group, conveniently called inmates, and a small supervisory staff. Inmates typically live in the institution and have restricted contact with the world outside the walls. The staff often operates on

[1] Arie Rimmerman, *Social inclusion of people with disabilities: National and international perspectives* (New York: Cambridge University Press, 2013).
[2] The UNCRPD can be retrieved from www.un.org/disabilities/convention/conventionfull.shtml.
[3] See Erving Goffman, *Asylums: Essays on the social situation of mental patients and other inmates* (New York: Anchor Books-Doubleday, 1961), p. 18.

an eight-hour day and is socially integrated into the outside world. Each grouping tends to conceive of the other in terms of narrow hostile stereotypes."

Another powerful book, published at the same time, was *Christmas in purgatory: A photographic essay on mental retardation*, by Prof. Burton Blatt and Fred Kaplan in August 1966. I still remember the first shocking sentence that opens the introduction: "There is a hell on earth, and in America there is a special inferno," which reflects the shocking evidence of abuse and neglect in large state institution.[4]

One of the first academics to predict the closure of institutions was Wolf Wolfensberger, a world-renowned advocate and expert on the care of people with intellectual disabilities.[5] He impressed me with his prediction of five positive trends: development of nonresidential community services; new conceptualizations of and attitudes toward residential services; increased usage of individual rather than group residential placements; provision of small, specialized group residences; and a decline in the incidence and prevalence of severe and profound retardation due to reduction in the birthrate of high-risk groups, improvement of health services for the population generally and for high-risk groups specifically, increased practice of abortion, general environmental betterment, and early childhood education.

My first involvement with deinstitutionalization was through my participation in the "Brick Government Committee" of 1987, which examined the feasibility of transitioning 100 individuals with intellectual disabilities from institutions to community-based programs.[6] The committee raised concerns about the lack of infrastructure and readiness in the community and recommended gradual transition over time.

In 2007, I was asked by Bizchut, The Israel Human Rights Center for People with Disabilities, to submit my professional testimony to Israel's Supreme Court regarding the right of persons with disabilities to live in the community. The testimony provided a scientific international base for the right of all people with disabilities, regardless of their functional level, to live in the community.[7] However, the catalyst for writing the book was my recent involvement in assisting in the formation of the new Israeli community living policy. In 2011, I was asked by the former minister of

---

[4] Burton Blatt and Fred Kaplan, *Christmas in purgatory: A photographic essay on mental retardation* (Boston: Allyn and Bacon, 1966), p. v. The first part of the book depicted horribly overcrowded wards, naked and half-clothed residents, and barren rooms. The second part of the book showed the relatively positive scenes from Seaside. The book's back cover included testimonials as to its importance from Senator Edward Kennedy, Governor George Romney of Michigan, and Governor Karl Rolvaag of Minnesota.

[5] Wolf Wolfensberger, "Will there always be an institution? Part 1: The impact of epidemiological trends," *Mental Retardation* 15 (1971), 14–20.

[6] Ministry of Welfare and Labor, *Report on the feasibility of transitioning people with Intellectual Disabilities from institutions to community-based programs ("the Brick Committee")* (Jerusalem: Ministry of Welfare and Labor, 1987).

[7] Arie Rimmerman, *The right of persons with disabilities to live in the community: National and international evidence* (Testimony to Supreme Court case 3304/2007).

Labor and Social Affairs Isaac Herzog to convene an international committee of experts in order to obtain evidence-based data and various opinions concerning Israel's services as compared to other Western countries.[8] The committee's report, discussed extensively in Chapter 7, is in my opinion one of the early efforts to implement Article 19 of the UNCRPD. It recommended that Israel should ultimately and gradually close all the institutions for persons with intellectual disability and focus on creating community-based services and housing for this population. The report was adopted by the Israeli government and became the new community living policy. In fact, Israel has begun transitioning 900 people with intellectual disabilities from institutions to community-based programs over a period of three years.

A significant conceptual contribution to the book was a seminar organized by Prof. Gerard Quinn at Haifa on May 4, 2015: *Just being me: My right to be in the world (community living) and my right to make my own decisions in the world (legal capacity)* addressed the important link between Article 12 (legal capacity) and Article 19 (community living). The seminar assisted in the writing of my closing remarks and particularly in addressing the importance of person-centered planning and personal budget and core instruments in community-living policies.

The book's underlying message is that deinstitutionalization and community living cannot be examined only in terms of number of institutions or hospitals that have been closed or number of people who live in supported housing. The challenge is substantial change in values, legislation, and policies supporting personal choices and social participation. One of the most important challenges of the book is in clarifying concurrent theological, traditional, and utilitarian values, such as new eugenics ideas that raise doubts as to whether persons with severe disabilities are persons. The belief is that such values encourage the worst practices, such as infanticide, sterilization, denial of human rights, and segregation.

A significant contribution of the book is in comparing US nondiscrimination legislation with European social welfare policies toward deinstitutionalization and community living. It demonstrates that although the two have different paths to community living, both recognize the importance of personal services and budget. Finally, the book provides the reader with information regarding the importance of implementing Articles 12 and 19 of the UNCRPD in promoting community-living policies and the challenges and resistance of implementing them in the United States and Europe. It recognizes the prevailing rationale that the Americans with Disabilities Act (ADA) of 1990 and the US Supreme Court's *Olmstead* decision are sufficient in guaranteeing nondiscrimination in existing US law. It provides insight

---

[8] The panel which was held in June 2011 consisted of Prof. Arie Rimmerman, University of Haifa, Israel; Prof. Gerard Quinn, University of Ireland (Galway School of Law); Dr. Joel Levy, former CEO of YAI Network, New York; Prof. Peter Blanck, Syracuse University, New York; and Prof. Meindert Haveman, TU Dortmund University, Germany. The committee's coordinator was Dr. Michal Soffer, University of Haifa.

into the skepticism in Europe regarding the failure of the Structural Funds strategy in changing community-living policies in Central and Eastern Europe. Finally, it recognizes that real challenge is the implementation of personal assistance schemes (Article 19(b)) requiring states to ensure that people with disabilities have access to community support services.

Acknowledgments

The book was made possible by generous support from the research staff of my Richard Crossman Endowed Chair of Social Planning at the University of Haifa, and particularly Dr. Ayelet Gur who prepared a comprehensive international literature review on deinstitutionalization. Special thanks to Prof. Gerard Quinn for his significant conceptual contribution to the book, primarily linking deinstitutionalization and community living policy to the UNCRPD. He was a leading expert in the International Panel of Experts' Report on Community Living in Israel together with Prof. Meindert Haveman, Prof. Peter Blanck, and Dr. Michal Soffer who drafted the report (reviewed in Chapter 7). Prof. Quinn, who spent part of his sabbatical year at the University of Haifa, initiated and organized an international seminar on May 4, 2015, on the link between Article 12 (legal capacity) and Article 19 (living in the community). Ideas discussed in the seminar about the importance of personhood in community living are integrated in my concluding remarks (Chapter 8). Special thanks to Mr. Yossi Silman, director general of the Ministry of Welfare and Social Affairs, and Mr. Gideon Shalom, director of Division of ID/DD at MOLSA, for allowing me to take part in shaping Israeli community living policy and sharing with me their thoughts and concerns.

I would like to thank my colleagues with whom I informally discussed some of the ideas examined in the book. Finally, I am grateful to my family for facilitating this important project; they have been a tremendous support for me.

1

Introduction

The twenty-first century finds a significant decline in the number of people with disabilities living in institutional care on both sides of the Atlantic. The US Supreme Court's *Olmstead* decision of 1999 is considered a milestone in establishing non-discrimination policy on community living of people with intellectual disability/developmental disability (ID/DD).[1] European deinstitutionalization community living policies are more scattered because of core differences in the social welfare approaches of social democratic, liberal, and conservative countries, and particularly between them and the former Communist states of Central and Eastern Europe. The book provides eight chapters of updated comparative analyses of community living between the United States and Europe with respect to changes in values and ideologies, policies, and legislation, and particularly to their response to the UNCRPD.

This Introduction presents the structure and scope of the book, assuming that the nature of change toward people with disabilities is rooted in our personal and societal values. This is the assumption of Chapter 2: that it is impossible to comprehend the legal and civic rights of people with disabilities, whether they have legal capacity or are considered part of society, without studying the way that Judeo-Christian theologies treat people with physical and mental impairments.[2] Interestingly, current Judeo-Christian scholars have looked for modern interpretations to bridge the dissonance between the biblical texts and progressive ideas of equality and inclusion of people with disabilities. One of the most important milestones of ancient times was the Roman law of guardianship which has had a remarkable impact on Western civilization and Western legal thought. Although

---

[1]   Mary Beth Musumeci and Henry Claypool, *Olmstead's role in community integration for people with disabilities under Medicaid: 15 years after the Supreme Court's Olmstead decision* (The Kaiser Commission on Medicaid and the Uninsured, June 2014).

[2]   See Carmelo Masala and Donatella Rita Petretto, "From disablement to enablement: Conceptual models of disability in the twentieth century," *Disability and Rehabilitation* 30 (2008), 1233–44. The article provides a general view of the conceptual elaborations on disablement in the twentieth century and discusses the role of these different contributions in developing the current concepts of disablement.

it is paternalistic in nature, it recognizes the need of certain people who are unable to take care of themselves to be protected by the law. The principles of the guardianship law exist in current Anglo-American legislation, such as a guardian's responsibilities, a commitment to keep inventory of the property, and liability when inappropriate decisions are made.

Chapter 3 discusses and provides updated analysis of the UNCRPD, and in particular Article 12 (legal capacity) and Article 19 (living in the community). Article 12 expresses the fundamental right of persons with disabilities to exercise their legal capacity on an equal basis with others. Article 19(a) of the UNCRPD, as well as Article 3(a), addressing individual autonomy,[3] is closely linked to the right to legal capacity, primarily because the person's needs to be recognized before the law is crucial for making decisions about place of residence and where and with whom he or she will live. Each person has the right to legal capacity on an equal basis with others.[4] There is no doubt that the state has an important duty in ensuring that persons with disabilities exercise their right to legal capacity by providing support when needed.[5] It demonstrates the link between with Article 19 regarding the person's choice of where and with whom he or she prefers to live. The chapter suggests that Articles 12 and 19 of the UNCRPD go hand in hand, and progress in one area positively affects the other area. Challenging institutionalization is thus interwoven with challenging the legitimacy of guardianship and developing alternative models for supported decisions.

Chapter 4 provides a comprehensive evidence-based view of the US institutionalization era, the emergence of deinstitutionalization in the second half of the twentieth century, and discusses in depth the impact of the latter on life of people with psychiatric and intellectual disabilities. The focus of the chapter is naturally the ADA (Title II) and the Supreme Court's *Olmstead* decision, including the litigations related to this landmark determination. It presents the debate that is still ongoing in the twenty-first century, that is, whether its nondiscrimination strategy has brought about the desired outcome. Finally, the chapter introduces the distinctive difference between the *Olmstead* Supreme Court decision and the UNCRPD,[6] regarding deinstitutionalization and community living policy. The conclusion is that while the *Olmstead* nondiscrimination decision allows states the freedom to determine the pace and cost of deinstitutionalization, the UNCRPD refers to the absolute right of persons with disabilities to choose where and with whom they prefer to live in the community. In this regard, the convention's human rights champions the needs and desires of the individual over financial or political concerns.

Chapter 5 presents institutionalization in Europe until World War II. It analyzes the differences and variations among countries, including the eugenics influence

---

[3] Article 3(a) is as follows: "Respect for inherent dignity, individual autonomy including the freedom to make one's own choices, and independence of persons."

[4] Article 12(2) of the UNCRPD.   [5] Article 12(3) of the UNCRPD.

[6] In particular, Articles 12 and 19 of the UNCRPD.

that has been associated with sterilization and segregation policies to the extreme of the killing of the "unfit" in Germany. The chapter focuses in particular on thorough examination of mental health policies in Italy and the United Kingdom, demonstrating the different commitment of transitioning from segregated hospitals to community living programs. Similar analysis, but with different models of welfare states, is presented with respect to intellectual disabilities. The chapter summarizes core longitudinal studies on deinstitutionalization of people with mental illness and intellectual and developmental disabilities (IDD). Furthermore, it discusses in depth the role of the Council of Europe and the EU in promoting community living policies, with their challenge to narrow the disparities between Western and former Communist states of Central and Eastern Europe regarding institutionalization and the lack of community living programs.

There is a very comprehensive review and analysis of the use of the Structural Funds to promote change in the former Communist states of Central and Eastern Europe, including the concern that the changes may fail. In addition, the chapter examines the impact of the UNCRPD on European community living policy. The European Court of Human Rights (ECHR) was influenced in the 2010s by the UNCRPD in ruling against violations and denial of civil rights in institutions in the former Communist states of Central and Eastern Europe. There are examples demonstrating the linkage between the European Court of Human Rights (ECHR) and the UNCRPD. Similarly, the EU 2010–2020 Strategy reflects commitment to the implementation of the UNCRPD.

Chapter 6 includes a comprehensive comparison between US and European policies and discusses their challenges in promoting community living for all people with disabilities. It demonstrates the different paths to implementing the deinstitutionalization policy in mental health and intellectual disabilities on both sides of the Atlantic. The chapter explores the core differences between the two, which reflect the conceptual and political views of human rights and social policy. US nondiscrimination legislation guides deinstitutionalization and community living. Class litigations (such as *Olmstead*) are essential in interpreting the ADA and in guiding policy implementation. The European path reflects welfare policy first and anti-discrimination legislation and litigations second.[7] The chapter also clarifies the differences in their political systems and in their core policies toward disability. European disability policy is collective and based on the social model and the responsibility of the social and political systems to correct evils and problems. A regulatory policy such as the Structural Funds is dominant, as litigation in the ECHR's is secondary.

Another difference that is introduced broadly is that the fundamental difference between EU and US community living policies is related to their differing

---

7 Gerard Quinn and Eilionóir Flynn, "Transatlantic borrowings: The past and future of EU non-discrimination law and policy on the ground of disability," *The American Journal of Comparative Law* 60 (2012), 23–48.

approaches toward the UNCRPD. The EU ratified the UNCRPD in 2011,[8] and, in fact, used it as a road map for the European Disability Strategy of 2014–2020. The United States has not ratified the UNCRPD and has instead based its community living policy on the *Olmstead* anti-discrimination interpretation of ADA Title II.

Chapter 7 presents the case of Israel in transitioning from a mixed policy of institutional and community care to community living policy. The case of Israel is interesting because it provides an insightful look at the report written by the panel of International Committee of Experts on Community Living of People with Intellectual Disabilities (ID), based on Articles 12 and 19 of the UNCRPD.[9] The panel demonstrated how the convention could be used as an effective instrument at the national level, examining the current Israeli system and offering progressive changes toward future community living policy.

The book ends with final thoughts (Chapter 8) about deinstitutionalization and community living policies in the United States and Europe. One of the important conclusions is that deinstitutionalization and community living policies cannot be examined only in terms of number of institutions or hospitals that have been closed or number of people who are living in community settings. The significant change has to be in values, legislation, and policies that contribute to personal choices and social participation.

In terms of values, the chapter suggests that it is difficult to believe in substantial change without recognizing past and prevailing theological and eugenics ideas. While earlier conceptualization, such as the medical model, normalization and the social model, and the nondiscrimination approach dealt with deficits and barriers, the convention is actually the first call for a person-centered approach. The major effort of deinstitutionalization in the twentieth century was the transition of people with intellectual and psychiatric disabilities from institutions to community-based programs, current in Europe and the United States. The shift toward human rights and personhood is reflected in a growing recognition that services have to be personalized in terms of planning and budgeting.[10] This means that funding of

[8] EU ratifies UN Convention on disability rights, January 5, 2011; available at http://europa.eu/rapid/pressReleasesAction.do?reference=IP/11/4.

[9] The panel report is reviewed in a forthcoming publication by Arie Rimmerman and Michal Soffer, "The making of disability policy in Israel: Ad-hoc advisory experts panels." In *Policy analysis in Israel*. Edited by Gila Menahem and Amos Zehavi (University of Bristol: Policy Press, 2016) pp. 109–120.

[10] See, for example, Simon J. Duffy, "Person centred planning and system change," *Learning Disability Practice* 7 (2004), 15–19; Simon J. Duffy and Helen Sanderson, "Person-centred planning and care management," *Learning Disability Practice* 7 (2004), 12–16; David Felce, "Can person-centered planning fulfill a strategic planning role?" Comments on Mansell & Beadle-Brown, *Journal of Applied Research in Intellectual Disabilities* 17 (2004), 27–30; Jim Mansell and Julie Beadle-Brown, "Person-centered planning or person-centered action? Policy and practices in intellectual disability services," *Journal of Applied Research in Intellectual Disabilities* 17 (2004), 1–9; Jim Mansell and Julie Beadle-Brown, "Person-centered planning or person-centered action? A response to the commentaries," *Journal of Applied Research in Intellectual Disabilities* 17 (2004), 31–35. In the response, Mansell and Beadle-Brown argue that extending person-centered planning for all people

services follows the person and not the service provider, and that users are free to choose their preferred degree of personal control over service delivery according to their needs, capabilities, current life circumstances, preferences, and aspirations.

In conclusion, the author believes that the UNCRPD is not only the road map for creating progressive community living but a challenge for Western countries in examining their current legislations, policies, and practices. Europe has to deal with significant gaps in deinstitutionalization policies and lack of community-based services in EEL countries. The United States, which has not ratified the UNCRPD, has to examine the benefits of the UNCRPD to its domestic policy. In terms of legal capacity and people's autonomy, it is evident that the guardianship laws are uneven among states. Therefore, if the United States ratifies the UNCRPD, many states will need to amend their guardianship laws to bring them in line with Article 12.

with disabilities in the United Kingdom is too ambitious. They express concerns that the plans are not feasible and are far from being an effective way of changing the lives of people with intellectual disabilities. There are current budgetary control mechanisms that undermine the individualized, tailored nature of planning and, therefore, the introduction of a new model of planning will not in itself be likely to change the experience of service users.

2

Theology, Eugenics, and the Roots of Change

In *Social inclusion of people with disabilities*,[1] I recognized the importance of Judeo-Christian and Greco-Roman roots, particularly in the Bible (the Old Testament), the New Testament, and ancient, medieval, and modern times. I concluded that current views of disability grew from victimization and marginalization in ancient times. The past reflects the changes in societal perception of disability, and in particular the role that religion, values, culture, and the legal and economic infrastructures played in their inclusion.[2]

Religion plays an important role in the lives of millions of people worldwide and directly or indirectly influences the status of people with disabilities in their societies. The chapter introduces disability in the Bible, New Testament, and the Koran, and discusses theological interpretations of disability in Judaism, Christianity, Islam, Buddhism, and Hinduism. It discusses ancient eugenics approaches as well as their expressions in the United States and Germany and their impact on medicalization and exclusionary practices of people with disabilities, including institutionalization. Finally, the chapter introduces and discusses the shift toward disability rights and a social model of disability that may have relevance to community living and legal capacity policies and practices.[3]

[1] Rimmerman, *Social inclusion*. In Chapter 2, I express my personal belief that the clues to current policies and practices are hidden in these roots. Core obstacles expressed are ambivalent regarding paternalistic views of self-determination and the ability to make the right choices.

[2] See Darta Schumm and Michael Stoltzfus, *Disability in Judaism, Christianity and Islam: Sacred texts, historical traditions and social analysis* (London: Palgrave Macmillan, 2011). Their volume of essays covers a wide range of voices, disabilities, and historical periods, expressing their view that religious and cultural attitudes guide us in our day-to-day life.

[3] See Wolf Wolfensberger, *The origin and nature of our institutional models* (Syracuse: Human Policy Press, 1975). In his essay, Wolfensberger provides an unusual historical perspective on the way the United States viewed and cared for individuals with intellectual disabilities in the boom period of large institutions. It is not only the person's impairment or behavior that is responsible for his or her exclusion but the actual design of the institution buildings sent a message to the public and the residents. There are at least three dimensions of attitudes and philosophies that can be discerned in building design. They are: (1) the role expectancies the building design and atmosphere impose upon prospective residents; (2) the meaning embodied in or conveyed by a building; and (3) the focus of convenience designed into the building, i.e., whether the building was designed primarily with the convenience of the residents in mind.

EXPRESSIONS OF DISABILITY IN THE BIBLE
AND JEWISH THEOLOGY

"Persons with disabilities have always been *in* but not *part of* society":[4] their unclear social standing in ancient society is expressed in the Bible and New Testament. The most common diseases mentioned in the Bible (*Tanakh*) are blindness, deafness, dumbness, leprosy, and paralysis. The first disability narrative is the metaphorical blindness of Isaac, which set the stage for deception and for the struggle of two brothers (Jacob and Esau) over a birthright and a blessing. God, out of mercy, caused Isaac's eyes to grow weak to protect him from the painful situation.[5] Blindness is cited in the blessing of Jacob to his sons; Jacob told Joseph that he had not thought to see his face, and now God had let him see his children.[6] These narratives of visual impairment of old age appear also in I Samuel and I Kings.[7] In all cases, the blindness is associated with God's involvement and message. In some cases, the disability is presented as a punishment for disobedience. For example, in Lev 26:14–16: "I will bring upon you sudden terror, wasting diseases and fever that will destroy your sight and drain away your life. In the case of Samson . . . the Philistines seized him, gorged out his eyes."[8] It is imperative that the Bible views blindness as a body defect, sometimes caused by the Lord and sometimes pitied by Him.

However, the Bible is less clear about people with mental illness. For example, among the curses threatened for faithlessness to the covenant is "*so that thou shalt be mad* [Heb. *meshugga*] *for the sake of thine eyes which thou shalt see.*"[9] Other illustrations involve King Saul, who was terrified by an evil spirit (David was invited to play the harp for him so that he could find relief);[10] and David, who feigned madness when he fled to the court of Achish, the king of Gath.[11] A midrashic interpretation is that David questions why God would have created such a purposeless state as insanity. But when he saves his life by pretending to be mad, David understands that madness also has a purpose. However, the term is often used differently. Hosea, the prophet is ironically described as "mad."[12]

However, disability is not always seen as a negative response, as in the case of Moses' speech disability, which did not disqualify him from leading the Israelites out of Egypt. In the Book of Exodus, when asked to lead the Israelites, Moses initially objects that he is "heavy of mouth and heavy of tongue"[13] – a phrase that has led many rabbinic interpreters to assume that he spoke with a stutter or lisp. In response, God affirms Moses' many capabilities and notes that his brother Aaron can offer any support that Moses needs to fulfill his responsibilities.

Another anecdote that reflects the status of people with disability (physical) is David's attitudes to Mephiboshet[14] – Jonathan's son and Saul's grandchild – who became disabled at the age of five after his nurse dropped him while fleeing after

[4] Rimmerman, *Social inclusion*, p. 9.   [5] Gen 27:1.   [6] Gen 48:10.
[7] I Sam 3:2 and 4:15; I Kgs 14:4.   [8] Judg 16:21.   [9] Deut 28:34.   [10] I Sam 16:14–23.
[11] See I Sam 21:13–16; Ps 31:1.   [12] Hos 9:7.   [13] Exod 4:10–15.   [14] II Sam 9.

learning that both the father and grandfather had died at the Battle of Mount Gilboa. David was complimented for returning the lands that had belonged to Mephibosheth's grandfather. By granting him the legal capacity to determine how his household and finances were to be run, David restored Mephibosheth's dignity and assured him of equal social status with those who could work. David's insistence that Mephibosheth always eat at the king's table also reinforced Mephibosheth's social status and indicated that he valued Mephibosheth's counsel and advice.

It appears that David's attitude to Mephiboshet was the exception, as people with disabilities were excluded from communal life. Mephiboshet saw himself as a "dead dog," perceiving his life as a disabled person as a fate worse than death.[15]

The two narratives that indicate the contradictory meaning of disability are presented in Lev 19:14: "Thou shalt not curse the deaf nor put a stumbling block before the blind, nor maketh the blind to wander out of [his] path." Also,

> The Lord spoke further to Moses: Speak to Aaron and say: No man of your offspring throughout the ages who has a defect shall be qualified to offer the food of his God. No one at all who has a defect shall be qualified: no man who is blind, or lame, or has a limb too short or too long; no man who has a broken leg or a broken arm; or who is a hunchback, or a dwarf, or who has a growth in his eye, or who has a boil-scar, or scurvy, or crushed testes. No man among the offspring of Aaron the priest who has a defect shall be qualified to offer the Lord's offering by fire; having a defect, he shall not be qualified to offer the food of his God. He may eat of the food of his God, of the most holy as well as of the holy; but he shall not enter behind the curtain or come near the altar, for he has a defect. He shall not profane these places sacred to Me, for I the Lord have sanctified them. (Lev 21:16–23)

While the Bible stands strongly against the exploitation of those with disabilities, Jewish law also places religious obstacles to the full integration of people with disabilities into the Jewish community. Is it possible that the Bible presents such an ambivalent approach, recognizing the obligation to remove barriers from blind people but at the same time prevents them from serving Lord? It appears that the Bible reflects the common approach that was prevalent at that time about the code of purity and holiness, namely, that every *kohen* ("priest"; pl. *kohanim*) who suffered a physical blemish was disqualified by virtue of his disability from performing the sacrificial ritual. The barring of people with disabilities from practices has its roots in David's heroic capture of Jerusalem, confirming that it was the common approach: ". . . And David said on that day: 'Whoever smites the Jebusites and reaches the tower, and [removes] the lame and the blind, despised by the soul of David.' Therefore they say: 'The blind and the lame shall not come into the house.'"[16]

---

[15] II Sam 9:8: "What is thy servant, that thou shouldest look upon such a dead dog as I am?"
[16] II Sam 5:8.

Although the text does not explain the rationale behind this exclusion, it is clear that a blemished priest was regarded as unholy, since he was forbidden to eat from the holy food in the holy portions. This distinguished persons with disabilities from their colleagues, treating them as totally unfit or as impure to carry out the priestly tasks or share in the priestly emoluments.

After the destruction of the Second Temple, most of the people of Israel lived in exile and in congregations, and there have since been efforts to explain the exclusion of the blemished kohen. Most of these interpretations justified the disqualification but offered a new explanation, that blemished priests would be a distraction for the congregants:[17]

> A priest whose hands have blemishes may not raise his hands. Rabbi Yehuda says, "Moreover, one whose hands are stained with a woad (a blue dye) or madder (a red dye) may not lift his hands, because the people will gaze at him.[18]

Moses ben Maimon ("Maimonides"), one of the leading Jewish scholars of the eleventh century, explained that priests should not gaze at the people to ensure that they do not become distracted. A priest with superficial blemishes is likely to attract attention, and he is therefore disqualified from blessing people.[19]

These negative expressions toward disability challenged Jewish scholars of modern times to offer a different interpretation. Elliot Dorff believes that everything is relative, and there is no doubt that the Hebrew Bible is more progressive than the philosophies of Plato and Aristotle, both of whom advocated infanticide for babies born with disabilities.[20] Tzvi Marx acknowledges the dissonance in Jewish tradition between the ethical and compassionate spirit of the Bible and the status of people with disabilities.[21] This ambivalence is visible as the ". . . heroes, the patriarchs and matriarchs of Israel – Isaac, who is blind; Jacob, who limps; the initially childless matriarchs Sarah, Rebecca and Rachel, and the speech-disabled Moses – are no less esteemed because of disability."[22] On the one hand, it guides us not to place obstacles before the blind, or curse the deaf, but at the same time excludes people with disabilities from obligations and rights. Marx challenges us to explore an internal ambivalence and to consider whether and how the law can better express the tradition's ethical mandate with respect to the disabled.

[17] Mishna (also spelled mishnah; Heb.: "repeated study"; pl. *mishnayot*), the oldest authoritative post-biblical collection and codification of Jewish oral laws, systematically compiled by numerous scholars (called tanna'im) over a period of about two centuries.

[18] In *m. Meg* 4:7.

[19] Moses ben Maimon (RaMBaM; usually called Maimonides), a Talmudist, philosopher of religion, astronomer, and physician born in Cordova, March 30, 1135, wrote numerous books. The Rambam wrote his classic compilation of Jewish law (halakha) called *Mishneh Torah* or *Yad Hahazaka*. *Tef* 14:7 addresses kohanic customs.

[20] E. Dorff, "Mishaneh Ha-Briyyot: A new Jewish approach to disabilities," *The United Synagogue of Conservative Judaism* (2007).

[21] Tzvi Marx, *Disability in Jewish Law* (New York: Routledge, 2002), p. 1.   [22] Ibid., p. 2.

DISABLED PEOPLE IN THE NEW TESTAMENT CHRISTIAN THEOLOGY AND CHRISTIAN THEOLOGY

There are more than seventy passages in which Jesus cures an illness, raises a person from the dead, or removes the disability. Approximately twenty-six stories relate to paralysis, blindness, hearing impairment and deafness, or mobility disabilities. The most cited cases appear in Matthew:

> When Jesus had entered Capernaum, a centurion came to him, asking for help. "Lord," he said, "my servant lies at home paralyzed, suffering terribly." Jesus said to him, "Shall I come and heal him?" The centurion replied, "Lord, I do not deserve to have you come under my roof. But just say the word, and my servant will be healed. For I myself am a man under authority, with soldiers under me. I tell this one, 'Go,' and he goes; and that one, 'Come,' and he comes. I say to my servant, 'Do this,' and he does it."[23]
>
> And getting into a boat he crossed over and came to his own city. And behold, some people brought to him a paralytic, lying on a bed. And when Jesus saw their faith, he said to the paralytic, "Take heart, my son, your sins are forgiven."[24]

In the case of the Canaanite woman:[25]

> Leaving that place, Jesus withdrew to the region of Tyre and Sidon. A Canaanite woman from that vicinity came to him, crying out, "Lord, Son of David, have mercy on me! My daughter is demon-possessed and suffering terribly..." Then Jesus said to her, "Woman, you have great faith! Your request is granted." And her daughter was healed at that moment.

In these passages, the book introduces healing of anonymous people with paralysis and demon-possession. In the second citation (Matt 9:1–8), it is clear that the cause of the disability is a sin.

It is clear that the case of Bartimaeus is different; he has been born blind, and therefore the healing is not associated with a sin but is a positive response for having faith in God.

> ... A blind beggar by the name of Bartimaeus son of Timaeus was sitting beside the road. When he heard that it was Jesus from Nazareth, he shouted, "Jesus, Son of David, have pity on me!" Many people told the man to stop, but he shouted even louder, "Son of David, have pity on me!"... Jesus told him, "You may go. Your eyes are healed because of your faith." Right away the man could see, and he went down the road with Jesus. (Mark 10: 52)

The New Testament reflects "disabling theology" of sin, suffering, and charity. All three reflect tremendous challenges to the inclusion of people with disabilities in community living. Viewing them as sinners mean that disability is a punishment for wrongdoing and justification for denying their participation in community life as

---

[23] Matt 8:5–8.   [24] Ibid., 9:1–8.   [25] Ibid., 15:21–28.

equal members. Perceiving disability as suffering in order to purify the righteous is recognizing that they are inferior and cannot challenge their destiny. The third theme perceives persons with disabilities as cases of charity. The charitable approach means creating justice, but also denies equity and natural participation.

It appears that early Christianity was influenced by Augustine, bishop of Hippo (354–430 CE).[26] Grace is the free gift of God to man, who was hopelessly corrupted by the fall of Adam. Most Christians thought that disability or disease was neither a disgrace nor a punishment for sin but, on the contrary, a means of purification and a path to grace. Some even believed that enough prayer and ritual could eliminate the disability. Responses to disability and disabled people during the first fifteen centuries of Church history seem to have been an odd mixture of doctrinal problematics and exclusions, practical kindliness, and rather grim-faced care, the balance often being tipped heavily toward one side or another. The Middle Ages brought increased views of supernaturalism as people became fearful of the mighty power of those with disabilities. People with disabilities, such as the court jester, who was actually someone with a humped back, were ridiculed. Ridicule often turned to persecution and "impurity" turned into a vision of disability as a manifestation of evil.[27] Surprisingly, the reformism of the sixteenth and seventeenth centuries did not change the views of the people during this period, and many of the disabled became victims of the prevailing demonism.

Deborah Beth Creamer sees the roots of these views in religious communities in the United States that have been less enthusiastic about disability rights legislation and in embracing inclusive practices and accessibility.[28] Similarly, Wolfensberger

---

[26] Tim Stainton, "Reason, grace and charity: Augustine and the impact of church doctrine on the construction of intellectual disability," *Disability and Society* 23 (2008), 485–96. The article examines how early church doctrine influenced the construction of and response to intellectual disability, and in particular the views of Augustine, bishop of Hippo. Stainton thought that while church doctrine mitigated the stark association of reason and human value found in classical Greek thought, it did not engender an attitude of equality in this world. The ideas of grace and the "divine plan," while opening up a limited space for acceptance and broad equality in the eyes of God, also reinforced and legitimated an inferior position in this world, leaving those considered to have an intellectual disability on the margins of social life and subject to a charity ultimately undertaken for the salvation of the giver, rather than for the welfare of the recipient. Subsidiary themes relate to the construction of intellectual disability, such as "object lessons to the wise" or as "monsters," to be used as sources of amusement; innocence and their association with children and the charity ethic are also examined.

[27] See, for example, "Accessibility guidelines for Unitarian Universalist Congregations: Creating Welcoming Congregations for People of all Abilities." www.uua.org/sites/live-new.uua.org/files/documents/equualaccess/accessibility_guidelines.pdf.

[28] Deborah Beth Creamer, "Disability theology," *Religion Compass* 6 (2012), 342. In this important article, Creamer's disability theology explores the ways in which religious traditions have engaged (or failed to engage) notions of disability and impairment, and offers constructive possibilities for inclusive theological work in the future. She reviews four primary models of disability (moral model, medical model, social model, and limits model) and explores how these relate to religious understandings and practices. The image of *The disabled god* is highlighted, as are the ways this field has come to engage varieties of disability experience (including cognitive disabilities and autism) and diversity more broadly. Philosophical notions (such as those around normalcy or human flourishing)

believed that the seeds of neglect and exclusion of people with disability were sown in the early days of the Christian church. In this respect, the church was as vulnerable to the same human and social dynamics as other social institutions.[29]

Modern scholars of religion looked for progressive interpretation of disability in pastoral care and religious education. One of the most remarkable works, *The disabled god*, written by Nancy L Eiesland offers a different image of disability in the New Testament. She points out that the scene described in Luke 24:36–39 in which the risen Jesus invites his disciples to touch his wounds represented Jesus' impaired body to his startled friends, and, made Jesus in fact, *The disabled god*. She argued that the injury was part of him, neither a divine punishment nor an opportunity for healing.[30] According to Creamer, Eiesland's proposal for *The disabled god* is not only a change in image and tone: Jesus did not sin and yet became disabled. In fact, the invitation to touch Jesus' scars shows that the attitudes against disabled people are inappropriate.

Eiesland's innovative approach to disability has been followed by additional scholars offering further inclusive interpretations. Kathy Black proposes what she calls the "theology of interdependence – "we are all interconnected and interdependent upon one another so that what we do affects the lives of others and the earth itself" (p. 34).[31] For Black, the stories of Jesus, especially the story of the resurrection, emphasize this connection. God is present in the midst of life and in the midst of suffering, offering possibilities for transformation. She argues that "the universe is interdependent, and God is a part of this interdependence" (p. 37). Black sees the community as a place "where people can be accepted for who they are as children of God, the place where dependency is acknowledged and interdependency is valued."[32]

Finally, Jennie Weiss Block offered in her book *Copious Hosting* "a theology of access," the goal of which is to ensure "that people with disabilities take their rightful place within the Christian community."[33] This theology of access assumes that

are explored alongside advocacy and access issues (particularly with regard to religious practices such as preaching, religious education, and biblical interpretation).

[29] See Rimmerman, *Social inclusion*, p. 12.

[30] Nancy L. Eiesland, *The disabled god: Toward a liberatory theology of disability* (Nashville: Abingdon Press, 1994).

[31] Kathy Black, *A healing homiletic preaching and disability* (Abingdon, MD: Abingdon Press, 1996), p. 37. In her book, Black offers a unique and effective approach for preaching about disabilities. By going to the heart of the gospel and drawing on the healing narratives or miracle stories, Black shows how preaching affects the inclusion or exclusion of millions of persons with disabilities in the community.

[32] Ibid., pp. 41–42.

[33] Jennie Weiss Block, *Copious hosting: A theology of access for people with disabilities* (Camden: Bloomsbury Academic, 2002), p. 11. The purpose of her book is to acquaint church and synagogue leaders with the history and philosophy of the disability movement and to provide resources from scripture and theology for thinking and preaching about disability in a new way. After treating the history and philosophy of the disability movement, Block offers a critique of the Christian tradition from the perspective of the disabled, examining, for example, the images used in Christian hymns.

people with disabilities are a unique group not because they are in any way inferior to nondisabled people but rather because they are oppressed by society. For the Roman Catholic Block, while God cannot be fully known, the lens of disability highlights a God who is unfailingly committed to inclusion and access.

INTERPRETATION OF DISABILITY IN QURAN AND ISLAM THEOLOGY

In my earlier book,[34] I explored the image of disability in the Quran concluding that that there is no specific reference to specific impairment, physical, cognitive, or mental. The closest interpretation appears among descriptions of disadvantageous conditions that are created within society. Islam recognizes the fact that disability can lead to disadvantage – that society disables an individual by not creating exclusive norms and being accessible. There are several generalized adjectives to describe classes of disadvantaged individuals, including the orphan, the weak, the oppressed, the sick, or the needy.

In the Western view, Muslims are sometimes said to be fatalistic because Islam requires submission to the will of Allah. However, there is very little evidence of this approach in the Quran. The core message of the Quran is that "with every hardship there is relief,"[35] and that "no person shall have a burden laid on him greater than he can bear."[36] In Surah Yusuf, the Quran states, "truly no one despairs of Allah's soothing mercy, except those who have no faith."[37]

One of the rare places that the Quran mentions disabled people is in the context of jihad: "Not equal are those of the believers who sit (at home), except those who are disabled, and those who strive hard and fight in the Cause of Allah with their wealth and their lives."[38]

In Surah Abasa,[39] the Prophet is not being admonished for his insensitivity toward the blind Abdullah ibn Umm Maktum but rather for his negligence toward someone who came to him to learn. As far as the Prophet was concerned, Abdullah ibn Umm Maktum's blindness was not a hindrance in his ability to carry out his duties.

There are a few people with disabilities in early Islam who have been companions of the Prophet, among them "Ataa" ibn Abi Rabah, paralyzed and blind who dedicated his life to seeking knowledge from the companions of the Prophet and later became the mufti of Mecca;[40] Abu Ubaidah Ibnul Jarrah had a deformed leg,

---

[34] Rimmerman, *Social inclusion.*   [35] Quran 94:5.   [36] Ibid., 2:286.   [37] Ibid., 12:87.
[38] Ibid., 4:95.   [39] Ibid., 80:1–10.
[40] Ibid., Vol. 7, Book 70, Hadith Number 555, translated as follows: Narrated 'Ata bin Abi Rabah:
   Ibn 'Abbas said to me, "Shall I show you a woman of the people of Paradise?"
   I said, "Yes." He said, "This black lady came to the Prophet and said, 'I get attacks of epilepsy and my body becomes uncovered; please invoke Allah for me.'" The Prophet said (to her), "If you wish, be patient and you will have (enter) Paradise; and if you wish, I will invoke Allah to cure you." She said, "I will remain patient," and added, "but I become uncovered, so please invoke Allah for me that I may not become uncovered." So he invoked Allah for her.

yet insisted on joining the battles with Prophet Mohammed. Probably, the best known is Julaybib, deformed in appearance but companion to Muhammad. When Julaybib wanted to marry, the Prophet approached the resisting family and convinced the daughter to marry him.[41]

A 2008 review and analysis of theology of disability in Islam is presented by Dr. Mohammed M. I. Ghaly, a lecturer of Islamic studies at Leiden University.[42] He addressed three theological questions raised by Muslim scholars: why does disability exist if God is the most merciful; why does He allow disability to exist if He has control over everything; does having a disability automatically indicate a sign of God's wrath and punishment? In Ghaly's opinion the key theological concept is *"talil,"* literally causation, or the search for causes, which refers to the logical relationship between cause and effect.[43] Based on interpretations of talil there are three standpoints in Islam: anti-theodicy,[44] pro-theodicy, and the mainstream approach. Those in favor of the anti-theodicy approach think that God is in charge of all activities.[45] Therefore, if it is God's will, there is no need to question or justify disability. Opponents (holding pro-theodicy perspective), for whom the starting point of pro-theodicy advocates is God's justice rather than God's omnipotence, challenge this view and accuse the anti-theodicy proponents of creating a tyrant image for God.[46]

According to those believing in God's justice there are three types of disabilities: (1) self-inflicted disability; (2) disability inflicted by humans or animals; and (3) disability inflicted by God. The latter is acceptable as it is always good, because it is either deserved punishment, or involving a profit or benefit.[47]

[41] See "Disability in Islam" by EquallyAble Foundation, Chantilly, VA. Retrieved May 2, 2016 from www.isna.net/uploads/1/5/7/4/15744382/equallyable_broch_proof_6.pdf.

[42] For further reading, see Mohammad M. I. Ghaly. "Islam and disability: Perspectives in Islamic theology and jurisprudence." Doctoral dissertation, Islamic Theology, Faculty of Religious Studies, Leiden University, 2008. His dissertation focuses on the status of people with disabilities within two Islamic sciences, Islamic Theology and Islamic Jurisprudence as reflected in the early and modern writings of Muslim scholars.

[43] Mohammad Hashim Kamali, *Principles of Islamic jurisprudence* (Cambridge: The Islamic Texts Society, 2003). The book offers the first detailed presentation available in English of the theory of Muslim law (*usul al-fiqh*). Often regarded as the most sophisticated of the traditional Islamic disciplines, Islamic jurisprudence is concerned with the way in which the rituals and laws of religion are derived from the Quran and the *Sunnah* – the precedents of the Prophet.

[44] Theodicy is the branch of theology concerned with defending the attributes of God against objections resulting from physical and moral evil.

[45] Taqi ad-Din Ahmad Ibn Taymiyyah, *Majmu al-Rasail* (Cairo: Al-Maktabah As-Salafiyah, 1974), p. 125, is considered a controversial Syrian thinker and theologian advocating for the supremacy and authoritativeness of the Quran and Sunnah of Muhammad and the early Muslim community. He encouraged a literal interpretation of scripture and condemned the popular practices of saint worship and pilgrimages to saints' tombs as worship of other than God. He rejected theology, philosophy, and metaphysical Sufism, although he encouraged pietistic Sufism, and was opposed to blind obedience to tradition (*taqlid*), favoring *ijtihad* (independent reasoning).

[46] See, for example, Daniel Gimaret, *Théories de l'acte humain en théologie Musulmane* (Paris: J. Vrin, 1980), pp. 281–83.

[47] Margaretha T. Heemskerk, *Pain and compensation in Mu'tazilite doctrine: Abd al-Jabbar's teaching* (Nijmegen: University of Nijmegen, 1995), pp. 161–67.

Mainstreamers adopt the middle ground approach, rejecting anti- and pro-theodicy approaches as interpreted by Ibn Al-Qayyim:

> ... it would be possible that each thing would create for itself such states and characteristics as are the best and most beautiful, and, so, by doing this, it would be false to say that moral and physical evils exist. But the fact of their existence shows that the existence of the world came about by something other than itself ...[48]

This approach maintains that disability *can be* – but does not necessarily *have to be* – a sort of punishment, meaning that disability can be also a source of rewards and an opportunity even to reach Paradise.[49] As stated by Bujayramiyy: "Blindness does not cause any harm for one's religion. What is harmful is blindness befalling one's heart that moves the person away from God."[50] Citing Rispler-Chaim,[51] Mohammed M. I. Ghaly concluded that "Against the abusive attitudes to the disabled in the Roman and Byzantine empires as well as in the dark Middle Ages in Europe, the attitudes in Islamic law were in every way enlightened and far-seeing."

DISABILITY IN EASTERN RELIGIONS

Theology of disability reflects primarily Judeo-Christian ethics and philosophy, overlooking Islam and particularly Eastern religions. It is important to review and obtain insights into two dominant religions – Buddhism and Hinduism – relevant to large portions of the world's population.

A central concept in Buddhism and Hinduism is karma, which is particularly relevant to disability. Karma in Buddhism is the law of moral causation that may explain inequality. The latter is due not only to heredity, environment, "nature and nurture," but also to karma. In other words, it is the result of our own past and current actions. Disability is a result of bad deeds, evil, and/or immorality in a past life, and thus based on retribution.[52] However, the law of karma is complicated and it is impossible to pinpoint or trace how and why a disability resulted from a specific karmic event, the focus is on the present and future challenges or responsibilities of the person with disability.

---

[48] Muhammad ibn Abi Bakr ibn Saad Ibn al-Qayyim, *Shifa al-Alil fi Masail al-Qada wa al-Qadar wa al-Hikma wa al-Talil* (Beirut: Dar al-Fikr, 1984), Vol. 1, pp. 51–52.

[49] Zidan. Abd al-Karim, *Al-Sunan Al-Ilahiyyah fi Al-Umam wa Al-Jamat wa Al-Afrad fi Al-Shariah Al-Islamiyyah* (Beirut: Muassasat al-Risalah, 1994), p. 213.

[50] Sulayman b. Muhammad Al-Bujayramiyy, *Hashiyat al-Bijirmi ala al-Khatib* (Beirut: Dar al-Fikr, 1951), p. 427.

[51] Vardit Rispler-Chaim, *Disability in Islamic law* (New York: Springer, 2006), p. 95.

[52] See two articles by independent researcher M. Miles: "Disability in an eastern religious context: Historical perspectives," *Disability & Society* 10 (1995), 49–70; "Disability on a different model: Glimpses of an Asian heritage," *Disability & Society* 15 (2000), 603–18.

Hinduism offers a different interpretation of karma, i.e., that a person's earlier deeds bear fruit (*karmaphala*), both good and bad.[53] It is linked to the belief in reincarnation, meaning that deeds performed in previous lives stay with the soul as it transmigrates from one life to the other. In this regard, bad karma is similar to sin. However, unlike the Western way of thinking which focuses on a single deed, in Hinduism every event is immutably determined by an unbroken chain of prior events, though people can change their fate by praying and performing good deeds (*karma-phala*).[54] Those with disability can mitigate the results of previous karma and accumulate good karma by performing righteous and pious actions.

Two additional core terms in Buddhism that may be related to disability are *suffering* and *self*. *Suffering* is a core concept in Buddhism thought and a critical term in understanding existence and experience of disability.[55] There are three types of suffering: physical and mental pain, the change related to growing of dying through our life cycle, and pervasive suffering, i.e., moment-to-moment suffering. As it is clear that suffering is here to stay and cannot be avoided or reduced, the person with disability can benefit from the experience in gaining wisdom and compassion.

Self in Buddhism is reflected through our being, on relationships that we have with others. It is based on the past, on hopes, connections, reactions, perceptions, needs, dreams, and desires. It is therefore crucial that people with disabilities create their own self.

GUARDIANSHIP: FROM ROMAN TO ENGLISH LAW

While the Romans practiced social exclusion and marginalization of people with disabilities, they were the first to offer them some legal support. The Roman law, known as the "Twelve Tables," is dated 449 BC and reflects the first secular effort to

53 See Vidya Bhushan Gupta, "How Hindus cope with disability," *Journal of Religion, Disability & Health* 15 (2011), 72–78. The article reviews how the belief in the law of karma helps Hindus cope with disability. Karma is neither divine retribution nor inevitable fate. One can mitigate the results of past karma and improve present and future karma by acts of piety and good deeds. Although the law of karma sometimes causes negative coping by evoking feelings of guilt for having brought on the condition due to past misdeeds, it generally helps in accepting the condition with equanimity. Equipoise and surrender to the will of God also help Hindus in coping with disability. The coping strategy of Hindus is compared to that of other Eastern religions such as Buddhism, Jainism, and Sikhism.

54 *Karma-phala* is a just consequence of one's own actions, and loosely translates into "fruits of actions." There are three types of karma phalas – Prarabda, Sancita, and Agami. They are accumulated, present life, and accidental fruits of actions.

55 Thomas G. Couser, *Recovering bodies: Illness, disability, and life writing* (Madison: University of Wisconsin Press, 1997). In *Recovering Bodies*, Couser coined the term *autopathography* to categorize autobiographical narratives of illness or disability. The book explores illness narrative as life writing and its potential to engage contemporary politics of the body (pp. 14–15) and to represent an entire life "to the degree that the writer identifies the self with the body" (p. 14). *Recovering Bodies* devoted considerable attention to subjectivity on conditions that "have been ... particularly stigmatizing or marginalizing" (p. 15), although mental illness narratives were omitted, partly because "dysfunctions like schizophrenia and depression raise complex and largely independent issues – such as the representations of altered consciousness – that [Couser] was ill-equipped to address" (p. 17).

define private law.[56] The Roman law of guardianship grew out of the family organization and is also quite closely connected with the law of inheritance. The power of a guardian is that form of family power which ordinarily takes the place of paternal power when there is no one to exercise the latter.

Although the legislation is still paternalistic, it was considered revolutionary at the time, because it recognized the needs of certain people who were unable to take care of themselves to be protected by the law.[57] It safeguarded the property rights of people with intellectual disabilities, offering them guardians to assist and manage their affairs.[58] This important law authorized deaf people capable of speech to integrate into civic and social society. They could marry, own property, and make decisions about their personal and economic life. Later Roman law was even more progressive as the Justinian code classified persons with disabilities according to the severity of their disability.

Anglo-American laws of guardianship took a number of principles from Roman legislation: guardian's duties, registering inventory of the property, and liability in wrong doing. However, the core difference between them is that the power of the guardian in Rome was derived from paternalistic power, whereas English law addressed the protection of body and property.

EUGENICS AND DISABILITY

The rise of eugenics restrictions in the early twentieth century had a tremendous impact on the personal and civic rights of people with disabilities. Eugenics rights restrictions emerged intertwined with the medicalization of people with mental and

---

[56] William Warwick Buckland, *A textbook of Roman law from Augustus to Justinian* (Cambridge: Cambridge University Press, 1933), pp. 1–2. Roman Law, since the earliest days of the Twelve Tables, to the Justinian code more than 1,000 years later, is arguably the most influential body of law ever developed, remaining at the core of European legal systems until the end of the eighteenth century and informing civil law and (to a lesser extent) common law to this day.

[57] The history of guardianship reform is lengthy and complex. For in-depth review, see Frank A. Johns and Vicki Joiner Bowers, "Guardianship folly: The misgovernment of *parens patriae* and the forecast of its crumbling linkage to unprotected older Americans in the twenty-first century–a march of folly? Or just a mask of virtual reality?" *Stetson Law Review* 27 (1997), 1–90. In their article, Johns and Bowers state that adult guardianship is a coercive exercise of the state's power over an innocent individual. It is justified only by the ward's incapacity and the need to protect the ward's well-being. However, studies of actual guardianship proceedings have long indicated serious ongoing concerns with the process. They challenge the presumption that guardianship, when not abused, is in the best interests of an incapacitated adult, presenting data indicating that guardianship itself can have significant negative effects on the physical and mental well-being of respondents and wards. They conclude that the guardianship system must be reformed to maximize the therapeutic effects of guardianship and to minimize the unnecessarily anti-therapeutic effects.

[58] See Margret A. Winzer, *The history of special education: From isolation to integration* (Washington, DC: Gallaudet University Press, 1993). In Chapter 1 (pp. 6–37), Winzer reviews disability and society before the eighteenth century, demonstrating the lessons of a dark past when people with disabilities were exposed to abuse, condemnation, or destruction, including rare practices of remedial learning and guardianship.

intellectual disability and the tendency to define them as genetically unfit and
deviant; they were therefore committed to institutions.[59] However, the roots of
eugenics ideology and exclusion practices can be found in ancient Greece
(368 BC), in Plato's work in particular, in order to create an ideal society free of
inferior classes.[60]

ANCIENT EUGENICS

Plato proposed that marriage for the guardian classes be abolished and that provision
be made for men and women of the same natural capacities to mate. Inferior
members of the guardian classes should be discouraged from reproducing.
Although Plato did not recommend infanticide of children with disabilities, he
thought that they should be excluded from community living. A similar approach
was advocated by Aristotle in his book *Politics*; however, unlike Plato he went further
by supporting their infanticide.[61]

AMERICAN EUGENICS

The first to use of the term "eugenics" was Sir Francis Galton in 1883.[62] The motive
was a positive one: to encourage the building of a healthy human race by encouraging capable people of above-average intelligence to bear more children. It is
noteworthy that Galton's proposal[63] avoided mentioning Plato's or Aristotle's early
writings, although their purpose was been similar, to encourage a superior society,
free of disabled people. Galtonian eugenics was popular in England and focused on
using statistical tools to quantify biological insights.[64] The eugenicists of the 1930s
included socialists, communists, and progressives who saw sterilization as a humane
way to prevent "crippling disabilities" believed to be genetic.

---

[59] James W. Trent, *Inventing the* feebleminded: *A history of mental retardation in the United States*
      (Berkeley: University of California Press, 1994). In his book, Trent explores the changing perceptions
      of intellectual disabilities in the nineteenth and twentieth centuries, claiming that economic vulner-
      ability was responsible for their institutionalization rather than their intellectual or social limitations.

[60] Plato, *The republic* (Oxford: Oxford University Press, 1955).

[61] Aristotle, *Politics* (London: J. M. Dent and Sons, 1964).

[62] Galton was Charles Darwin's cousin and was very familiar with the theory of evolution by natural
      selection. Galton argued that early marriage between healthy, mentally strong families should be
      encouraged by financial incentives, and reproduction by the "feeble-minded" should be curtailed. In
      his mind, superior mental and physical capabilities were advantageous not only to an individual but
      essential for the well-being of society as a whole.

[63] Francis Galton, *Inquiries into human faculty and its development* (London: J. M. Dent and Sons,
      1943), p. 17.

[64] See, for example, Daniel J. Kevles, *In the name of eugenics: Genetics and the uses of human* (New
      York: Alfred A. Knopf, 1985), pp. 37–40. Daniel Kevles traces the study and practice of eugenics in
      England and the efforts to "improve" the human species by exploiting theories of heredity, from its
      inception in the late nineteenth century to its twenty-first-century manifestation within the field of
      genetic engineering.

Attitudes toward Nazi totalitarianism varied widely between 1933 and 1939. Many American eugenicists were emphatically opposed to Nazi totalitarianism, while others were quite supportive of the Hitler government.[65] Charles R. Stockard, president of the board of the Rockefeller Institute for Medical Research between 1935 and 1939, thought that forced sterilization practice was a matter of urgency. At a roundtable discussion at the New York Academy of Medicine in 1937, he said that the human race faced "ultimate extermination" unless propagation of "low grade and defective stocks" could be "absolutely prevented."[66]

The scientific assumption was that all disabilities had a defective genetic origin. The most scientific-based theory of the time was the genetics law of heredity by George Mendel,[67] whose ideas led to a national movement encouraging American to bear healthier babies through "Better Baby Contests," or sought "Fitter Families for Future Firesides."[68] Eugenics ideology turned to portraying fictitious inferior families such as the Jukes and Kallikaks, the Zeros, the Nams, the Happy Hickories, and the Doolittles in their books and reports to illustrate that these people were degenerate, shiftless, and useless to society.[69]

[65] See Barry Mehler, "Sources in the study of eugenics, I: Inventory of the American Eugenics Society papers," *Mendel Newsletter* 14 (1977), 9–14; Mark H. Haller, *Eugenics: Hereditarian attitudes in American thought* (Brunswick, NJ: Rutgers, 1963), pp. 117, 174. Kenneth Ludmerer, *Genetics and American society: A historical appraisal* (Baltimore: The Johns Hopkins University Press, 1972), p. 174.

[66] The remarks were made in April 21, 1937. See American Eugenics Society Papers, BK 6. Can be retrieved on special request from American Eugenics Society Records (1916–1973) from http://amphilsoc.org/collections/view?docId=ead/Mss.575.06.Am3-ead.xml.

[67] Paul A. Lombardo, "Disability, eugenics, and the culture wars," *Saint Louis University Journal of Health Law & Policy* 2 (2009), 57–80. Lombardo encourages the reading of the history of eugenics and reminds modern society how fear, greed, and hate can be exploited to enable bigotry to flourish against the poor, the disabled, and the merely different.

[68] Steven Selden, *Inheriting shame: The story of eugenics and racism in America* (New York: Columbia University Teachers College Press, 1999). Selden relates the story of the eugenics movement in America during the early decades of the twentieth century. Complete with archival photographs, *Inheriting shame* provides a powerful historical account and refutation of biological determinist ideas. Selden discusses the role played by America's foremost socialists and scientists, popular media, and most importantly, the school textbook, in shaping public consciousness regarding the "truth" of biological determinism. Much more than simply an historical overview, *Inheriting shame* concludes with a trenchant analysis of contemporary research evidence of the role that inheritance plays in complex human behavior – including traits ranging from Down's syndrome to violent behavior and homosexuality.

[69] See, for example, Henry Herbert Goddard, *The Kallikak family: A study of the heredity of feeble-mindedness* (New York: Macmillan, 1913). Goddard, a pioneering psychologist and educator in the early twentieth century, published his most important book of "family" in upstate New York – actually a grouping of people possibly but not definitely related – and concluded that they were all descended from a single Continental Army soldier. Martin Kallikak first married a Quaker woman and all of the offspring that came from the marriage were intelligent and resourceful and demonstrated no indications of mental defectiveness. Goddard discovered that Kallikak's liaison with a feebleminded girl, however, resulted in "a race of defective degenerates." *The Kallikak family* attracted widespread criticism for its careless and imprecise research methodology and conclusions. Within a decade, Goddard himself considered the book unsound and its conclusions to be neither accurate nor defensible; Nicole Hahn Rafter, *White trash: The eugenic family studies, 1877–1919* (Boston: Northeastern University Press, 1988). Rafter reviews and analyzes family studies that have been

STERILIZATION LAWS

The eugenics sentiment developed into the first eugenical sterilization law in America.[70] Laws requiring sterilization of citizens deemed "unfit" were passed throughout the twentieth century. The first state sterilization law was passed in Indiana in 1907 to prevent "... the procreation of confirmed criminals, idiots, imbeciles, and rapists."[71]

By 1911, Washington, California, Connecticut, and New Jersey enacted involuntary sterilization laws. By 1930, a total of thirty-three states had enacted such laws, although in three states – New Jersey in 1913, New York in 1918, and Indiana in 1921 – the laws were struck down as unconstitutional. In 1914, the Eugenics Record Office (ERO) in Cold Spring Harbor, New York attempted to put an end to ongoing court challenges by designing a model eugenics law.

Unfortunately, between 1907 and 1939, more than 30,000 people in twenty-nine states were sterilized, most of them poor or residents of government institutions, proving that there was an economic reason for the mass sterilizations. It took years to reverse the sterilization laws. And, in the early years of the twenty-first century Virginia, Oregon, North Carolina, South Carolina, California, Georgia, and Minnesota apologized for passing these laws in the first place.

GERMAN EUGENICS

The earliest interest in eugenics can be traced to Dr. Alfred Ploetz's work, who founded the Archives of Race-Theory and Social Biology in 1904 and the German Society of Racial Hygiene in 1905.[72] The German term *Rassenhygiene* or race

central to the eugenics movement that so powerfully shaped the intellectual and social landscape of the late nineteenth and early twentieth centuries. These studies of the Jukes, Nams, Kallikaks, and Zeros present families with inferior genes. The stories tell the history of degenerate clans which transmitted through the generations a host of socially undesirable traits including alcoholism, crime, feeblemindedness, "pauperism," sexual promiscuity, and even loquacity. In her extensive introduction, Rafter analyzes what the family studies reveal about social construction knowledge, using them to examine ways in which information is created, received, and used, and discusses the contribution of the family studies to the ideology of eugenics and to social policy. She also explores the reasons why the studies, produced over five decades by authors from background as diverse as biology and the ministry, consistently singled out as the rural poor – the "white trash" of the book's title – as threats to the American gene pool.

70 Indiana 1907 Penal Institutions – Surgical Operation. Retrieved April 1, 2016 from www.iupui.edu/~eugenics/1907%20Sterilization%20Law.pdf; see also Richard Feldman and Jeff Bennett, "The most useful citizen of Indiana: John Hurtly and the public health movement," *Traces of Indiana and Midwestern History* 12 (2000), 34–41.

71 The Indiana University – Purdue University, Indianapolis (IUPUI) Center for Bioethics and Program in Medical Humanities & Health Studies, Indiana Eugenics: History and Legacy, 1907–2007, Indiana University – Purdue University, 2007. Retrieved April 19, 2016 from www.iupui.edu/~eugenics/.

72 Paul Weindling, *Health, race, and German politics between national unification and Nazism, 1870–1945* (Cambridge: Cambridge University Press, 1993), p. 74. Weindling studied in depth the origins, social composition, and impact of eugenics in the context of the social and political tension of the rapidly industrializing Nazi empire. It provides broader analysis of eugenics beyond the Holocaust

hygiene encompassed more than the word "eugenics"; it included all attempts to improve hereditary qualities as well as measures directed at population increase. German scientists and politicians were inspired by the American eugenics movement and legislation.[73] Between 1928 and 1936, a number of European nations also passed sterilization laws, including Denmark (1929), Germany (1933), Sweden and Norway (1934), Finland and Danzig (1935), and Estonia (1936).

In Germany, the National Socialists introduced the Law for the Prevention of Hereditarily Diseased Offspring on July 14, 1933.[74] The law stated that people suffering from particular illnesses could be forcibly sterilized in order to prevent the spread of hereditary diseases. The new law listed the types of "illness" that warranted the sterilization of carriers, including congenital mental deficiency, schizophrenia, epilepsy, hereditary deafness and blindness, as well as people with "any severe hereditary deformity" and alcoholics. As a result, hundreds of thousands of people were forcibly sterilized. Others were murdered. Followers of the eugenics movement believed that the German population could be genetically "improved" and welcomed the law. For the victims of forced sterilization, this violent physical intrusion meant a life without the possibility of having children. Many were heavily traumatized and suffered their entire lives.

The transition from sterilization to euthanasia and killing of children and adults born with physical deformities, intellectual disabilities, or suffering from mental illness was a natural one for Adolf Hitler in order to maintain his eugenics ideology. He initiated the T4 program that emanated from the office located in Tiergartenstrasse 4 in Berlin. Hitler placed the operation under the control of the chief of the State Chancellery, Philipp Bouhler and D. M. Karl Brandt. "Defective" children were removed from their families and taken to "hospitals," where the exterminations were carried out at the Hartheim and Hadamar killing centers.

One of the most important and well-known books about the Nazi euthanasia "aktion" was written by Ernst Klee,[75] in which he describes the extermination "hospitals" such as Grafeneck or Hartheim, where the first gas chambers were

claiming that German racism had an effect on biology, the medical profession and on public health services.

[73] See Marie E. Kopp, "Eugenic sterilization laws in Europe," *American Journal of Obstetrics and Gynecology* 34 (1937), p. 499. She notes that German law was much more comprehensive than all other similar laws and bills.

[74] Law for the Prevention of Genetically Diseased Offspring (Ger. *Gesetz zur Verhütung erbkranken Nachwuchses*) or "Sterilisation Law" was a statute in Nazi Germany enacted on July 14, 1933 (and activated in January 1934).

[75] Ernst Klee, *Euthanasie im NS-Staat: Die Vernichtung lebensunwerten Lebens* (Frankfurt am Main: Fischer Taschenbuch, 2009); see also Ernst Klee, *Dokumente zur Euthanasie* (Frankfurt am Main: Fischer Taschenbuch Verlag, 1985). Klee became well known in the 1980s by virtue of his numerous books and newspaper articles about the scandals of the Nazi doctors, especially those involved with the so-called euthanasia programs, as well as about the Nazi lawyers and what became of them later. Euthanasia exposed the willing participation of German medics in identifying and rounding up the men, women, and children who fell victim to the extermination program carried out in specially created gas chambers in isolated mental hospitals in many parts of Germany.

built, before the Holocaust, and where mostly adult victims were suffocated with carbon monoxide. Klee describes further the killing by doctors of crippled children with lethal injections and the starvation of patients marked for extermination.

Klee also describes the resistance from the churches and the relatives of the victims, which led to a slowdown and greater secrecy surrounding the operation, but did not stop it.

The operation was conducted still more covertly after August 1941, when 70,000 people had already died in the gas chambers of Grafeneck, Hartheim, Hadamar, Bernburg, Brandenburg, and Sonnenstein. By that time, every third inmate of a psychiatric institution in Germany had already died, either by being actively killed or by starvation, leading to about 93,000 "free beds" – to use the Nazi terminology – by the end of 1941.

EUGENICS AND GUARDIANSHIP

The test case for Virginia's Eugenical Sterilization Act of 1924 was introduced in *Buck v. Bell* in Virginia in 1927,[76] in which the court addressed the case of Carrie Buck, a resident of the State of Virginia, a "feeble-minded" eighteen-year-old woman, whose mother was similarly feebleminded. Buck was sent to the Virginia State Colony for Epileptics and Feebleminded, where she took an IQ test that showed she had a mental age of a nine-year-old, which classified her as a "moron." Ms. Buck, who was not married, was also the mother of a daughter, Mary, likewise described by the State of Virginia as feebleminded and therefore "unfit."

In 1924, Virginia passed a statute authorizing the superintendents of institutions for certain classes of persons afflicted with hereditary conditions causing insanity or imbecility to order the sterilization of such persons. In order for the sterilization procedure to proceed, superintendents were required to present a petition to the board of directors for their institutions, notify the inmate and their guardian, and convene a hearing to present evidence for and against conducting the procedure. In this case, Dr. John Hendren Bell conducted the proceedings against Buck after her first physician passed away during the progress of her case. Bell similarly pushed for sterilization under the statute, based on the same justification.[77]

The Supreme Court had to decide whether the state could order the sterilization of a feebleminded woman. Justice Oliver Wendell Holmes for the Court infamously justified its decision as follows:

[76] *Buck v. Bell*, 47 S.Ct. 584, 584 (1927). Retrieved July 2, 2015 from http://faculty.law.miami.edu/zfenton/documents/Buckv.Bell.pdf.

[77] See Julius Paul, *"Three generations of imbeciles are enough: State eugenic sterilization in American thought and practice"* (1965). *Buck v. Bell Documents*, Paper 95. Retrieved November 9, 2015 from http://readingroom.law.gsu.edu/buckvbell/95.

We have seen more than once that the public welfare may call upon the best citizens for their lives. It would be strange if it could not call upon those who already sap the strength of the State for these lesser sacrifices, often not felt to be such by those concerned, in order to prevent our being swamped with incompetence. It is better for all the world if, instead of waiting to execute degenerate offspring for crime or to let them starve for their imbecility, society can prevent those who are manifestly unfit from continuing their kind ... *Three generations of imbeciles are enough.*[78]

Both Carrie and Mary were subsequently sterilized.

Early cases tended to support the rights of parents and other guardians to approve the sterilizations of people who were considered incapable of making their own decisions, sometimes using the Fourteenth Amendment to justify its ruling, arguing that since institutionalized adults were being sterilized with the approval of substitute decision makers, denying the same "right" to people living in the community violated the right to equal protection.[79]

EUGENICS, MEDICALIZATION, AND INSTITUTIONALIZATION

The eugenics movement endorsed the notion that human beings can be profiled as products of heredity, like stock. Therefore, the medicalized approach tended to classify people as socially unfit or in need of institutionalization care and medical treatment.[80] This attitude built up negative sentiments toward people with disabilities, and particularly those with mental illness and intellectual disabilities. Eugenics tried to control groups of people who were considered to be inferior and the cause of many social problems, and therefore needed to be removed from society. The expansion of institutional care is attributed not only to eugenics and prevailing medicalization approaches but also to urbanization, manufacturing, and changing demographics, including massive immigration. However, a different explanation is that institutionalization reflects the need to control deviant members of a growing society or, in the case of people with intellectual disability, the segregation into institutional setting was to control their productive lives.[81]

---

[78] *Buck v. Bell*, 274 U.S. 200 (1927), 208. Retrieved July 13, 2015 from https://supreme.justia.com/cases/federal/us/274/200/case.html.

[79] See The Right to Self-Determination: Freedom from Involuntary Sterilization, *Disability justice*, http://disabilityjustice.org/right-to-self-determination-freedom-from-involuntary-sterilization/.

[80] Lori B. Andrews, "Past as prologue: Sobering thoughts on genetic enthusiasm," *Seton Hall Law Review* 27 (1997), 893, 904 (describing practice of clinical genetic testing without disclosure to patients).

[81] David J. Rothman, *The discovery of the asylum: Social order and disorder in the new republic* (Hawthorne, NY: Aldine De Gruyter, 2002). Rothman presents the historical social contexts of the prison and asylum in the United States, identifying the salient influences that converged in the tumultuous 1820s and 1830s that led to a particular ideology in the development of prisons and asylums. He demonstrates that meaningful historical interpretation must be based upon not one but a series of historical events and circumstances, their connections and ultimate consequences.

There is no doubt that these custodial institutions were essentially manifestations of eugenically driven social policy.

SOCIAL EXCLUSION

The eugenics movement in the United States and Europe was associated with exclusion practice and stigmatization toward people with disabilities who are perceived as "genetically inferior." The experience of being marginalized and excluded is often associated with negative emotions and feelings and a sense of sadness, loneliness, anger, shame, and anxiety.[82] Rejection of an entire group of people, such as people with disabilities, can have negative effects, particularly when it results in social avoidance or isolation.

The media has an extremely important role in integrating or excluding people with disabilities. These negative attitudes are reflected by depicted images of disability (pitiable, sinister or evil, super cripple, a burden) and how media culture constructs the current portrayals of disability.[83] Printed and, primarily, digital media such as movies and TV shows play important roles in shaping public attitudes toward people with disabilities, viewing them as capable (or incapable) of making decisions about themselves or as equal participants in society. The path to change is in recognizing the sensitive role of the media in society and in creating a progressive image of people with disabilities.

THE ROOTS OF CHANGE

The roots of change grew from victimization and marginalization in ancient times to inclusion and recognition of rights in our times. The past reflects the changes in societal perception of disability, and, in particular the role that religion, values, culture, and the legal and economic infrastructures played in defining disability.

The second half of the twentieth century in the United States witnessed significant changes in values and attitudes toward persons with disabilities.[84] The civil rights movement of the Sixties in the United States encouraged people with disabilities to become organized. In the early 1970s, they lobbied Congress to include civil rights language for people with disabilities in the 1972 Rehabilitation Act, an act which was vetoed by President Richard Nixon. After a group of people with disabilities marched on Washington, a revised 1973 Rehabilitation Act was passed. Parallel to the disability rights movement, parents and advocates of children with

---

[82] See Marc. R. Leary, *Interpersonal rejection* (New York: Oxford University Press, 2001), an overview of the cutting edge work of leading scholars on rejection research.

[83] Rimmerman, *Social inclusion*, pp. 55–56.

[84] For a complete review, see Richard K. Scotch, "American disability policy in the twentieth century." In *The new disability history: American perspectives (History of disability)*. Edited by Paul K. Longmore and Lauri Umansky (New York: New York University Press, 2001), pp. 375–392.

disabilities struggled for access to educational services. The Individuals with Disabilities Education Act (IDEA) of 1990 called for a free and appropriate public education for every child with a disability, to be delivered in the least restrictive and most integrated environment appropriate.[85]

Despite changes in rehabilitation and education law, people with disabilities did not achieve broad civil rights until the enactment of the ADA in 1990.[86] This landmark federal anti-discrimination law ensured equal access to employment opportunities and public accommodations for people with disabilities. With this act, Congress identified as a national goal the full participation, inclusion, and integration of people with disabilities into society.

Similar developments were recorded in the late twentieth and early twenty-first centuries. Countries such as the United Kingdom, Australia, Canada, and Israel passed laws aimed at reducing discrimination against people with disabilities. These civil rights became the milestones for global anti-discrimination and equal opportunity legislation.

There is no doubt that the most remarkable international development was the UNCRPD[87] which acknowledges equality, dignity, autonomy, independence, accessibility, and inclusion as the keys to ensuring that people with disabilities are able to fully realize equal citizenship in the world. The convention came into force on May 3, 2008 and articulates a bold human rights framework for removing the barriers facing people with disabilities in Canada and around the world. As the first convention of the twenty-first century, it is quickly becoming one of the most ratified treaties in the human rights system.

THE CONCEPTUAL SHIFT: FROM DISABLEMENT TO ENABLEMENT[88]

Although the twentieth century departed from traditional approaches, it traced concepts of pathology and mercy. Toward the end of the second half of the twentieth century, there was a significant shift toward a socio-functional approach, emphasizing the role of the physical and social environment in conceptualizing disability.

The moral or religious model was influenced by the Judeo-Christians theology of disability.[89] It perceived disability as an act of God and a sin or punishment inflicted upon an individual or family by an external, usually supernatural force. Birth conditions were associated with actions committed in a previous reincarnation. There was a link between a sin or immoral behavior and the cause of psychosis or

---

[85] Rimmerman, *Social inclusion*, p. 26.   [86] ADA 42 USC §§ 12101 et seq.

[87] See the official website of the UNCRPD, www.un.org/disabilities/convention.

[88] Rimmerman, *Social inclusion*, pp. 23–31.

[89] See Jayne Clapton and Jennifer Fitzgerald, "The history of disability: A history of otherness," *New Renaissance Magazine* 7 (1997). Retrieved November 15, 2011 from www.ru.org/human-rights/the-history-of-disability-a-history-of-otherness.html.

another mental illness. Therefore, the latter could be cured by acts of exorcism or sacrifice, or by justifying the persecution or even the death of the sinner. The moral/religious model viewed disability as a personal tragedy.[90] Human beings could not fully understand the reason for suffering or choosing certain persons, but took comfort in recognizing that it was God's will.

The medical model of disability emerged toward the middle of the eighteenth century, and it has been associated partially with the eugenics approach. The first disability model was offered by Nagi disagreeing with the assumption that the presence of impairment was enough to determine disability.[91] He renamed the process whereby the person with a given disability has some functional limitations and some disabilities, calling it "disablement" to highlight its dynamic nature.

The best-known medical model of disability was the International Classification of Impairments, Disabilities and Handicaps (ICIDH).[92] The model includes three central terms: (1) "impairment" – "any loss or abnormality of psychological, physiological, or anatomical structure or function"; (2) "disability" – "any restriction or lack (resulting from impairment) of ability to perform an activity in the manner or within the range considered normal for human being; and (3) "handicap" – "a disadvantage for a given individual, resulting from an impairment or a disability, that limits or prevents the fulfilment of a role that is normal (depending on age, gender, and social and cultural factors) for that individual."

The model proposes multiple links among the three levels instead of linear connection. As it offers integration between medical components and the consequences of disease, it therefore provides a common international terminology for all, applicable to individual assessment as well as to surveys and research.[93] The main criticism against the ICIDH is that it focuses on the individual, on his or her personal experiences, with physical and social environments being interpreted through personal eyes.

The social model arose in response to the shortcomings of the medical model of disability. One of the most significant critiques was written by Mike Oliver, who thought that disability "as a category can only be understood within the framework which suggests that it is culturally produced and socially structured."[94] The social model was based on the struggle of two important movements: the Independent Living Movement and the Disability Rights Movement in the United States.

[90] Michael Oliver, *Understanding disability: From theory to practice* (Basingstoke: Macmillan, 1996).

[91] S. Z. Nagi, "Some conceptual issues in disability and rehabilitation." In *Sociology and rehabilitation*. Edited by M. B. Sussman (Washington, DC: American Sociological Association, 1965), pp. 100–13.

[92] In 1980, the World Health Organization (WHO) published a tool for the classification of the consequences of disease, the International Classification of Impairments, Disabilities and Handicaps (ICIDH). It was field-tested in several countries and a revision process was begun in 1995 to address, inter alia, the need to use the classification as a framework for reporting on the health status of populations.

[93] Mary Chamie, "Survey design strategy for the study of disability," *World Health Statistics Quarterly* 42 (1989), 122–40.

[94] Mike Oliver, *The politics of disablement* (London: Macmillan, 1990), p. 22.

However, from a socio-political standpoint, the social model has been viewed as a Minority Group Model of Disability, keeping society responsible for denying the needs and aspirations of people with disabilities.

The International Classification of Functioning, Disability and Health (ICF) identifies three levels of human function: functioning at the level of body or body parts, the whole person, and the whole person in his or her complete environment. These levels, in turn, contain three domains of human function: body functions and structures, activities, and participation. The term "disability" is used to denote a decrement at each level, impairment, an activity limitation, and a participation restriction.[95]

The model defines the activity and participation domains in the context of health experience: *activity* is the execution of a task or action by an individual; *activity limitations* are defined as difficulties an individual may have in executing activities. *Participation* is involvement in a life situation, while *participation restrictions* are problems an individual may experience in involvement in life situations

The ICF can be applied at the individual, institutional, and social levels. At the individual level, it is used for the assessment of an individual's level of functioning, treatment planning and maximization of intervention. At the institutional level, the ICF can be used for education and training, planning, and development, and as a management and outcome evaluation instrument. Finally, at the social level, the ICF is expected to be used for eligibility criteria for state entitlements such as social security benefits, disability pensions, workers' compensation and insurance, social policy development, including legislative reviews, model legislation, regulations and guidelines, and definitions for anti-discrimination legislation and for needs assessment. However, the social model has been criticized by specialists for minimizing the importance of the medical perspective of disability and in particular the importance of the emotional and bodily experiences of people with disabilities. There is also a concern about the clash between the social model and social welfare legislation and entitlements.[96] The concern is one of impracticality as the current qualifying standards for benefits are primarily medical. It is unclear how these extreme manifestations can be bridged.

CONCLUSION

We cannot understand legal and civic rights of people with disabilities, whether they have legal capacity or are considered part of society, without studying the way that Judeo-Christian theologies treat people with physical and mental impairments.[97] Henri-Jacques Striker believes that the clues are hidden in the Bible (the Old Testament) and the New Testament, as the original texts tend to see disability as

---

[95]   Alan M. Jette, "Toward a common language for function, disability, and health," *Physical Therapy* 86 (2006), 726–34.
[96]   Masala and Petretto, "From disablement to enablement," 1242–44.   [97]   Ibid.

God's will.[98] They are often treated with mercy and compassion but also as sinners deserving punishment. Although the Quran does not refer specifically to people with disabilities in the same way as do the Bible and the New Testament, it portrays them as disadvantaged together with the orphan, the weak, or the needy. Eastern religions, in particular Buddhism, see disability as related to Karma – the result of past life bad deeds, evil, and/or immorality, and thus based on retribution. People with disability therefore have to experience suffering and must experience their living through their own selves.

Interestingly, current Judeo-Christian scholars look for modern interpretations to bridge the dissonance between the biblical texts and progressive ideas of equality and inclusion of people with disabilities. Tzvi Marx acknowledged the gap between the ethical and compassionate spirit of the Bible and the marginal status of people with disabilities. He argued that respected figures with disability had a central role in biblical text: Isaac was blind, Jacob limped, and Moses led the people of Israel in the desert regardless of his speech disorder.[99] Similarly, Nancy L. Eiesland offered a new interpretation for disability, viewing Jesus as "the disabled God." The injury is part of him, and therefore disability is not a sin or a condition that is expected to be healed.[100] In the second half of the twentieth century, we have seen new interpretations of disability in Islam and Buddhism, a departure from fatalism and a perception of difficulties or deprivation as opportunities to get closer to God.[101]

One of the most important milestones of ancient times is the Roman law of guardianship which has had a remarkable impact on Western civilization and Western legal thought. Although it is paternalistic in nature, it recognizes the need of certain people who are unable to take care of themselves to be protected by the law. The principles of the guardianship law exist in current Anglo-American legislation, such as guardian's responsibilities and a commitment to keep inventory of property and liabilities in case inappropriate decisions are made.

While there has been tremendous progress and increased commitment to disability rights in the last twenty-five years, and although Western society has reversed eugenic practices, it appears that medicalization and genetic human engineering approaches are still prevalent today. One of the debated areas of concern is the "new eugenics," using reproductive and genetic technologies in order to allow parents to enhance human characteristics and capabilities or prevent the birth of a disabled baby. A potential concern raised by disability activists is that the new eugenics sends a negative message to people with disability that they are less welcome in society and create a class of fit and unfit families as did the old eugenics.[102] They particularly

[98]   Henri-Jacques Striker, *History of disability* (Ann Arbor: University of Michigan, 2000).   [99]   Ibid.
[100] Eiesland, *The disabled god.*   [101]   Zidan, *Al-Sunan Al-Ilahiyyah.*
[102] Annette Patterson and Martha Satz, "Genetic counseling and the disabled: Feminism examines the stance of those who stand at the gate," *Hypatia: Journal of Feminist Philosophy* 17 (2002), 118–42, explores the possible systematic bias against people with disability in the structure and practice of genetic counseling. The authors recommend that methodology developed by feminist standpoint

reject Peter Singer's extreme infanticide approach justifying the killing of babies with severe disabilities.[103] The reason for justifying infanticide in such cases is their lack of enjoyment and adequate quality of life. Singer recommended parents so choose, and replace them with "normal" ones."[104]

The progressive anti-discrimination and equal opportunities laws and policies of the 1990s are remarkable because they change completely the status of people with disabilities in most Western countries. The most important milestone is the UNCRPD which set challenges to the international community in two core areas, the right of people with disabilities to be recognized as full persons before the law (legal capacity) and the right to live in the community as equal citizens (Article 19). The hope is that earlier theological and secular approaches will not prevent them from exercising their human and civil rights.

---

epistemology be used to incorporate the perspective of disabled individuals in genetic counselors' education and practice, thereby reforming society's view of the disabled and preventing possible negative effects of genetic counseling on the self-concept and material circumstances of disabled individuals.

[103] See Peter Singer and Helga Kushe, *Bioethics*, 2nd edn. (Oxford: Blackwell Publishing, 2006). Singer and Kushe cover issues such as reproduction, genetics, life and death, and animal experimentation, as well as genetic screening, the use of embryonic human stem cells, and resource allocation between patients.

[104] Peter Singer, *Practical ethics*, 2nd edn. (Cambridge: Cambridge University Press, 1993), 175–217. In probably one of the most controversial books in bioethics, Singer justified infanticide arguing that severely disabled newborns lacked the essential characteristics of personhood – rationality, autonomy, and self-consciousness.

3

The Paradigm Shift of Articles 12 and 19
of the UN Convention on the Rights of Persons
with Disabilities (UNCRPD)

The UN Convention on the Rights of Persons with Disabilities (UNCRPD) was adopted by the UN General Assembly on December 13, 2006. The treaty was opened for signature on March 30, 2007, and entered into force on May 3, 2008. It is considered the first new human rights convention of the twenty-first century and the most updated human rights instrument with an explicit social development dimension. Although the UNCRPD does not create new rights, it marks a change of paradigm from medical and social welfare to human rights and social functional models. It is important to note that the convention takes into consideration previous international human rights documents, including early designated instruments in the disability area.

INTERNATIONAL DISABILITY HUMAN RIGHTS INSTRUMENTS PRIOR TO THE UNCRPD

Since the 1950s there have been efforts to promote prevention and rehabilitation measures of disability, but they were based on the medical model. There was some progress in the 1970s, and particularly in the 1980s and 1990s, in developing disability human rights instruments to promote the status of people with disabilities worldwide. Table 3.1 summarizes key disability human rights instruments prior the UNCRPD.

CENTRAL RESOLUTIONS OF THE 1970s

Two major resolutions in the 1970s reflected the early signs of a disability rights approach: the 1971 Declaration on the Rights of Mentally Retarded Persons and the 1975 Declaration on the Rights of Disabled Persons. In 1971, the General Assembly of the United Nations, in resolution 2856 (XXVI), proclaimed the Declaration on the Rights of Mentally Retarded Persons. The declaration establishes that "mentally retarded persons" have the same rights as other human beings. Specifically, they have the right to: proper medical care, physical therapy, education, training,

TABLE 3.1 *Key Disability Rights Instruments Prior to the UN Convention on the Rights of Persons with Disabilities (UNCRPD)*

Year	Disability Human Rights Instrument
1971	Declaration on the Rights of Mentally Retarded Persons
1975	Declaration on the Rights of Disabled Persons
1982	World Programme of Action concerning Disabled Persons
1990	Tallinn Guidelines for Action on Human Resources Development in the Field of Disability
1991	Principles for the Protection of Persons with Mental Illness and the Improvement of Mental Health Care
1993	Standard Rules on the Equalization of Opportunities for Persons with Disabilities

rehabilitation, and guidance to develop their ability and maximum potential; economic security and decent standards of living; to perform productive work and engage on any meaningful occupation; to live with their own families or foster care, and to participate in community life; a qualified guardian when required to protect their personal well-being and interest; protection from exploitation, abuse, and degrading treatment; and to due process of law.

The Declaration on the Rights of Disabled Persons, proclaimed by General Assembly resolution 3447 (XXX) of December 9, 1975, reiterates the commitments and principles established in earlier United Nations instruments,[1] and reaffirms the rights of persons with disabilities, set forth in the declaration, without discrimination on any basis.[2] It also reiterates the necessity of preventing physical and mental disabilities and of assisting persons with disabilities "to develop their abilities in the most varied fields of activities and of promoting their integration as far as possible in normal life."[3] It states: "Disabled persons have the inherent right to respect for their human dignity. Disabled persons, whatever the origin, nature and seriousness of their handicaps and disabilities, have the same fundamental rights as their fellow-citizens of the same age, which implies first and foremost the right to enjoy a decent life, as normal and full as possible,"[4] to include civil and political rights.

THE 1982 WORLD PROGRAMME OF ACTION CONCERNING DISABLED PERSONS

The human rights of persons with disabilities became an important part of the international policy agenda of the 1980s. The World Programme of Action concerning

---

[1] Declaration on the Rights of Disabled Persons, Preamble paragraphs.
[2] Declaration on the Rights of Disabled Persons, Operative paragraph 2.
[3] Declaration on the Rights of Disabled Persons, Preamble paragraphs.
[4] Declaration on the Rights of Disabled Persons, Operative paragraph.

Disabled Persons,[5] adopted by General Assembly resolution 37/52 in 1982 at the end of the International Year of Disabled Persons,[6] also reiterates the equality of rights of all human beings. It is considered a comprehensive global strategy that utilized equalizing of opportunities as a guiding principle for achieving full participation on the basis of equality in all aspects of social and economic life and development. The strategy is perceived as a call for a social welfare agenda integrated into a human rights charter. It is the first declaration that recognizes that people with disabilities represent a diversified population that experiences "different barriers, of different kinds, which have to be overcome in different ways."[7] In terms of the language and concept, it is the first human rights declaration that departs from the traditional medical model, adopting human rights and social dimensions. Finally, it calls on governments to be instrumental in their integration into ordinary schools and competitive jobs. It is important to note that the action program identifies persons with mental and psychiatric disabilities as the most neglected and in need of special planning and supplement care.

THE 1990s: STANDARDIZATION AND PRINCIPLES OF DISABILITY RIGHTS

Another resolution adopted by the United Nations General Assembly was the Tallinn Guidelines for Action on Human Resources Development in the Field of Disability in 1989 (General Assembly resolution 38/28). The guidelines provide a framework for promoting participation, training, and employment of disabled persons within all government ministries and at all levels of national policymaking in order to equalize opportunities for persons with disabilities.

In 1991, the General Assembly adopted a key resolution entitled "Principles for the protection of persons with mental illness and the improvement of mental health

[5] Retrieved April 12, 2016 from www.independentliving.org/files/WPACDP.pdf. The main argument for declaring the World Program of Action concerning Disabled Persons is the recognition that more than 500 million people with disabilities cope with physical and social barriers in their own societies that hamper their full participation. Because of this millions of children and adults in all parts of the world often face a life that is segregated and debased.

[6] In 1976, the General Assembly proclaimed 1981 as the International Year of Disabled Persons (General Assembly resolution 31/123). It called for a plan of action at the national, regional and international levels, with an emphasis on equalization of opportunities, rehabilitation and prevention of disabilities. The main theme was full participation and equality, defined as the right of persons with disabilities to take part fully in the life and development of their societies, enjoy living conditions equal to those of other citizens, and have an equal share in improved conditions resulting from socio-economic development. Other objectives of the International Year of Disabled Persons included: increasing public awareness; understanding and acceptance of persons who are disabled; and encouraging persons with disabilities to form organizations through which they can express their views and promote action to improve their situation. A major lesson of the International Year of Disabled Persons was that the image of persons with disabilities depends to an important extent on social attitudes, which were a major barrier to the realization of the goal of full participation and equality in society by persons with disabilities.

[7] World Program of Action concerning Disabled Persons, paragraph 8.

care."[8] These principles focus on quality of care more than on human rights such as the right to liberty and equality.[9] The twenty-five principles that cover all personal rights provide agreed upon but non-legally binding basic standards that mental health systems should meet and rights that people diagnosed with mental disorders should have. Although the document underwent extensive drafting over twenty years and remains the international human rights agreement most specifically concerned with mental health, it has been criticized for not offering stronger protections in some areas.

Among the major outcomes of the United Nations Decade of Disabled Persons[10] was the adoption of the Standard Rules on the Equalization of Opportunities for Persons with Disabilities[11] by the General Assembly on December 20, 1993 (resolution 48/96 annex). These rules do not form part of a treaty and therefore lack legal effect; however, they reflect the strong moral and political commitment of governments to take action to attain equalization of opportunities for persons with disabilities. The Standard Rules consists of twenty-two rules summarizing the message of the World Programme of Action incorporating the human rights perspective which had developed during the decade. These rules concerning persons of disabilities consist of four chapters – preconditions for equal participation, target areas for equal participation, implementation measures, and the monitoring mechanism – and cover all aspects of life of persons with disabilities.

Michael Stein is skeptical about the enforceability of international human rights treaties.[12] He believes that disability human rights international instruments lack

8   The General Assembly resolution 46/119 of December 17, 1991. Retrieved March 1, 2016 from www.un
     .org/documents/ga/res/46/a46r119.htm.
9   See article by Eric Rosenthal and Leonard S. Rubenstein, "International human rights advocacy
     under the 'Principles for the Protection of Persons with Mental Illness,'" *International Journal of Law
     and Psychiatry* 16 (1993), 257.
10   In order to provide a timeframe during which governments and organizations could implement the
     activities recommended in the World Program of Action, the General Assembly proclaimed
     1983–1992 the United Nations Decade of Disabled Persons (General Assembly resolution 37/52).
     With regard to education and employment of persons with disabilities, the General Assembly adopted
     the "Tallinn Guidelines for Action on Human Resources Development in the Field of Disability," in
     1989 (General Assembly resolution 38/28), which provide a framework for promoting participation,
     training and employment of disabled persons within all government ministries and at all levels of
     national policymaking in order to equalize opportunities for persons with disabilities.
11   Retrieved March 5, 2016 from www.un.org/esa/socdev/enable/dissreoo.htm.
12   See, for example, Oona A. Hathaway, "Do human rights treaties make a difference?" (2002). Faculty
     Scholarship Series. Paper Number 839; http://digitalcommons.law.yale.edu/fss_papers/839. The arti-
     cle is based on a retrospective study of human rights treaties, concluding that external pressure on
     countries to demonstrate a commitment to human rights norms creates strong incentives to engage in
     favorable expressive behavior by ratifying human rights treaties. But because human rights treaties are
     generally only minimally monitored and enforced, there is little incentive for ratifying countries to
     make the costly changes in actual policy that would be necessary to meet their treaty commitments.
     Given this, it is perhaps not so surprising that the empirical analysis demonstrates that ratifying
     a human rights treaty can relieve pressure for change imposed by international actors who may rely
     more heavily on positions than effects in evaluating countries' records. This reduction in pressure may
     in turn lead a ratifying country to improve its practices less than it otherwise might.

legally binding power and are therefore considered as soft measures. In his opinion, the only significant instrument is the Standard Rules on the Equalization of Opportunities for Persons with Disabilities.[13] He believes the hard laws are United Nations universal treaties, and the preferred among them are the International Bill of Human Rights, the International Covenant on Civil and Political Rights (ICCPR),[14] and the International Covenant on Economic, Social, and Cultural Rights (ICESCR).[15]

The establishment of the Ad Hoc Committee to examine the feasibility of enacting a new disability-based human rights instrument marked the beginning of the UNCRPD.[16] The Ad Hoc Committee working group prepared the basis of future negotiations.[17] On January 16, 2004, the working group issued draft UNCRPD articles for consideration beginning with the next ad hoc session; on August 25, 2006, the last day for negotiating and amending the proposed convention at the eighth session, the Ad Hoc Committee adopted the UNCRPD.

THE UN CONVENTION ON THE RIGHTS OF PERSONS WITH DISABILITIES (UNCRPD)

The UNCRPD marks the gradual shift in international perceptions toward persons with disabilities from dependent and people needy of medical treatment and social protection to persons with fundamental rights who are able to make life decisions based on free and informed consent and as active members of society. In its holistic approach, it resembles United Nations human rights conventions, particularly the Convention on the Rights of the Child, reflecting a broad platform containing civil and political rights together with economic, social, and cultural rights.[18]

[13] See Michael Ashley Stein, "Disability human rights," GLADNET Collection, Cornell University ILR School. Retrieved January 9, 2016 from http://digitalcommons.ilr.cornell.edu/cgi/viewcontent.cgi?article=1452&context=gladnetcollect.

[14] Retrieved January 3, 2016 from www.ohchr.org/en/professionalinterest/pages/ccpr.aspx.

[15] Retrieved January 3, 2016 from www.ohchr.org/EN/ProfessionalInterest/Pages/CESCR.aspx.

[16] Ad Hoc Comm. on a Comprehensive and Integral International Convention on the Prot. & Promotion of the Rights & Dignity of Pers. with Disabilities, Report of the Working Group to the Ad Hoc Committee, U.N. Doc. A/AC.265/2004/WG.1 paragraph 1 (Jan. 27, 2004).

[17] According to Stein, the working group included twelve nongovernmental organizations ("NGOs"). See "Disability human rights," paragraph 2. The inclusion of NGOs at this stage was unprecedented in the normal course of treaty development at the United Nations, and can be interpreted as acquiescence to NGOs' assertion of "nothing about us without us."

[18] See Michael Ashley Stein and Penelope J. S. Stein, "Beyond disability civil rights" (2007). Faculty Publications. Paper 263, http://scholarship.law.wm.edu/facpubs/263. This article claims that civil rights alone cannot ensure social and economic equality for persons with disabilities worldwide. It recommends that states apply a holistic and integrated human rights approach as set forth in the disability human rights paradigm, recognizing the importance of both first- and second-generation rights, and so embraces anti-discrimination as well as equality measures. In their opinion, the Convention has a similar orientation and will obligate states to take this approach.

The purpose of the UNCRPD as presented in Article 1 is "to promote, protect and ensure the full and equal enjoyment of all human rights and fundamental freedoms by all persons with disabilities, and to promote respect for their inherent dignity. Persons with disabilities include those who have long-term physical, mental, intellectual, or sensory impairments which in interaction with various barriers may hinder their full and effective participation in society on an equal basis with others."[19] Articles 2 to 5 address definitions, general principles, and general obligations, and equality and nondiscrimination. Article 2 defines core key terms used in the convention including communication, discrimination on the basis of disability, reasonable accommodation, and universal design. Article 3 presents the principles of respect for dignity, nondiscrimination, participation, and inclusion, respect for difference, equality of opportunity, accessibility, equality between men and women, and respect for children. Article 4 introduces the measures that countries must adopt, including active involvement of people with disabilities, and ensuring and promoting the full realization of all human rights and fundamental freedoms for all persons with disabilities without discrimination of any kind. Article 5 address equality and nondiscrimination, meaning that everyone is equal before and under the law and is entitled to equal protection and benefit of the law without discrimination.

Articles 6 and 7 introduce two target vulnerable sub-populations requiring special attention. Article 6 identified women with disabilities as experiencing multiple discrimination and called on the states to ensure that women with disabilities are able to fully enjoy the rights and freedoms set out in the convention. Article 7 states that children with disabilities have the same human rights as all other children. The best interests of the child must be a primary consideration in all actions concerning children with disabilities, and children with disabilities have the right to express their views on all matters affecting them.

Article 8, awareness-raising, is considered to be one of the core missions of the convention, and is fundamental for any progress. Therefore, it calls on countries to raise awareness of the rights, capabilities, and contributions of people with disabilities. They must challenge stereotypes and prejudices relating to people with disabilities through campaigning, education, media, and awareness-raising programs.

Article 9, accessibility, states that people with disabilities have the right to access all aspects of society on an equal basis with others including the physical environment, transportation, information, and communications, and other facilities and services provided to the public.

Article 10 addresses the right to life and directs that states must take all necessary measures to ensure that people with disabilities are able to effectively enjoy this right on an equal basis with others. Article 11 calls on the countries to take all necessary measures to ensure the protection and safety of all persons with disabilities

[19] UNCRPD Article 1, 2006, www.un.org/disabilities/convention/conventionfull.shtml.

in situations of risk, including armed conflict, humanitarian emergencies, and natural disasters.

Article 12, equal recognition before the law, is central to this book and will be presented separately. It states that people with disabilities have the right to recognition as persons before the law and have legal capacity on an equal basis with others in all aspects of life. Countries must take appropriate measures to provide support to people with disabilities so that they can effectively exercise their legal capacity. Article 13, access to justice, calls on states to ensure that people with disabilities will have the right to effective access to justice on an equal basis with others, including through the provision of appropriate accommodations. Article 14 addresses the right of people with disabilities to liberty and security on an equal basis with others. Article 15 states that people with disabilities have the right to be free from torture and from cruel, inhuman or degrading treatment or punishment and that none will be subjected to medical or scientific experimentation without his or her free consent. Article 16, states that people with disabilities have the right to be protected from all forms of exploitation, violence and abuse, including gender-based aspects, within and outside the home. Article 17 addresses the right of persons with disabilities to respect for their physical and mental integrity on an equal basis with others. Article 18 covers the right of people with disabilities to a nationality, including children with disabilities who have the right to a name and to know and be cared for by their parents.

Article 19, the right to live independently in the community, is the topic of this book and will be addressed separately in this chapter. Countries must ensure that people with disabilities have the opportunity to choose where they live and with whom they live and are provided with the support necessary to do this.

Article 20 addresses personal mobility and instructs states to take effective and appropriate measures to ensure personal mobility for people with disabilities in the manner and time of their choice, and at affordable cost. People with disabilities also have the right to access quality mobility aids, assistive technologies, and forms of live assistance and intermediaries. Article 21 states that people with disabilities have the right to express themselves, including the freedom to give and receive information and ideas through all forms of communication, including through accessible formats and technologies, sign languages, Braille, augmentative and alternative communication, mass media, and all other accessible means of communication. Article 22 addresses the right of people with disabilities to privacy, including that personal information and information about their health should be protected.

Article 23 is the only one that addresses the role of the family. It states that people with disabilities have the right to marry and to found a family. Countries must provide effective and appropriate support to people with disabilities in bringing up children and provide alternative care for children with disabilities when the immediate family is unable to care for them.

Article 24 deals with the right to education without discrimination. Countries must ensure that people with disabilities can access an inclusive, quality, and free primary and secondary education in their own community, and provide reasonable accommodation and individualized support to maximize academic and social development. Article 25 focuses on health, stating the right to the enjoyment of the highest attainable standard of health without discrimination. Countries must take all appropriate measures, including measures that are gender-sensitive, to ensure that people with disabilities have access to the same range, quality, and standard of health care that is available to everyone else, and which are close to their own communities. Article 26 calls on states to take effective and appropriate measures to enable people with disabilities to develop, attain, and maintain maximum ability, independence, and participation through the provision of habilitation and rehabilitation services and program. Article 27 addresses employment, the right to work, including the right to work in an environment that is open, inclusive, and accessible. Countries must take appropriate steps to promote employment opportunities and career advancement for people with disabilities. Article 28 deals with the right to an adequate standard of living including food, water, clothing, and housing, and to effective social protection including poverty reduction and public housing programs.

Article 29 focuses on the right to participate in politics and in public affairs, as well as to vote and to be elected; and Article 30 addresses the right to participation in cultural life, recreation, leisure, and sport. Article 31, statistics and data collection, addresses the collection of information about people with disabilities, with the active involvement of people with disabilities, so that they can better understand the barriers they experience and make the convention rights real. Finally, Articles 32 to 50 explain how the countries bound by the convention must give it full effect. They also explain the responsibility of countries to report to the United Nations Committee on the Rights of Persons with Disabilities on how they are putting the convention into effect.

The core Articles 19 and 12 of the UNCRPD are pivotal to the community living policy of people with disability. Article 19 addresses the right to live independently in the community and is pro-choice in nature, ensuring that "persons with disabilities have the opportunity to choose their place of residence and where and with whom they live on an equal basis with others and are not obliged to live in a particular living arrangement."[20] Article 12 supports the person's legal capacity to make decisions, including those regarding their residence. The two articles are interlinked, as legal capacity is fundamental for making choices about where and with whom the person wishes to live. However, living in the community facilitates legal capacity and making choices compared to those living in institutional or congregate care. The two are introduced and discussed with respect to community living policies.

[20] Article 19(a) of the UNCRPD, www.un.org/disabilities/default.asp?id=279.

FOCUS ON ARTICLE 12: EQUAL RECOGNITION
BEFORE THE LAW

The Roman law of guardianship grew out of the family organization and was closely related to the law of inheritance. The power of a guardian is based on paternal power when there is no one to exercise the latter. Roman legislation was considered a breakthrough then and a departure from the old eugenics approaches of the ancient world.

The English law of guardianship represents a transition toward the principle of protecting the bodily and mental immaturity of youth. It is clear that Article 12 challenges the concept of guardianship and replaces it with a progressive civil rights approach and the provision of supported decision-making.[21]

ARTICLE 12: EQUAL RECOGNITION BEFORE THE LAW[22]

1. States Parties reaffirm that persons with disabilities have the right to recognition everywhere as persons before the law.
2. States Parties shall recognize that persons with disabilities enjoy legal capacity on an equal basis with others in all aspects of life.
3. States Parties shall take appropriate measures to provide access by persons with disabilities to the support they may require in exercising their legal capacity.
4. States Parties shall ensure that all measures that relate to the exercise of legal capacity provide for appropriate and effective safeguards to prevent abuse in accordance with international human rights law. Such safeguards shall ensure that measures relating to the exercise of legal capacity respect the rights, will and preferences of the person, are free of conflict of interest and undue influence, are proportional and tailored to the person's circumstances, apply for the shortest time possible and are subject to regular review by a competent, independent and impartial authority or judicial body. The safeguards shall be proportional to the degree to which such measures affect the person's rights and interests.
5. Subject to the provisions of this article, States Parties shall take all appropriate and effective measures to ensure the equal right of persons with disabilities to own or inherit property, to control their own financial affairs and to have equal access to bank loans, mortgages and other forms of financial credit, and shall ensure that persons with disabilities are not arbitrarily deprived of their property.

---

[21] See, for example, Amita Dhanda, "Legal capacity in the disability rights convention: Stranglehold of the past or lodestar for the future?" *Syracuse Journal of International Law and Commerce* 34 (2007), 429–62; Eilionóir Flynn and Anna Arstein-Kerslak, "The support model of legal capacity: Fact, fiction or fantasy?" *Berkeley Journal of International Law* 32 (2014), 124–43.

[22] www.un.org/disabilities/default.asp?id=272.

Article 12 (see above) consists of five paragraphs. Paragraph 12(1) focuses on the right of persons with disabilities to be recognized before the law. It guarantees that every human being possesses legal personality, which is a prerequisite for the recognition of a person's legal capacity.

Paragraph 12(2) is central, recognizing that persons with disabilities enjoy legal capacity on an equal basis with others in all areas of life and be holders and actors under the law. As holders of rights they are entitled to full protection of their rights by the legal system. As actors under the law, they are recognized as agents who can perform acts with legal effect. The right to recognition as a legal agent is provided for in Article 12, paragraph 5, of the convention, which outlines the duty of states to "take all appropriate and effective measures to ensure the equal right of persons with disabilities to own or inherit property, to control their own financial affairs and to have equal access to bank loans, mortgages and other forms of financial credit, and shall ensure that persons with disabilities are not arbitrarily deprived of their property."

Article 12(3) recognizes the right of persons with disabilities to support, in broad terms, in the exercise of their legal capacity. It demands that countries ensure that persons with disabilities will not be denied their legal capacity, providing them with access to the support that may be necessary to enable them to make decisions that have legal effect. Support in the exercise of legal capacity must respect the rights, will, and preferences of persons with disabilities and should never amount to substitute decision-making.

Article 12(4) outlines the safeguards that must be present in a system of support in the exercise of legal capacity. It requires states parties to create appropriate and effective safeguards for the exercise of legal capacity. These safeguards have to ensure the respect of the person's rights, will, and preferences and provide protection from abuse on an equal basis with others.

Article 12(5) requires that states parties take legislative, administrative, judicial, and any other measures to ensure the financial and economic rights of persons with disabilities on an equal basis with others. There is recognition that persons with disabilities have been denied access to finance and property. This approach of denying persons with disabilities legal capacity in financial matters must be replaced with support to exercise legal capacity in accordance with Article 12, paragraph 3.

ARTICLE 12 DEBATED

Article 12 challenges the frequent use and appropriateness of guardianship for persons with disabilities by offering the concept of supported decision-making. Guardianship laws are considered as restricting civil rights and civil liberties, and in many cases guardianships are imposed on people with disabilities without enough evidence of their decision-making incapability. In some cases, disability alone appears to be used as a sufficient justification for the imposition of guardianship.[23]

Gerard Quinn believes that Article 12 reflects a paradigm shift from the traditional guardianship approach to supported decision-making. According to Quinn, it is a major change in terms of status of persons with disabilities.[24] The specific reference to persons with disabilities was inserted because they were treated until the twentieth century as "sinners" and incapable of making their own choices.

The article is nondiscriminatory in recognizing personhood and legal capacity and functionalist in terms of access to support in order to exercise legal capacity in all areas. The underlying assumption is that all people, regardless of their disability or type of impairment, have self-determination and capability.[25] The role of the state is clear: not to restrict or remove the right to legal capacity, but to provide access to support. Article 12(3) bridges the distinction between civil and political and socio-economical rights,[26] while Article 12(4) requires that any measures relating to the exercise of legal capacity must "provide for appropriate and effective safeguards to prevent abuse"[27] and must "respect the rights, will and preferences of the person."[28] They have to be short, independent, be proportional and tailored to the person's needs, and free from conflict of interest.

There is no doubt that Article 12 challenges historical and traditional approaches to legal capacity, and in particular guardianship. Therefore, it is no surprise that the CRPD Committee raised concerns about its formulation and legal interpretations.[29] One of the most conceptual issues is that "support to exercise legal capacity" in

[23] See Dorothy Squatrito Millar, "Age of majority, transfer of rights and guardianship: Consideration for families and educators," *Education and Training in Developmental Disabilities* 38 (2003), 378–97. Under the Individuals with Disabilities Education Act (IDEA), when youths reach the age of majority they become responsible for their educational program unless they are determined to be incompetent. Millar examined guardianship inconsistencies and found that (a) a disability label limited the ability to make decisions, and youth reaching the age of majority were main reasons that petitions were filed; (b) evidence used to "prove" incompetence was unclear; (c) a ward's "conditions" remained constant following the guardian's appointment; and (d) guardianship did not necessarily resolve the areas of concern.

[24] Gerard Quinn, "Personhood and legal capacity: Perspectives on the paradigm shift of Article 12 CRPD." A concept paper presented at HPOD, Harvard Law School, February 20, 2010.

[25] Penny Weller, "Supported decision-making and the achievement of non-Discrimination: The promise and paradox of the disabilities convention," *Law in Context* 26 (2008), 85, 103. Weller argues that the UNCRPD has the potential to limit involuntary medical treatment through requiring the development of genuine processes of supported decision-making in health care. She argues that the emphasis on nondiscrimination in the UNCRPD envisages supported decision-making processes in health as central to the effective operation of nondiscriminatory environments and the achievement of full social participation.

[26] Sandra Fredman, *Discrimination law* (Oxford: Oxford University Press 2011), 67–70.

[27] UNCRPD (n 1) Art 12(4).   [28] Ibid.

[29] The seventy-three comments submitted to the UNCRPD Committee in response to its draft General Comment on Article 12 can be seen at the UN Office for the High Commission for Human Rights, "Submissions to the Draft General Comment on Article 12 of the Convention – Equal Recognition before the Law and Draft General Comment on Article 9 of the Convention – Accessibility," CRPD Committee Website, February 2014; available at www.ohchr.org/EN/HRBodies/CRPD/Pages/

Article 12(3) is defined broadly as encompassing "both informal and formal support arrangements, of verifying types and intensity." It is clear that supported decision-making is made by the person, on his or her behalf, with support to exercise legal capacity and excludes *substitute decision-making.*[30] In other words, Article 12(3) is viewed as contrasting with *supported decision-making.* However, there is debate in the literature as to whether supported decision-making can refer only to statutory arrangements alone.[31]

An interesting clarification has been offered by Browning, Bigby, and Douglas, differentiating between supported decision-making and *support with decision-making.*[32] In their opinion, the latter refers to a range of measures to assist persons who may require assistance to make decisions outside the context of directly exercising legal capacity, for example using simple or sign language. The sensitive obligation of the state is a real challenge: how to support the person's will and preference in complicated and unclear situations when the person is subject to special medical conditions. Therefore, Article 12 challenges current legislations of guardianship and mental capacity in different countries and the need to clarify the types of support arrangements that do not violate the person's basic rights.

THE CHALLENGE OF IMPLEMENTATION

As most of the current national laws impose barriers to the exercise of legal capacity by persons with disabilities, or deny access to needed supports for the exercise of legal capacity, it is necessary for states to modify these laws to bring them into

DGCArticles12And9.aspx. Retrieved January 10, 2015. Right to Legal Capacity _ 47 Retrieved June 16, 2015 at University of Haifa Library from http://hrlr.oxfordjournals.org/.

[30] CRPD Committee, supra n 3 at paragraph 23. Substitute decision-making regimes can take many different forms, including plenary guardianship, judicial interdiction, and partial guardianship. However, these regimes have certain common characteristics: they can be defined as systems where (i) legal capacity is removed from a person even if this is just in respect of a single decision; (ii) a substitute decision-maker can be appointed by someone other than the person concerned, and this can be done against his or her will; or (iii) any decision made by a substitute decision-maker is based on what is believed to be in the objective "best interests' of the person concerned, as opposed to being based on the person's own will and preferences.

[31] See Michael Bach and Lana Kerzner, "A new paradigm for protecting autonomy and the right to legal capacity." Prepared for the Law Commission of Ontario 2010. Retrieved June 1, 2016 from www.access-to-justice.org/mediabin/Article-Summary-Bach.pdf. This paper attempts to answer a question framed by the Law Commission of Ontario: "What principles and considerations should be applied when considering placing limitations on the ability of persons with disabilities to make their own choices?" In particular, the paper identifies persons with severe intellectual, cognitive, or psychosocial disabilities as most at risk of being considered "not capable" of decision-making by people caring for them.

[32] Michelle Browning, Christine Bigby, and Jacinta Douglas, "Supported decision making: Understanding how its conceptual link to legal capacity is influencing the development of practice," *Developmental Disabilities* 1 (2014), 34–45, clarifies the conceptual link between supported decision-making and legal capacity and how this influences the development of practice. It examines how the concept has been defined as a process of supporting a person with decision-making; a system that affords legal status; and a means of bringing a person's will and preference to the center of any substituted decision-making process.

consonance with Article 12. The first strategy that governments must implement is to replace existing substitute decision-making laws and policies with supported decision-making mechanisms that are recognized in legislation and have corresponding policies and programs to effectively implement a system of supported decision-making. In parallel, they are responsible for developing, supporting, and offering support services, and for establishing safeguards to ensure a high quality of support and compliance with standards such as respect for the rights, will, and preferences of the person, freedom from conflict of interest and undue influence, and tailoring them to individual circumstances.[33]

There is a wide range of informal supports that allow for personal choice among different options, including support networks, community services, peer support, and personal assistance and planning. It is equally important to dismantle widely used substitute decision-making policies and legislation and to abolish plenary guardianship, which imposes the continuation of guardianship against the person's will.

Under Article 4 of the UNCRPD, states parties are obligated to adopt all appropriate legislative, administrative, and other measures for the implementation of the rights in the UNCRPD, and to take all appropriate measures, including legislation, to modify or abolish existing laws, regulations, customs, and practices that constitute discrimination against persons with disabilities.[34] However, it seems that most of the countries that have ratified the convention have a long way to go in shifting from the guardianship system to supported decision-making.

Canada is among the pioneering countries to establish supported decision-making even before the UNCRPD. In 1996, British Columbia enacted the Representation Agreement Act which presumes persons with intellectual disabilities and persons with mental illness have capacity, and establishes a system to allow them to make advanced decisions on various issues without court involvement, while representation agreements allow persons to nominate a person to make decisions for them under certain circumstances.[35] However, British Columbia has not canceled the substitute decision-making model. A public guardian is authorized to make decisions for individuals who do not or, for some reason, cannot, enter into a representation agreement.

Sweden has stopped providing plenary guardianship but permits partial guardianship as a last resort. It offers a court-appointed tutor (in Swedish, a "god man"), often a friend or family member, who acts with the person's consent, and a trustee who, like a guardian, can make decisions for the person on financial and personal welfare

---

[33] See IDA Forum principle recommendations at http://social.un.org/ageing-working-group/docu ments/egm/Article12.pdf.

[34] UNCRPD, art. 4(1)(a), (b).

[35] This, of course, resembles powers of attorney and health care advance directives that are available in one form or another in every state in the United States. For a state-by-state survey of the availability of psychiatric advance directives, see www.nrc-pad.org/.

matters and is supposed to follow a "best interest" approach.[36] In Germany, the focus is on supported decision-making for persons with disabilities and with mental illness. The individual retains legal capacity even when limited (temporary) guardianships are instated for court-specified tasks, often financial matters.[37]

England still awards guardianship under the supervision of the Office of the Public Guardian.[38] The Mental Capacity Act of 2005 presumes capacity for everyone unless and until determined otherwise. The focus is on the individual and his or her social network instead of court-appointed support. If there is no social network, independent mental capacity advocates can provide support for making decisions. Thus, substitute decision-making and the "best interests" presumption still constrain advancement toward supported decision-making.[39]

The United States' guardianship system, which is state-based, seems stuck with the guardianship system.[40] On a positive note, there have been some efforts to limit guardianships as individual states enact amendments to better protect the rights of persons with disabilities through time- and task-specific guardianship orders. Michigan, for example, enacted a procedural bill in 2012 that preserves the individual's fundamental human rights by listing the powers of the guardian. The guardian's powers are tailored to the specific needs of the individual following a court determination of the person's decision-making ability regarding where to live, whether to take or refuse medication, obtain services, and handle financial matters.[41]

---

[36] Soumitra Pathare and Laura S. Shields, "Supported decision-making for persons with mental illness: A review," *Public Health Reviews* 2 (2012), 15, provides a comprehensive review of the global evidence on supported decision-making for persons with mental illness in both legislation and research, with a focus on low- and middle-income countries. There are only a few countries with supported decision-making policies and procedures for persons with mental illness. There is also a general paucity of research evidence for supported decision-making, with the majority of research focusing on shared decision-making for treatment decisions.

[37] Ibid., p. 13.   [38] Ibid., p. 12.

[39] See Generva Richardson, "Mental disabilities and the law: From substitute to supported decision-making? Current legal problems," *Current Legal Problems* 65 (2012), 333–54. There are two statutes in England and Wales dealing with the closely related concepts of mental disorder and mental capacity, and the relationship between them has proved to be difficult and controversial. The article examines two of the most familiar proposals which try to resolve the tension between the concepts. It concludes that while both may reduce the discriminatory aspects of the current law, they are both constrained by their reliance on substitute decision making and best interests. An alternative and more radical model based on universal capacity and supported decision making is provided by the UNCRPD.

[40] A. Frank Johns, "Person-centered planning in guardianship: A little hope for the future," *Utah Law Review* (2012), 1541–73, examined the potential for person-centered planning within the American system of guardianship. It concluded that guardians' current exercise of authority was not person-centered because it gave little attention to the person of those relegated to its paternalistic protections. It provided guidance on how person-centered planning could be incorporated into guardianship and included three case studies using person-centered tools in assessing the wants and needs of clients being served.

[41] Ibid. at 2.

FOCUS ON ARTICLE 19: LIVING INDEPENDENTLY AND BEING INCLUDED IN THE COMMUNITY

Article 19, below, recognizes the right of persons with disabilities to live independently and be included in society, and the responsibility of the state to provide support and structures that enable persons with disabilities to engage in community life. Living independently does not mean living alone or in isolation.[42] Rather, it means exercising freedom of choice and control over decisions affecting one's life with the same level of independence and interdependence within society on an equal basis with others. Consequently, Article 19 refers to "living independently and being included in the community" as one right, where autonomy and inclusion are mutually reinforcing and jointly avoid segregation.[43]

ARTICLE 19: LIVING INDEPENDENTLY AND BEING INCLUDED IN THE COMMUNITY

States Parties to the present Convention recognize the equal right of all persons with disabilities to live in the community, with choices equal to others, and shall take effective and appropriate measures to facilitate full enjoyment by persons with disabilities of this right and their full inclusion and participation in the community, including by ensuring that:

(a) Persons with disabilities have the opportunity to choose their place of residence and where and with whom they live on an equal basis with others and are not obliged to live in a particular living arrangement;

(b) Persons with disabilities have access to a range of in-home, residential and other community support services, including personal assistance necessary to support living and inclusion in the community, and to prevent isolation or segregation from the community;

(c) Community services and facilities for the general population are available on an equal basis to persons with disabilities and are responsive to their needs.

Article 19 of the UNCRPD (living independently and being included in the community) is the first international human rights treaty to expressly recognize the right of all people with disabilities to live and participate in the community and have the same equal choices as others as to where and with whom he or she prefers to live.

---

[42] See the contribution of the International Disability Alliance.

[43] See, for instance, the daily summaries of discussion at the seventh session of the Ad Hoc Committee on a Comprehensive and Integral International Convention on the Protection and Promotion of the Rights and Dignity of Persons with Disabilities, January 19–20, 2006, can be retrieved from www.un .org/esa/socdev/enable/rights/ahc7sum19jan.htm and www.un.org/esa/socdev/enable/rights/ahc7 sum20jan.htm. See also the report of the third session of the Ad Hoc Committee, footnote 53; available at www.un.org/esa/socdev/enable/rights/ahc3reporte.htm, and the daily summary of discussions related to Article 15 at the third session of the Ad Hoc Committee, can be retrieved from www.un .org/esa/socdev/enable/rights/ahc3sum15.htm.

Article 19 is related to provisions in other human rights treaties, including the International Covenant on Civil and Political Rights,[44] the International Covenant on Economic, Social and Cultural Rights[45] and the Convention on the Rights of the Child.[46] The right to live independently and to be included in the community has also been recognized in regional human rights documents such as the European Social Charter (art. 15) and the Inter-American Convention on the Elimination of All Forms of Discrimination against Persons with Disabilities (art. 4, para. 2 (b)).

Article 19 calls for the provision of support and structures enabling people with disabilities to engage in community life. This implies commitment of the countries that have ratified the convention to end the institutionalization of people with disabilities and replaces it with appropriate community-based services that promote social inclusion.

Article 19 is based on general principles of the convention (art. 3), in particular the principles concerning individual's autonomy and independence. It implies that society combats stereotypes and prejudices relating to persons with disabilities and raises awareness of their capabilities and contributions to society (art. 8). Additional articles associated with Article 19 are nondiscrimination (art. 5) and accessibility (art. 9) which are essential to ensure that community services and facilities for the general population are available on an equal basis to persons with disabilities and respond to their needs.[47]

ARTICLE 19: CORE CONCEPTS

Article 19 is based on three major mechanisms: choice (paragraph a), individualized support (paragraph b), and availability and accessibility of community services and facilities (paragraph c). Paragraph a, requires state parties to ensure that persons with disabilities have the opportunity to choose their place of residence and where and with whom they live on an equal basis. Therefore they need to offer a range of options for community living. As discussed earlier, Articles 12 and 19 are interlinked, as the right to exercise legal capacity underpins the right to live independently in the community and vice versa. Legal capacity consists of two inseparable elements: to be recognized as a legal person before the law and to exercise rights as a legal person under the law. The exercise of legal capacity as recognized in the UNCRPD

---

[44] See, for example, Articles 9, 12, 16, and 17.   [45] For instance, Articles 11 and 12.

[46] For instance, Articles 2, 9, 16, 20, 23, 25, and 27.

[47] *Thematic study of persons with disabilities to live independently and be included in the community.* Report of the Office of United Nations High Commissioner for Human Rights, December 12, 2014, Note 7. The study, developed under Human Rights Council resolution 25/20, is focused on the right to live independently and be included in the community, and the enjoyment, protection, and promotion of that right as a substantive means for the realization of other rights, as a condition for avoiding institutionalization and segregation in health and social settings, and as a prerequisite to provide for the full development of the capabilities of persons with disabilities and their meaningful participation in, and contribution to, society.

requires that the will and preferences of a person are respected, and allows for the exercise of free and informed consent.[48]

Although it is not specified, Article 19 rules out institutions and segregated places, primarily because they have control over day-to-day decisions and are insensitive to a person's personal preferences.[49] Therefore, the Committee on the Rights of Persons with Disabilities encourages states to adopt national deinstitutionalization policies. By shifting people with intellectual and mental disabilities from institutional to community-based housing, they can reclaim control over their lives and make personal choices.

Article 19 calls for action and the provision of community support services and personal assistance. Article 19(c) requires states parties to ensure that community services and facilities for the general population are available on an equal basis to persons with disabilities and are responsive to their needs. The services have to allow them all community rights, among them education, work, and transportation. It is clear that Article 19(c) flows from the general principles of Article 3, in particular those of full and effective participation and inclusion in society and of respect for difference and acceptance of persons with disabilities as part of human diversity. Building an inclusive community requires (a) the removal of barriers; (b) systemic transformation of mainstream services in society; and (c) an inclusive process in which persons with disabilities are actively involved. Article 19 emphasizes the importance of informal networks in building an inclusive society, particularly, the role of family, friends, neighbors, peers, and others in creating the proper climate and support system. Regardless of the nature of informal networks, Article 19 requires that persons with disabilities exercise full decision-making abilities, with the network playing a supportive role.[50] Networking does not replace the importance of personal assistance, including peer support and advocacy, crisis respite and planning, nonmedical support to deal with altered perceptions, and assistance to meet the practical needs of everyday life. The provision of access to personal assistance for persons with intellectual and psychosocial disabilities is essential to moving from a medical to a social approach concerning mental health issues with respect to personal autonomy.

THE CHALLENGES OF ARTICLE 19

Article 19 calls for adopting effective and appropriate measures on the part of the states. Each country has a different legal system and therefore requires adjustment to domestic law and social-political realities. In some countries, The UNCRPD (including Article 19), is already part of national law, but in other countries it requires significant changes in domestic legislation.

[48]   Ibid., note 16.   [49]   Ibid., note 21.
[50]   See, further, the discussion on choice and control in the section "International Disability Human Rights Instruments Prior to the UNCRPD" of this chapter.

The first challenge is choice of residence (Article 19(a)) which is related to recognition before the law and legal capacity. Unfortunately, many central and eastern European countries have restrictive guardianship schemes that prevent people from making personal decisions in a wide range of areas, including the right to where and with whom to live. They have a long way to go to adopt Article 12 and in particular to allow people with disabilities to exercise supported decision-making.[51] It is clear that the lack of legal capacity, autonomy, and choices is critical, and in particular the right of persons with disabilities to choose where and with whom they would like to live. Another challenge is access to a range of community support services (Article 19(b)). The lack of community-based services is crucial for states' compliance with Article 19, as people with disabilities have limited choices regarding their place of residence. This is particularly a major problem for countries that are dependent primarily on institutional and congregate care facilities.[52] In these countries, there is also a lack of equal access to mainstream community services, which limits the choice of residence. Although Article 19 does not address deinstitutionalization, its provisions make clear that the closure of institutions is required, together with the development of community-based alternatives. Article 19 emphasizes full inclusion and participation in the community, which can only be achieved when there are no more institutions.

In general, the United States is considered more progressive in deinstitutionalization and community-based legislation and policies than European countries. The ADA[53] prohibits discrimination against people with disabilities and calls for

---

[51]   Open Society Foundations, "A community for all: Implementing Article 19," December 2011, www
.opensocietyfoundations.org/sites/default/files/community-for-all-guide-20111202.pdf.
The "Community for All" Guide and Checklist were developed as part of a project of the Mental
Health Initiative and the Law and Health Initiative of the Open Society Public Health Program. They
offer a detailed look at the rights identified in the UNCRPD), especially Article 19 which provides for
the right to live independently and be included in the community.

[52]   See, for example, Jim Mansell et al., *Deinstitutionalization and community living — outcomes and
costs: Report of a European study.* Vol. 2: Main Report (Canterbury: Tizard Centre, University of Kent,
2007), p. 26. The authors estimated that nearly 1.2 million people were living in residential institutions
for people with disabilities in European Union member states.

[53]   The Americans with Disabilities Act was signed into law on July 26, 1990. Its overall purpose is to make
American society more accessible to people with disabilities. In 2008, the ADA Amendments Act
(ADAAA) was passed. Its purpose is to broaden the definition of disability, which had been narrowed
by US Supreme Court decisions. The ADA is divided into five titles:

    1.   EMPLOYMENT (TITLE I)
       Title I requires covered employers to provide reasonable accommodations for applicants and
       employees with disabilities and prohibits discrimination on the basis of disability in all aspects
       of employment. Reasonable accommodation includes, for example, restructuring jobs, making worksites and workstations accessible, modifying schedules, providing services such as
       interpreters, and modifying equipment and policies. Title I also regulates medical examinations and inquiries. For more information, see http://AskJAN.org/links/adalinks.htm#I.
    2.   PUBLIC SERVICES (TITLE II)
       Under Title II, public services (which include state and local government agencies, the National
       Railroad Passenger Corporation, and other commuter authorities) cannot deny services to people
       with disabilities or deny participation in programs or activities that are available to people without

reasonable accommodation in the community as opposed to institutional care. In *Olmstead v. LC*,[54] the Supreme Court decided that unjustified segregation of persons with disabilities constituted discrimination in violation of title II of the ADA. The court held that public entities must provide community-based services to persons with disabilities when (1) such services are appropriate; (2) the affected persons do not oppose community-based treatment; and (3) community-based services can be reasonably accommodated taking into account the resources available to the public entity and the needs of others who are receiving disability services from the entity. However, unlike the convention which mandates that states ensure that persons with disabilities live independently and in the community, the right as enunciated in *Olmstead* is not as strong.[55] The ADA suggested that any change has to be reasonable and take into account economic hardship.

The EU made a commitment to recognizing the rights of all people with disabilities living in the EU and to taking action to ensure that these rights are enforced, including the right to independent living. The EU effort, discussed fully in Chapter 5, is based on two instruments: the Structural Funds[56] and the availability of personal assistance schemes.[57] However, there are concerns raised since the

     disabilities. Public transportation systems, such as public transit buses, must also be accessible to individuals with disabilities. For more information, see http://AskJAN.org/links/adalinks.htm#II.

3.   PUBLIC ACCOMMODATIONS (TITLE III)
     Public accommodations include facilities such as restaurants, hotels, grocery stores, retail stores, etc., as well as privately owned transportation systems. Title III requires that all new construction and modifications must be accessible to individuals with disabilities. For existing facilities, barriers to services must be removed if readily achievable. For more information, see http://AskJAN.org/links/adalinks.htm#III.

4.   TELECOMMUNICATIONS (TITLE IV)
     Telecommunications companies offering telephone service to the general public must have telephone relay services for individuals who use telecommunication devices for the deaf (TTYs) or similar devices.

5.   MISCELLANEOUS (TITLE V)
     This title includes a provision prohibiting either (a) coercing or threatening or (b) retaliating against individuals with disabilities or those attempting to aid people with disabilities in asserting their rights under the ADA.

54   *Olmstead v. L C* (98–536) 527 U.S. 581 (1999). Retrieved January 16, 2016 from https://supreme.justia .com/cases/federal/us/527/581/case.html.

55   Anita Silvers and Michael Ashley Stein, "Disability, equal protection, and the Supreme Court: Standing at the crossroads of progressive and retrogressive logic in constitutional classification" (2001). Faculty Publications. Paper 703; http://scholarship.law.wm.edu/facpubs/703. Silvers and Stein demonstrate that current disability law resembles the abandoned, sexist framework for determining sex equality and argue that disability equality cases should receive similar analysis as the more progressive, current sex equality standard. As such, the article attempts to synthesize case law (14th Amendment Equal Protection jurisprudence) and statutory law (Title VII and the ADA) into a comprehensive overview of the state of current disability law viewed within the context of discrimination law in general.

56   The Structural Funds is a financial tool set up to implement the regional policy of the European Union. The funds are intended to reduce regional disparities in income, wealth, and opportunities.

57   See Commission Staff Working Document, Report on the implementation of the UNCRPD by the European Union, June 2014. See: http://ec.europa.eu/justice/discrimination/files/swd_2014_182_en.pdf. The commission staff working document 4. I highlights the promotion of the rights of persons with

beginning of the twenty-first century by the European Coalition for Community Living (ECCL) regarding the implementation of Article 19 in the European Union.[58] The coalition identified insufficient data on institutional care, adverse impact of austerity measures on people with disabilities, insufficient action to raise awareness about institutions of people with disabilities, and slow progress in developing community-based alternatives to institutional care. Additional obstacles are related to the European Structural Funds and particularly the decision of state members to transfer them from institutional to community-based programs, and promoting personal assistance as an essential component of independent living.

CONCLUSION

Article 12 expresses the fundamental right of persons with disabilities to exercise their legal capacity on an equal basis with others. Article 19(a) of the UNCRPD, as well as Article 3(a), addresses individual autonomy,[59] closely linked to the right to legal capacity, primarily because the person's need to be recognized before the law is crucial for making decisions about place of residence and where and with whom he or she will live. Each person has the right to legal capacity on an equal basis with others.[60] There is no doubt that the state has an important duty in ensuring persons with disabilities are able to exercise their legal capacity, by providing support when needed.[61]

It is clear that the optimal condition for making choices is when they live independently in the community, as provided for in Article 19. The less desirable condition is when they live in institutional or congregate care, controlled by others and by regulations that restrict their legal capacity.

The implementation of Articles 12 and 19 of the UNCRPD go hand in hand, and progress in one area positively affects the other area. Challenging institutionalization is thus interwoven with challenging the legitimacy of guardianship and developing alternative models for supported decisions. The overwhelming opinion in the United States is that its domestic laws and policies are compatible with the UNCRPD. However, the debate regarding US ratification of the UNCRPD and the treaty's possible impact on US sovereignty has been a key area of concern. Critics of the convention maintain that treaties are the supreme "law of the land" under the Constitution, and that US ratification of the UNCRPD could supersede federal, state, and local laws. Supporters assert that the UNCRPD is a nondiscrimination

---

disabilities in line with the CRPD in the development and implementation of EU policies and legislation.

[58] ENIL-ECCL Shadow Report on the Implementation of Article 19 of the UNCRPD in the European Union, October 2014, pp. 7–10, www.enil.eu/wp-content/uploads/2012/06/Shadow-Report-11-04-2014-final-WEB-1-1.pdf.

[59] Article 3(a) states: "Respect for inherent dignity, individual autonomy including the freedom to make one's own choices, and independence of persons."

[60] Article 12(2) of the UNCRPD.   [61] Article 12(3) of the UNCRPD.

treaty that does not create new obligations. They contend that US laws meet, and in some cases exceed, the UNCRPD requirements.[62] The United States is moving progressively from substitute to supported decision-making practices and in terms of deinstitutionalization it is much more advanced than most European countries.

The EU is more diversified in adopting Articles 12 and 19, regardless of the European Commissioner for Human Rights' call on member states of the Council of Europe to abolish mechanisms for full incapacitation and plenary guardianship and adopt supported decision-making standards.[63] Deinstitutionalization and community-based policies are slower in several European states and is considered one of the most challenging goals.

The next two chapters (4 and 5) review and discuss community living policies in the United States and EU, and in particular how they handle the deinstitutionalization of people with disabilities. The United States has an ongoing experience of promoting community-living policies based on a civil-rights approach, underpinning US disability discrimination law, which views institutions as violating the American Disabilities Act. On the other hand, the European model leans toward the social welfare and new social models that are gradually adopting American anti-discrimination legislation. Europe is now at a crossroads, trying to implement the 2014–2020 programming period by using the Structural Funds to ease the transition to community living for persons with disabilities.

---

[62] CRS Report prepared by Congressional Research Service on the United Nations Convention on the Rights of People with Disabilities, www.fas.org/sgp/crs/misc/R42749.pdf.

[63] See Commissioners Report: *Who gets to decide? Right to legal capacity for persons with intellectual and psychosocial disabilities.* Council of Europe, Strasbourg, February 20, 2012, https://wcd.coe.int /ViewDoc.jsp?id=1908555.

4

US Policy toward Community Living as Aspects
of Nondiscrimination

The United States is considered a frontrunner in promoting anti-discrimination legislation for people with disabilities.[1] This is marked by the Americans with Disabilities Act (ADA) in 1990 and particularly the Supreme Court decision on *Olmstead v. LC* (1999),[2] the landmark decision that the unnecessary segregation of individuals with disabilities may constitute discrimination based on disability. It is important to trace the roots of community living policy and legislation for people with disabilities in the United States by reviewing and discussing institutionalization, deinstitutionalization, and the civil and legislative milestones contributing to community living policies, and, particularly, the *Olmstead* court decision followed by additional decisions regarding the right to live in the community. There is growing research examining the impact of deinstitutionalization and whether the transition to community-based programs has improved the life of people with disabilities. However, there is no doubt that the seminal *Olmstead* Supreme Court decision is the most important indication of the United States' nondiscriminatory approach to community living.

INSTITUTIONALIZATION OF PEOPLE WITH MENTAL ILLNESS

In Chapter 2, we noted the impact of the American Eugenics Movement on the life of people with disabilities during the nineteenth and twentieth centuries. Almost all people with intellectual, psychiatric, and physical disabilities were then considered genetically inferior and seen as a threat to society. In many states, support for the eugenics movement resulted in legislation requiring mandatory sterilization, incarceration, and in many cases the castration of persons with disabilities who were

---

[1] Theresia Degener and Gerard Quinn, "A survey of international, comparative and regional disability law reform." In Breslin and Yee, *Disability rights law and policy*, 3–129. Degener and Quinn identify and categorize disability anti-discrimination law and policy, including instruments adopted by the United Nations, legislation and constitutional reforms at the level of individual countries, and recent regional reforms.

[2] *Olmstead v. LC.*

placed in large institutions.[3] In the 1940s, new genetic research demonstrated unequivocally that the founding precepts of the eugenics movement were invalid.[4] However, by that time hundreds of thousands of people with intellectual disabilities or psychiatric disabilities had been admitted to state institutions.

Until the nineteenth century, people with psychiatric disabilities were cared for by family members, particularly in rural areas. Mental hospitals were considered as progressive and humanitarian institutions intended to treat people with acute mental illness. Therefore, until 1890 the number of long-term patients in mental institutions was considerably low as compared to acute cases.[5] There is no doubt that the end of the nineteenth century reflects a gradual change in the number of long-term patients, which reached its peak in the early 1950s.[6] One of the reasons for this tremendous change was urbanization, industrialization, and the change in the American workforce that reflected the shift from family to institutional care.

The eugenics movement created the climate of demonizing people with mental illness and encouraging the state to protect society from their threat to public safety. Many states had opened public and state psychiatric hospitals that rapidly became crowded by the poor, since the better-off patients could take refuge in the private philanthropic asylums, such as McLean Hospital in Massachusetts, which required patients to pay their own way.[7]

Several scattered reports from the first half of the twentieth century confirm the change in the character of mental hospitals.[8] Before then, hospitals had significant turnover rates, even though they retained patients who failed to improve or recover.

[3] Philip Reilly, *The surgical solution: A history of involuntary sterilization in the United States* (Baltimore: The Johns Hopkins University Press, 1991), pp. 94–110. The book documented chronically and statistically the sad saga of the involuntary sterilization between 1907 and the early 1960s, of 60,000 in the United States.

[4] Paul A. Lombardo, "Medicine, eugenics, and the Supreme Court: From coercive sterilization to reproductive freedom," *The Journal of Contemporary Health and Law Policy* 13 (1996), 1–25. Lombardo challenges the scientific and legal legitimacy of eugenics in responding to the following questions: do the mentally ill have rights equivalent to the general population in the area of reproduction or anywhere else in civic life, or are they disqualified by their "social inadequacies?" What roles do low IQ or other inherited characteristics play in determining a future criminal career? And, how does the racial composition of the citizenry affect the health of society? He claims that the eugenicists answer incorrectly every time. However, they have been successful in imprinting the laws, and reaction to their legacy played a major part in grounding the case law that now defines reproductive rights.

[5] See Gerald N. Grob, "Mental health policy in America: Myths and realities," *Health Affairs* I (Fall 1992). He reported figures from Worcester State Hospital, the oldest and most important public institution in Massachusetts. In 1842 (a decade after it opened), 46.4 percent of its patients had been hospitalized for less than a year; only 13.2 percent had been in the hospital for five or more years. The comparable figures in 1870 were 49.6 percent and 13.9 percent.

[6] Ibid.   [7] Ibid.

[8] See Ellen Dwyer, *Homes for the mad: Life inside two nineteenth-century asylums* (New Brunswick, NJ: Rutgers University Press, 1987), p. 116. Dwyer evaluated the creation of two New York asylums with distinctly different purposes: the Willard State Hospital and the Utica Asylum. By 1890, New York decided to use Willard as an institution for the incurable insane and Utica as a hospital only for those who showed promise of responding to treatment. Dwyer suggests that approach had a major impact on the nineteenth-century insane asylum and the preference of large hospitals; similar evidence is

In the four decades following the opening of Utica State Lunatic Asylum in the 1840s, the proportion of patients who left the New York institution fluctuated at around 40 percent. The proportion of short-term cases fell and those of long-term increased. For example, 27.8 percent of the nation's total patient population in 1904 had been institutionalized for twelve months or less. This percentage fell to 12.7 by 1910 and to 17.4 in 1923. By the 1930s nearly 80 percent of its mental hospital beds were occupied by chronic patients.

However, the changes were also in the type of patients admitted to state mental hospitals; by 1920, about 18 percent of all first admissions to New York State mental hospitals were diagnosed as psychotic because of senility or arteriosclerosis. Twenty years later the rate had risen to 31 percent. Furthermore, in 1930, 40 percent of all first admissions were aged sixty and over, compared with only 13.2 percent of the state population. A similar pattern was reported by Herbert Goldhamer and Andrew Marshall in their institutionalization study. As late as 1958 nearly one-third of all resident state hospital patients in the nation were over the age of sixty-five.[9]

It is evident that the focus of public policy was on the severely and chronically mentally ill; however, due to the Great Depression (1929–1940), the financial crisis was a burden on state hospitals, and the conditions in them continued to worsen.

Most of the mental hospitals in the United States in the mid-1940s were transformed into permanent custodial care facilities for aged patients suffering from very serious somatic and psychiatric disabilities.

DEINSTITUTIONALIZATION OF PEOPLE WITH MENTAL ILLNESS

A number of factors led to the adoption of deinstitutionalization policy and transition to community care. The first catalyst was growing dissatisfaction with the quality of care in psychiatric hospitals, a major matter of concern to mental health advocates as well as policy-makers. In parallel, the development of new psychotropic drugs,

---

presented in N. A. Dayton, *New facts on mental disorders: Study of 89,190 cases* (Springfield, IL: Charles Thomas, 1940), 414–29.

9   See the following reports: Benjamin Malzberg, "A statistical analysis of the ages of first admissions to hospitals for mental disease in New York State," *Psychiatric Quarterly* 20 (1949), 344–66; Benjamin Malzberg, "A comparison of first admissions to the New York civil state hospitals during 1919–1921 and 1949–1951," *Psychiatric Quarterly* 28 (1954), 312–19; idem, "Trends of mental disease in New York State, 1920–1950," Proceedings of the *American Philosophical Society* 99 (1955), 174–75. Malzberg demonstrated that the rate of hospital admissions for mental disorders was unquestionably rising. In 1903, 186.2 patients out of 100,000 suffered from psychiatric ill health; in 1952, that rate was 386.8. Herbert Goldhamer and Andrew W. Marshall, *Psychosis and civilization: Two studies in the frequency of mental disease* (Glencoe, IL: Free Press, 1953). Goldhamer and Marshall found that for about one hundred years, from the middle of the nineteenth century to the 1950s, there was a remarkable stability in the rates of mental illness in the United States. Changes in public awareness of problems appear to be much more volatile than the changes in the actual state of affairs in many areas

and particularly the widespread use of thorazine in 1955, reduced the need for extended hospitalization.[10]

An additional catalyst was a number of court decisions. What has become known as the "least restrictive alternative," called for involuntary admission to psychiatric hospitals only if there were no other treatment options. Until the 1975 decision in *O'Connor v. Donaldson*, there had been no Supreme Court ruling on the due process rights of involuntary civilly committed mental patients except in cases involving criminal convictions of mentally ill persons. The court in *O'Connor* held that mentally ill persons were entitled to due process. Thus, to confine a person involuntarily violates due process if it cannot be shown that he or she is dangerous to himself/herself or to others.[11] This historical decision affected most of those hospitalized against their will, since very few of them were actually found to be dangerous at the time of their commitment.

Other remarkable milestones were the passage of the National Mental Health Act, which provided federal funding for psychiatric education and research,[12] and the Community Mental Health Act of 1963[13] which provided funding for community living and programs.

THE DEVELOPMENT OF DEINSTITUTIONALIZATION COMMUNITY SUPPORT POLICIES

A historical and conceptual analysis of deinstitutionalization reveals that the goals have been changed over time. The first era (from 1950 to 1970) marked the growing impact of the civil rights movement and the Rehabilitation Act of 1973 ("Rehab Act"). Disability rights advocates protested against the inhumane conditions in institutions and, more importantly, there was a new focus on personal autonomy

[10]   Randall G. Krieg, "An interdisciplinary look at the deinstitutionalization of the mentally ill," *The Social Science Journal* 38 (2001), 367–68.

[11]   "[A] State cannot constitutionally confine without more a non-dangerous individual who is capable of surviving safely in freedom by himself or with the help of willing and responsible family members or friends." 422 U.S. at 576.

[12]   The National Mental Health Act was designed to improve the mental health of US citizens through research into the causes, diagnosis, and treatment of psychiatric disorders. It authorized the surgeon general to support research, training, and assistance to state mental health programs (PL 79–487, 60 Stat. L. 421.) (The National Institute of Mental Health was established under the authority of this law on April 15, 1949).

[13]   Congress in 1963 enacted the Community Mental Health Centers Act authorizing appropriations of $150 million over fiscal years 1965–1967 for grants to the states to pay from one-third to two-thirds of the costs of constructing public and private nonprofit community mental health centers for the prevention, diagnosis, treatment, and rehabilitation of mentally ill patients in their own communities. The Act was part of a comprehensive mental health package, the Mental Retardation Facilities and Community Mental Health Centers Construction Act of 1963 (PL 88–164), proposed by the Kennedy administration and in large part endorsed by Congress. An administration-backed section providing federal assistance for staffing centers was included in the Senate version, but was deleted in the House and in conference between the Senate and House.

and individual rights.[14] The most important concept used at the time was the "normalization principle" which means living in the Least Restrictive Environment (LRE).[15] The key legislative impetus behind this movement was the Rehab Act, and in particular Section 504 which addresses discrimination against people with physical and mental disabilities.[16] Specifically, it prohibited federal programs from excluding persons on the basis of disability and provided the framework for vocational rehabilitation and independent living.

The second era is characterized by increased advocacy and the growing importance of research and empirical research that demonstrated the preference of community-based placements over institutional care.[17] Despite the progress, this period is not free of setbacks, such as the 1981 Supreme Court refusal to find an articulated right to treatment in the least restrictive environment under the Developmental Disabilities Assistance and Bill of Rights Act ("DDA Act"[18]) in

---

[14]   Advocates realized that this new law would need regulations in order to be implemented and enforced. By 1977, Presidents Richard Nixon and Gerald Ford had come and gone. Jimmy Carter had become president and had appointed Joseph Califano as his secretary of Health, Education, and Welfare (HEW). Califano refused to issue regulations and was given an ultimatum and deadline of April 4, 1977. April 4 went by with no regulations and no word from Califano. On April 5, demonstrations by people with disabilities took place in ten cities across the country. In San Francisco, protesters refused to disband. Demonstrators, more than 150 people with disabilities, had taken over the federal office building and refused to leave. They stayed until May 1. Califano had issued regulations by April 28, but the protesters remained until they had reviewed the regulations and approved of them.

[15]   Least Restrictive Environment (LRE) refers to the Individuals with Disabilities Education Act [20 United States Code (U.S.C.) Sec. 1412(a)(5)(A); 34 Code of Federal Regulations (C.F.R.) Sec. 300.114.] mandate that students with disabilities should be educated to the maximum extent appropriate for peers without disabilities. The LRE mandate ensures that schools educate students with disabilities in integrated settings, alongside students with and without disabilities, to the maximum extent appropriate. Least restrictive environment is not a particular setting. The term the "Least Restrictive Environment Continuum" was also used in the late 1960s and early 1970s to reflect a progressive approach of transitioning institutionalized disabled persons to least restrictive settings. LRE appears in *Pennhurst State School and Hospital v. Halderman*, 451 U.S. 1, 5 (1981), as a guiding treatment and habilitation principle to provide the service in the setting that is least restrictive of the person's personal liberty.

[16]   Section 504 of the Rehabilitation Act of 1973, Pub. L. No. 93–112, 87 Stat. 394 (Sept. 26, 1973), codified at 29 U.S.C. § 701 et seq.

[17]   See, for example, Charlie C. Lakin, *Demographic studies of residential facilities for mentally retarded people: An historical review of methodologies and findings* (Minneapolis: University of Minnesota, Center for Residential Services and Community Living, 1979); Heather Hemming, "Follow up of adults with mental retardation transferred from large institutions to new small units," *Mental Retardation* 24 (1986), 229–35.

[18]   The Developmentally Disabled Assistance and Bill of Rights Act (Act) established a federal-state grant program whereby the Federal Government provides financial assistance to participating states to aid them in creating programs to care for and treat the developmentally disabled. The Act is voluntary, and the states are given the choice of complying with the conditions set forth in the Act or forgoing the benefits of federal funding. The "bill of rights" provision of the Act, 42 U.S.C. §§ 6010(1) and(2), states that mentally retarded persons "have a right to appropriate treatment, services, and habilitation" in "the setting that is least restrictive of . . . personal liberty."

Pennhurst State School and Hospital v. Halderman.[19] The third era marked the most significant change after the enactment of the ADA.[20]

THE FIRST ERA OF DEINSTITUTIONALIZATION

During the early years, effort was concentrated on moving individuals out of state public mental hospitals. The first stage was transitioning the hospitalized population from asylums to community-based residences. The number of residents of state institutions was reduced from 559,000 in 1955 to 154,000 in 1980.[21] From the beginning of 1980s, the focus changed to improving and expanding the range of services and supports for those living in the community. The closure of whole institutions began in the early 1990s, recognizing the importance of human and civil rights and societal and community inclusion. This trend has been strengthened in the twenty-first century.

Initially, the states focused on emptying state institutions by transferring those individuals who could be treated in the community. The core reason for this policy was an economic one, reducing the cost of state hospitals, which required a 300 percent increase in spending in the 1980s.[22] In practice, the process was slow[23] and only accelerated into a full-scale project in the late 1960s and 1970s when the federal government stepped in. The establishment of the Joint Commission on Mental Health marked the formal change.

The report released to Congress known as *Action for Mental Health* called for the assessment of mental health conditions and resources in an effort to arrive at a national program that would approach adequacy in meeting the individual needs of America's mentally ill.[24] The commission called for a doubling of the

[19] See *Pennhurst State School and Hospital v. Halderman* (No. 79–1404)1981, www.law.cornell.edu /supremecourt/text/451/1. Terri Lee Halderman, an intellectually disabled resident of Pennhurst, brought a class action in the Federal District Court on behalf of herself and all other Pennhurst residents against Pennhurst State School and various officials responsible for its operation. It was alleged, inter alia, that conditions at Pennhurst were unsanitary, inhumane, and dangerous, and that such conditions denied the class members various specified constitutional and statutory rights, including rights under the Act, and, in addition to seeking injunctive and monetary relief, it was urged that Pennhurst be closed and that community living arrangements be established for its residents. The District Court found that certain of the claimed rights were violated and granted the relief sought. The Court of Appeals substantially affirmed, but avoided the constitutional claims and instead held that § 6010 created substantive rights in favor of the intellectually disabled, that persons with intellectual disabilities had an implied cause of action to enforce those rights, and that the conditions at Pennhurst violated those rights. The court further found that Congress enacted the Act pursuant to both § 5 of the Fourteenth Amendment and the spending power.
[20] Americans with Disabilities Act of 1990 as Amended, www.ada.gov/pubs/adastatute08.pdf.
[21] Chris Koyanagi, *Learning from history: Deinstitutionalization of people with mental illness as precursor to long-term care reform* (Menlo Park, CA: The Kaiser Family Foundation, 2007), p. 1.
[22] See Harry A. Foley and Steven S. Sharfstein, *Madness and government: Who cares for the mentally ill?* (Washington, DC: American Psychiatric Press, 1983), p. 33.
[23] From 1956 to 1962, the resident population in institutions reduced from 559,000 to 505,000.
[24] Joint Commission on Mental Illness and Health, *Action for mental health* (New York: Basic Books, 1961).

budget on mental health services in five years, and tripling it in ten years. It also requested increases in training to ensure availability of the necessary workforce to serve this population.

There is always a discrepancy between policy recommendations and actual implementation by government. President John F. Kennedy's message in 1963 to Congress marks an evident change in the federal government's deinstitutionalization policy. He called to replace institutions with community programs, including outpatient care, day treatment, rehabilitation, foster-home services, and public education on mental health. The president made it clear that the funding, spending, and allocation of responsibilities had to be changed. He tripled the budget allocated to local and nonprofit agencies and allowed them to be responsible for community-based programs. In his view, the states would remain responsible for long-term institutional services, with the hidden assumption that state hospitals would be replaced by the community programs.[25]

In 1963, the federal government provided funds for the construction of facilities to serve as community mental health centers (CMHCs).[26] The Community Mental Health Centers Construction Act Amendments of 1965[27] was intended to provide federal support for eight years and beyond. In addition, the states had to offer similar funding for community mental health programs.[28]

Additional sources of funding for community mental health services came from the creation of Medicaid and Medicare in 1965. Medicaid coverage of general hospital psychiatric services allowed the addition of a significant number of acute care beds in the community for psychiatric patients. From 1955 to 1977 general hospitals more than doubled their psychiatric patient-care episodes, as state hospital

---

[25] Foley and Sharfstein, *Madness and government*, p. 50; deinstitutionalization could not exist without tremendous support from civil rights activists who challenged in court the poor civil rights conditions in mental health institutions. The centrality of court decisions against institutionalization and the preference for community placement will be discussed separately.

[26] The Community Mental Health Act of 1963 (CMHA) (also known as the Community Mental Health Centers Construction Act, Mental Retardation Facilities and Construction Act, Public Law 88–164, or the Mental Retardation and Community Mental Health Centers Construction Act of 1963) was an act to provide federal funding for community mental health centers in the United States. This legislation was passed as part of John F. Kennedy's New Frontier plan. It led to considerable deinstitutionalization.

[27] In 1965, Congress reversed itself on the staffing issue and enacted a law (PL 89–105) amending PL 88–164 by authorizing federal grants to help pay for the salaries of professional and technical staff in mental health centers. The measure was proposed by president Lyndon B. Johnson. It authorized appropriations of $19.5 million in fiscal 1966, $24 million in fiscal 1967, and $30 million in fiscal 1968 for the grants. Such sums as were necessary were authorized for follow-up grants during fiscal 1967–1972 to centers that had received initial staffing grants under the fiscal 1966–1968 specific authorizations.

[28] PL 89–105 required the provision of five core services: inpatient, outpatient, emergency, partial hospitalization, and consultation and education on mental health. A second list of services was recommended, but not required: pre-admission screening, post-discharge services, and rehabilitation for individuals with serious mental illnesses.

use declined by 30 percent over the same period.[29] General hospitals contributed to the deinstitutionalization policy by offering short-term hospitalization and follow-up outpatient services. However, Medicaid funding to nursing homes had a less positive effect, as it encouraged states to transfer state hospital patients into these settings.

The enactment of Supplemental Security Income (SSI) in 1972 was probably the most important step in deinstitutionalization efforts, allowing people with psychiatric disabilities to receive disability benefits and supporting living costs for many people discharged from state institutions.

Was the early phase of deinstitutionalization successful? If the main indicator is reduction in state hospital placement, the policy was considered a success. By 1977, there were 650 community mental health centers covering 43 percent of the population and serving 1.9 million individuals a year. In addition, most of the mental health episodes shifted from state hospitals to local general hospitals,[30] and the lengths of hospital stays dropped significantly from six months in 1954 to twenty-three days in 1980.[31]

However, the first phase of deinstitutionalization suffered from financial, organizational, and programmatic problems, as the focus was on preventing institutionalization rather than providing comprehensive community-based programs. In retrospect, it is evident that deinstitutionalization at the initial stage had been well intentioned but left many people in far worse conditions than they had endured back in the asylums. Massive deinstitutionalization in the 1970s and 1980s, well before communities had organized reasonable community services, contributed to neglect of people with mental illnesses and homelessness.

THE SECOND ERA: BUILDING UP COMMUNITY SUPPORT

Since the 1970s, there has been a shift in government policy to build up the community support system. The first efforts were credited to the National Institute of Mental Health which created in 1975 the Community Support Program (CSP),[32] providing grants to state mental health authorities for planning a comprehensive range of mental health services and other supports to help adults with serious mental illnesses live successfully in the community. However, the change of the locus of care was a necessary but insufficient step in successful deinstitutionalization. The funding for CSP was marginal: $6 million for 1980–1983 with an increase to $19 million in 1988.

---

[29] Leona L. Bachrach, "The effects of deinstitutionalization on general hospital psychiatry," *Hospital and Community Psychiatry* 32 (1981), 786.

[30] Foley and Sharfstein, *Madness and government*, p. 103.

[31] Carl A. Taube and Samuel A. Barrett, *Mental health, United States* (Washington, DC: US Government Printing Office, 1985), DHHS Pub. No (ADM), 85–1378.

[32] For further reading on the Community Support Program, see Judith C. Turner and William J. Ten Hoor, "The NIMH community support program: Pilot approach to a needed social reform," *Journal of Schizophrenia Bulletin* 4 (1978), 319–48.

The most important message came from President Carter's Commission on Mental Health,[33] which called for a new national priority for adults and children with serious mental disorders and recommended an orderly phase-down of state hospitals through performance contracts that would integrate federal and state funding. The Mental Health Systems Act of 1980 offered numerous changes to the federal CMHC program, including expanding services beyond clinical care alone.

Deinstitutionalization policy, based on the Mental Health Systems Act, was repealed and funds for community mental health shifted into a block grant to the states. Federal funding was also cut by 25 percent. A further cut in the 1980s during the Reagan administration significantly reduced federal spending on human service programs. The administration also slashed federal support for public housing. As low-income housing became less available, a substantial number of people with serious mental illnesses were left with no community support.

Although deinstitutionalization policy suffered tremendous cuts by state and federal governments, there was some progress during the 1980s. States discovered that, through the Rehabilitation Service category of Medicaid, reimbursement could be claimed for a range of services that improved the functioning of people with serious mental illnesses.[34] At the federal level, important recommendations in the National Plan began to take effect through changes to Medicaid. A new Medicaid service of targeted case management specifically allowed states to serve individuals with chronic and persistent mental illness, and Medicare was amended to equalize the co-payment for medication management services.[35]

The 1990s brought significant legal change through the enactment of the ADA in 1990[36] and, in 1988, amendments to the Fair Housing Act extended its protections to people with disabilities.[37]

[33] See White House Press Secretary Release, "Executive order, President's Commission on Mental Health," February 17, 1977, box 25, Presidential Commission on Mental Health Papers, record group 25, Carter Presidential Library.
[34] Medicaid is a federal-state health insurance program for persons with limited income and/or disabilities. Medicaid allows states to use federal dollars to match state dollars for defined services. One category of Medicaid services incorporates rehabilitative, community-based services to persons with psychiatric and co-occurring psychiatric-substance abuse diagnosis. This category is known as the Medicaid Rehabilitation Option or MRO. Medicaid also pays for behavioral health services through the Clinic Option and through Targeted Case Management (TCM). The MRO services have the advantages of being reimbursed for delivery in clients' natural settings as well as in offices. They focus specifically on assisting clients to gain skills and resources that allow them to live and function as independently as possible.
[35] Koyanagi, *Learning from history*, pp. 1–22.
[36] The ADA is the nation's first comprehensive civil rights law addressing the needs of people with disabilities, prohibiting discrimination in employment, public services, public accommodations, and telecommunications.
[37] The US Department of Housing and Urban Development (HUD) has played a leading role in the administration of the Fair Housing Act since its adoption in 1968. The 1988 amendments, however, have greatly increased the department's enforcement role. First, the newly protected classes have proven to be significant sources of new complaints. Second, HUD's expanded enforcement role took the department beyond investigation and conciliation into the mandatory enforcement area.

However, the focus on disability rights legislation has been associated with growing criticism of deinstitutionalization for focusing more on emptying state mental hospitals than improving the conditions and well-being of the persons themselves.[38] In a survey that examined the years 2004–2005, E. Fuller Torrey and colleagues found that the reduction in beds in mental hospitals[39] resulted in a significant increase in the number of seriously mentally ill persons in jails, with 16 percent of inmates in jails and prisons suffering from serious mental illness, compared to 6.4 percent in 1983. In other words, poorly planned deinstitutionalization indirectly caused the placement of more seriously mentally ill people in prisons and jails.

The situation has worsened due to tremendous cuts in public funding. From 2009 to 2011 there was a significant reduction in non-Medicaid state mental health spending of more than $1.8 billion dollars.[40] States have cut core services for tens of thousands of youths and adults living with the most serious mental illness.[41] These services included community- and hospital-based psychiatric care, housing, and access to medications. Medicaid funding of mental health services was also reduced, shifting financial responsibility to emergency rooms, community hospitals, law enforcement agencies, correctional facilities, and homeless shelters.

IMPACT OF DEINSTITUTIONALIZATION: LESSONS FROM RESEARCH STUDIES

There is a paucity of research on the impact of deinstitutionalization of people with mental illness in the United States. The "Vermont study"[42] – a follow up study of thirty-two years of 269 backward patients from Vermont State Hospital, released to

---

[38] For more details, see E. Fuller Torrey, *Nowhere to go: The tragic odyssey of the homeless mentally ill* (New York: Harper and Row, 1988). Torrey, a writer and psychiatrist, argues that there are now more mentally ill people living on the streets than in the nation's mental hospitals, and that an increasing proportion of them are filling up the prisons. He claims that while only a small proportion of mentally ill people ever become dangerous – and even potentially dangerous paranoid schizophrenics are unlikely to become violent if properly treated – people with serious mental illnesses are now routinely released from hospitals with no arrangement for continued treatment. As a result, Fuller says, the number of violent crimes they commit is rising rapidly.

[39] In 1955, there were 558,239 patients in the state mental hospitals; by the end of 1994, this figure had decreased to 71,619, meaning that 87 percent of the hospital beds had been closed.

[40] See a comprehensive report by NAMI documenting state-by-state funding changes for public mental health services since 2009 for youth and adults living with serious mental illness. The report also describes how states have chosen to implement these funding cuts. The report concludes with policy recommendations focused on the steps that should be taken to ensure that valuable public resources are spent wisely and effectively. It is written by Ron Honberg et al., *State mental health cuts: A national crisis*, National Alliance on Mental Illness (NAMI, March 2011). Retrieved December 20, 2015, from www2.nami.org/ContentManagement/ContentDisplay.cfm?ContentFileID=125018.

[41] California cut $587.4 million during this period, Kentucky $193.7 million, New York $132 million, and Illinois $113.7 million.

[42] M. Courtenay et al., "The Vermont longitudinal study of persons with severe mental illness, I: Methodology, study sample, and overall status 32 years later," *American Journal of Psychiatry* 144 (1987), 718–26.

the community in the mid-1950s – presents longitudinal data about those released in the early wave of deinstitutionalization. At their ten-year follow up it was found that about 70 percent of these patients remained out of the hospital but substantial numbers of them reported social isolation and recidivism. From twenty to twenty-five years after their index release, 262 of them were blindly assessed with structured and reliable protocols. Of the group, one-half to two-thirds had achieved considerable improvement or recovery.

In the beginning of the twenty-first century there has been a tendency to study the contribution of the deinstitutionalization of the people with mental illness to growth in the US incarceration rate. One of the most updated studies carried out by Raphael and Stoll assessed the degree to which this population, which would have been in mental hospitals in past years, was transinstitutionalized to prisons and jails.[43] They found no evidence of transinstitutionalization for any demographic groups for the period 1950–1980. However, for the twenty-year period 1980–2000, they identified significant transinstitutionalization rates for all men and women, with a relatively large transinstitutionalization rate for men in comparison to women and the largest transinstitutionalization rate observed for white men. Their estimates suggested that 4–7 percent of incarceration growth between 1980 and 2000 was attributable to deinstitutionalization.

DEINSTITUTIONALIZATION OF PEOPLE WITH INTELLECTUAL DISABILITIES

The general view of people with intellectual disabilities in the United States in the nineteenth century was dominated by efforts to educate the "poor idiots" and to make them socially competent. This was gradually transformed during the first half of the twentieth century by the eugenics approach, which intended to identify, sterilize, and segregate every feebleminded person in order to maintain racial purity and protect society.[44] The crack in this regressive approach began after 1950, and led to the adoption of the deinstitutionalization and human rights approaches, although traces of segregated and excluded elements still exist.

The first residential school for children with intellectual disabilities was opened in 1848 in Boston in a wing of the Perkins Institute for the Blind.[45] The overwhelming belief at that time was that intellectual disability was associated with the immoral behavior of one of the parents, as suggested in Howe's early study.[46] The 1850s and 1860s saw the opening of private residential schools in the

---

[43] Steven Raphael and Michael A. Stoll, "Assessing the contribution of the deinstitutionalization of the mentally ill to growth in the U.S. incarceration rate," *Journal of Legal Studies* 42 (2013), 187–222.

[44] President's Committee on Mental Retardation, *Mental retardation: Past and present* (Washington, DC: US Government Printing Office, 1977), p. 2.

[45] See Perkins School for the Blind's Legacy at www.perkins.org/history/legacy.

[46] Samuel Gridley Howe, *Report made to the legislature of Massachusetts, upon idiocy* (Boston: Printed from the state ed. by Coolidge & Wiley, 1948). Retrieved December 11, 2015 from http://archive.org

Northeast,[47] and the first institution for children with developmental and intellectual disabilities was opened in Syracuse in 1851.[48]

During that time, more experimental residential schools were opened, including in Pennsylvania, Ohio, Kentucky, and Illinois. In 1875, there were 1,041 persons with intellectual disabilities residing in public and private facilities in seven states. These residential schools were quite successful in training children with developmental disabilities and the majority returned to their homes and communities as productive young workers. However, by 1880 most of the residential schools were turned into custodial asylums, which reduced their educational and training programs to a minimum.[49]

Economic hardship was associated with less favorable attitudes toward people with disabilities and an acceptance by the majority of the professional community that custodial institutions might be the least negative solution. Economic pressures were making it more and more difficult for families to continue educating or caring for family members on their own, but it wasn't until the states promised funding that schools for the feebleminded began accepting those with more extensive care needs.

Not only was there more funding for custodial care over time, but economic fluctuations made it more and more difficult to place even trained individuals in the community. By the time that eugenics portrayed children and adults with intellectual disabilities as a threat to society, the idea of custodial and institutional care was already in place.[50] The rationale for institutional care, inspired by the concept of eugenics, was expressed by Mr. Edward R. Johnson's plan for Vineland Institution in New Jersey:[51]

1. All feebleminded children under the age of 12 (or until they become dangerous sexually or otherwise) excepting idiots, should be sent to the Special Classes in the public schools. The parents will thus bear the expense of housing, feeding, and clothing their own children for these years. The only public expense will be

/details/66450930R.nlm.nih.gov. In the same year, Samuel Gridley Howe established the Massachusetts School for Idiotic Children and Youth, one of the first of its kind in the United States.

47 For further reading, see Mary Bernie-Smith, James R. Patton and Shannon H. Kim, *Mental Retardation: An introduction to intellectual disabilities* (New York: Pearson, 2005, 7th edition).

48 The Syracuse State Institution for Feebleminded Children. The New York State Custodial Asylum for Feebleminded Women first opened in 1878 as a branch of the Syracuse State Institution for Feebleminded Children, but was made an independent institution and located at Newark in 1885. Additional information about the care in New York State between 1736 and 1912 can be retrieved from www.socialwelfarehistory.com/programs/mental-health/care-insane-new-york-1736-1912/.

49 Wolf Wolfersberger, "The origin and nature of our institutional models". In *Changing patterns in residential services for the mentally retarded*. Edited by R. B. Kugel and W. Wolfersberger (Washington, DC: President's Committee on Mental Retardation, 1969, pp. 59–171).

50 Walter E. Fernald thought that "feebleminded women are almost invariably immoral, and if at large usually become carriers of venereal disease and give birth to children who are as defective as themselves. The feebleminded woman who marries is twice as prolific as the normal woman." See Walter E. Fernald, "The burden of feeble mindedness," *Journal of Psycho-Asthenics* 17 (1912): 87–111.

51 Edward R. Johnstone, *A plan for the care of the feebleminded* (Vineland, NJ: The Training School, 1912), pp. 97–98.

that of the school, and if the training is largely physical and manual, much good will be accomplished.

2. Cities with a sufficient number of feebleminded children between the ages of 12 and 20 will establish municipal residential institutions which should be under the control of the educational authorities. Children from the Special Classes would be committed to the institution at the proper age. Here the expense must be borne by the municipality, the parents contributing what they are able, and the State assisting as it does in county care of the insane.

3. Those who are 21 years old and over "and the number have still further decreased," can be cared for by the State at its central custodial institutions at Vineland (women) and Skillman (men), and the transfers should be made directly from the institutions for children to the State – the parents contributing what they are able as they now do.

4. All idiotic cases – those whose personal habits are unclean and who need special care – should be cared for in the above institutions, or better still in the almshouses.

There is no doubt that the distorted images created more pressure to continue the trends, and between 1880 and 1900 the institutionalized intellectually disabled/developmentally disabled population rose from a little over 4,000 to 15,000.[52] The states continued building institutions and expanding custodial care in the existing ones, sending a clear message to society that they would be run efficiently to reduce spending. However, the attempt to completely segregate the population of persons with intellectual disabilities was an utter failure, and came at an appalling cost in dehumanization, exploitation, and degradation.

In 1925, there were about 40,000 in custodial institutions. Surprisingly, the greatest increase took place between 1925 and 1950 as the institutional populations grew to 128,000. After 1950, it reached a final peak of 190,000 in public institutions. Since that time, the deinstitutionalization movement, accompanied by the growth of community services, brought about a reduction for the first time since the institutional movement began. In 1975, the institutional population was estimated to be between 165,000 and 170,000, less than that of 1950.[53] It appears that the main reason

---

[52] For comprehensive reading on institutional care in the United States, see Steven Noll and James Trent, *Mental retardation in America: A historical reader* (New York: New York University Press, 2004). The book includes essays by a wide range of authors who approach the problems of intellectual disabilities from many differing points of view. This work is divided into five sections, each following in chronological order the major changes in the treatment of this population in the United States. It covers topics ranging from representations of the intellectual disability as social burdens and social menaces, Freudian-inspired ideas of adjustment and adaptation, the relationship between community care and institutional treatment, historical events such as the *Buck v. Bell* decision which upheld the opinion on eugenic sterilization, the evolution of the disability rights movement, and the passage of the ADA in 1990.

[53] President's Committee on Mental Retardation (PCMR). *Mental retardation past and present* (Washington, DC: US Government Printing Office, 1977), p. 15. The President's Panel saw clearly the need to develop the entire plan of action into a cohesive, flexible, dynamic, and effective attack on

for the tremendous increase in institutional care after the 1930s was the Great Depression, followed by World War II in the 1940s. These events had a major effect on the American family, which preferred to ease its economic burden by leaning toward out-of-home placement.

DEINSTITUTIONALIZATION OF PEOPLE WITH INTELLECTUAL DISABILITIES (ID)

The national deinstitutionalization movement for individuals with intellectual and developmental disabilities in the United States of America began in 1967 when the population of individuals with ID/DD living in isolated institutional settings peaked at 194,650 and has continuously declined ever since.[54] A major catalyst for the deinstitutionalization of the ID/DD population was a series of class action lawsuits and an increasingly growing protest against the inhuman conditions and practices in these institutions. These important and significant developments increased awareness of alternative care options, particularly for those residents who were capable of living in the community.

It is important to note that the early wave of lawsuits resulted in decrees requiring states to improve conditions at public institutions without expanding the option of community-based programs. The 1970s brought an additional challenge – to eliminate the unnecessary institutionalization of people with developmental disabilities who were capable of living in their own communities. The most important development came later when, in 1991, New Hampshire and the District of Columbia became the first state and jurisdiction to close their only public institutions for people with developmental disabilities and develop a delivery system based entirely on community-based services. Since then, six states – Alaska, Maine, New Mexico, Rhode Island, Vermont, and West Virginia – followed suit, and other states are using waivers and other innovative ways to reduce their dependence on institutional care.[55] The shift from institutional to community care is reflected in articles published in the *American Journal of Mental Deficiency* between 1970 and 1975 and 1980 and 1985. Over this decade, there was a twofold increase in the proportion of articles concerning community placement – from 7 percent to 14 percent – and a dramatic shift in the sources for all research subjects. In the early 1970s, nearly 74 percent of

the totality of problems concerning programs for the mentally retarded in the United States. To this end, the panel made several recommendations regarding organization, planning, and coordination of programs. The history of subsequent federal legislation to implement these recommendations during the administrations of presidents Kennedy, Johnson, and Nixon is introduced in the above report.

54 Naomi Scott, Charlie K. Lakin, and Sheryl A. Larson, "The 40th anniversary of deinstitutionalization in the United States: Decreasing state institutional populations, 1967–2007," *Intellectual and Developmental Disabilities* 46 (2008), 402–05.

55 David Braddock et al., "The state of the states in developmental disabilities: Summary of the study." In *The state of the states in developmental disabilities*. Edited by David Braddock et al. (Washington, DC: American Association of Mental Retardation, 1998), pp. 23–54.

the 83,771 subjects included in 544 research reports came from institutional populations; by the 1980s, only 13 percent of 136,074 subjects (456 articles) lived in public residential facilities.[56]

THE RIGHT TO HUMANE TREATMENT
IN INSTITUTIONAL SETTINGS

In the 1960s and 1970s, the public and the courts became concerned about the lack of therapeutic and habilitation services in public institutions for people with intellectual disabilities. The most important institutional rights case litigated in the 1970s was *Wyatt v. Stickney.*[57] A federal court in Alabama held for the first time that people who are involuntarily committed to state institutions because of mental illness or developmental disabilities have a constitutional right to treatment that would afford them a realistic opportunity to return to society. *Wyatt v. Stickney* was the seminal case in achieving drastic deinstitutionalization of previously committed patients. Following Judge Frank M. Johnson's decision, there was similar litigation in a number of states, among them Louisiana, Minnesota, and Ohio. Rather than face costly court-imposed standards, some of them impossible to meet (Alabama's efforts to recruit psychiatrists were unsuccessful), states rapidly emptied their hospitals. In the case of Alabama, the population at its state psychiatric hospitals was reduced by almost two-thirds between 1970 and 1975. The Wyatt litigation was also significant in giving birth to the Mental Health Law Project (known as the Bazelon Center for Mental Health Law).[58]

A typical example is *Welsch v. Likins,*[59] in which six residents of six different Minnesota state hospitals filed a lawsuit in the US District Court for the District of Minnesota alleging that conditions in the institutions violated their constitutional

---

56   Sharon Landesman and Earl Butterfield, "Normalization and deinstitutionalization of mentally retarded individuals: Controversy and facts," *American Psychologist* 42 (1987), 809–16. The article examines the sources of the controversy over normalization and deinstitutionalization, claiming that although they led the field of intellectual disability for more than two decades they lacked a substantial scientific base, particularly the impact of environmental change on functioning.

57   *Wyatt v. Stickney,* 325 F. Supp. 781 (M.D. Ala. 1971). Can be retrieved from http://law.justia.com /cases/federal/district-courts/FSupp/325/781/2594259/.

58   The Bazelon Center for Mental Health Law is a national legal-advocacy organization representing people with mental disabilities in the United States. Originally known as The Mental Health Law Project, the Center was founded as a national public-interest organization in 1972 by a group of specialized attorneys and mental disability professionals who were working to help the court define a constitutional right to treatment in terms of specific standards for services and protections. In 1993, the organization changed its name to the Judge David L. Bazelon Center for Mental Health Law to honor the legacy of Judge David L. Bazelon, whose decisions as chief judge of the United States Court of Appeals for the District of Columbia Circuit pioneered the field of mental health law.

59   See *Welsch v. Likins,* 373 F. Supp. 487, 490–91 (4th D. Minn. 1974). Retrieved July 2, 2015 from http://disabilityjustice.org/suits-involving-the-cambridge-state-hospital-cambridge-minnesota /welsch-v-likins/.

rights under the Eighth and Fourteenth Amendments to the Constitution.[60] Judge Earl Larson, who relied on the *Wyatt v. Stickney* court decision, ruled in favor of the plaintiffs.[61] He stated that a "growing body of law recognizing a constitutional right to treatment for persons confined in various settings without having been found culpable of criminal conduct,"[62] holding that "due process requires that civil commitment for reasons of mental retardation be accompanied by minimally adequate treatment designed to give each committed person a realistic opportunity to be cured or to improve his or her mental condition."[63]

Moreover, the Due Process Clause requires "that State officials charged with obligations for the care and custody of civilly committed persons make good faith attempts to place such persons in settings that will be suitable and appropriate to their mental and physical conditions while least restrictive of their liberties."[64]

One of the most important court decisions in the United States was associated with the abusive, inhumane living conditions of the residents with developmental disabilities at Pennhurst State School and Hospital, in Spring Hill, Pennsylvania.[65]

On May 30, 1974 a class action lawsuit was filed in the US District Court for the Eastern District of Pennsylvania on behalf of former and current residents of Pennhurst against the institution (known as *Halderman v. Pennhurst State School and Hospital*). The plaintiffs argued that the institutionalization of the residents violated their constitutional rights under the First, Eighth, Ninth, and Fourteenth Amendments, as well as under federal civil rights laws and the Pennsylvania Mental Health and Mental Retardation Act of 1966. They sought damages and equitable relief, including the closing of Pennhurst, and provision of education, training, and care in community settings.

US District Court Judge Raymond J. Broderick found that Pennhurst was overcrowded, understaffed, and lacked the programs needed for adequate habilitation. He also found that various unwarranted forms of restraints "were used as control measures in lieu of adequate staffing,"[66] including seclusion rooms, physical restraints, and psychotropic drugs. The physical environment was found to be "hazardous to the residents, both physically and psychologically"[67] and residents were found to have been subjected to abuse by both other residents and staff.[68] The decision ruled in the plaintiffs' favor. In a wide-ranging opinion, he found that

---

[60] Specifically, they claimed that the failure to provide an adequate program of habilitation violated their right to treatment under the Due Process Clause of the Fourteenth Amendment; that the failure to develop less restrictive, community-based alternatives for care and treatment violated the Due Process Clause of the Fourteenth Amendment; and that certain restrictions and conditions at the institution violated the Cruel and Unusual Punishment Clause of the Eighth Amendment.

[61] Ibid.   [62] Ibid. at 497.   [63] Ibid. at 499.   [64] Ibid. at 512.

[65] The conditions in this institution were brought to the public's attention in 1968 in a five-part television exposé by Bill Baldini called *Suffer the little children*. While the airing of the documentary resulted in some improvements, particularly related to the development of early community supports, conditions at Pennhurst continued to deteriorate.

[66] *Halderman v. Pennhurst State School and Hospital*, 446 F. Supp. 1295, 1306 (E.D. Pa. 1977).

[67] Ibid. at 1308.   [68] Ibid. at 1308–1309.

the residents of Pennhurst had three distinct sets of constitutional rights: the right to habilitation, the right to be free from harm, and the right to non-discriminatory habilitation.

Finally, the Supreme Court case decision in *Youngberg v. Romeo*, 457 U.S. 307 (1982) is probably one of the most significant decisions affirming certain substantive liberty rights of people with intellectual disabilities. The plaintiff was Nicholas Romeo, a person with profound ID, who was involuntarily and permanently committed to the Pennhurst State School and Hospital. Mrs. Romeo filed a federal lawsuit on her son's behalf, claiming that Pennhurst administrators knew about his recurrent injuries and did nothing. The institution violated the Eighth Amendment's prohibition of cruel and unusual punishment, and the Fourteenth Amendment's due process guarantee. The complaint requested both monetary damages and injunctive relief. Nicholas Romeo subsequently broke his arm and was transferred to the Pennhurst hospital ward, where he remained under physical restraint for parts of each day. However, the request for individual injunctive relief in Romeo's lawsuit was withdrawn because he was also a member of a class-action case in what would become another significant Supreme Court decision, *Pennhurst State School and Hospital v. Halderman*.

At trial, the jury issued a verdict in favor of defendant Pennhurst. The Court of Appeals for the Third Circuit reversed the jury verdict and remanded the case for a new trial. The US Supreme Court ruled that the Fourteenth Amendment's due process guarantee protected the rights of individuals with intellectual disabilities involuntarily committed to state institutions for reasonably safe conditions of confinement, freedom from unreasonable bodily restraints, and minimally adequate habilitation training at those facilities. *Youngberg v. Romeo* is notable as the first occasion in which the Supreme Court reviewed and affirmed the constitutional due process liberty rights of involuntarily committed individuals with IDD.

FOCUS ON WILLOWBROOK STATE SCHOOL

Willowbrook State School in Staten Island, New York is one of the symbols of huge public institutions that reflect institutionalization and institutionalization of children and adults with developmental disabilities. At its highest population, in 1969, 6,200 residents were living in buildings meant to house 4,000. Understaffed, overcrowded, and underfunded, it became a center of benign neglect and abuse. Hepatitis was so rampant that several researchers used it as an experiment site for their controversial medical study in which residents were intentionally exposed to the deadly virus, without their consent, in order to test the effectiveness of various vaccines.[69]

---

[69] See Geraldo Rivera, *Willowbrook: A report on how it is and why it doesn't have to be that way* (New York: Random House, 1972). Rivera relates the background to his now-famous investigative television report (January 6, 1972) and special (February 2, 1972). He includes the basic facts he

In 1966, Dr. Burton Blatt, a special educator and academic, published with Fred Kaplan the photographic exposé *Christmas in purgatory*, a searing portrait of life in a mental institution, including Willowbrook, which brought national attention to the abuse of people with mental retardation in America's institutions. Senator Robert Kennedy, who, when visiting the site, called it a "snake pit," finding thousands of residents "living in filth and dirt, their clothing in rags, in rooms less comfortable and cheerful than the cages in which we put animals in a zoo."[70] The visit brought conditions at Willowbrook into the national spotlight and the state of New York responded by developing a five-year improvement plan. However, after making minor adjustments, conditions at the institution quickly reverted to the inhumane conditions that had thrust it into the public consciousness.

In 1972, ABC News investigative reporter Geraldo Rivera drew national attention again to Willowbrook, with a television exposé that was watched by millions. *Willowbrook: The last great disgrace*[71] exposed the institution's serious overcrowding, dehumanizing practices, dangerous conditions, and regular abuse of residents. The public was again outraged. However, this time the outrage served to spur a parents advocacy group, the Association for the Help of Retarded Children (AHRC), to take action in federal court. AHRC filed a class action suit in the US District Court for the Eastern District of New York on March 17, 1972. The lawsuit alleged that the existing conditions violated the residents' constitutional right to treatment under the Due Process Clause of the Fourteenth Amendment and that their denial of a public education violated the Equal Protection Clause of the Fourteenth Amendment. Specifically, AHRC claimed that conditions at Willowbrook violated the constitutional rights of the residents.

Parents outlined multiple violations, including: confining residents for indefinite periods; failing to release residents eligible for release; failing to conduct periodic evaluations of residents to assess progress and refine goals and programming; failing to provide habilitation for residents; not providing adequate educational programs, or services such as speech, occupational, or physical therapy; overcrowding; lack of privacy; failure to provide protection from theft of personal property, assault, or injury; inadequate clothing, meals, and facilities, including toilet facilities; confining residents to beds or chairs, or to solitude; lack of compensation for work performed; inadequate medical facilities; and understaffing and incompetence in professional staff.

uncovered about Willowbrook and descriptions of other New York State institutions he visited (Letchworth Village and Suffolk State School). He also describes the surreptitious "raids" he made on Willowbrook to obtain footage and the protests organized in the aftermath of his first televised report.

70 Blatt and Kaplan, *Christmas in purgatory*.

71 Geraldo Rivera, *Willowbrook: The last great disgrace*, 1972, WABC-TV. Geraldo Rivera was one of the first journalists to expose realities on local TV. As the producers were putting the documentary together, they located a piece of film shot ten years earlier of Robert F. Kennedy after he completed a tour of Willowbrook, in which he said Willowbrook was a "disgrace." Despite Kennedy's anger and compassion, nothing was done about it.

In April 1973, US District Court Judge Orrin G. Judd rejected the plaintiffs' arguments that the Due Process Clause guaranteed a right to treatment and that the denial of public education violated the Equal Protection Clause. However, he did find that the conditions in Willowbrook violated the constitutional right of persons living in state custodial institutions to be protected from harm. According to the judge, the plaintiffs' constitutional right to protection from harm in a state institution meant that the residents of Willowbrook were "entitled to at least the same living conditions as prisoners."[72] This right, he continued, "may rest on the Eighth Amendment, the due process clause of the Fourteenth Amendment or the equal protection clause of the Fourteenth Amendment (based on irrational discrimination between prisoners and innocent mentally retarded persons)."[73] Accordingly, Judge Judd granted much of the requested injunctive relief, including prohibiting the use of seclusion and restraints, increasing medical, therapeutic, and recreational staffing, requiring maintenance, and requiring regular progress reports. With this injunctive order in place, the case proceeded to trial on October 1, 1974, with the parties continuing negotiations for months afterwards. The case was settled on April 30, 1975, when Judge Judd signed the *Willowbrook Consent Judgment: New York State Association for Retarded Children, Inc., et al. v. Hugh L. Carey*, 393 F. Supp. 715 (1975).

The Willowbrook Consent Judgment set forth guidelines and requirements for operating the institution and established new standards of care for all Willowbrook residents at the time of the settlement. The Consent Judgment outlined specific procedures and instructions for treatment of residents, covering issues such as resident living, the environment, programming and evaluation, hiring of personnel, education, recreation, food and nutrition, dental and medical care, therapy services, use of restraints, conditions for residents to provide labor to the facility, and conditions for research and experimental treatment. The Consent Judgment set a goal of reducing the number of residents living at Willowbrook to no more than 250 by 1981.[74] Although the parties ended up in court on many more occasions in disputes over the ongoing implementation of the Consent Decree, it was, in a sense, fully implemented in 1987, when the Willowbrook State School and Hospital officially closed.

THE ADA AND THE *OLMSTEAD* SUPREME COURT DECISION

In 1990, Congress enacted the Americans with Disabilities Act[75] which is considered to be the most comprehensive anti-discrimination measure against intolerance of

---

[72] *New York State Association for Retarded Children, Inc. v. Rockefeller*, 357 F. Supp. 752, 764 (1975). Retrieved May 26, 2015 from *New York State Association for Retarded Children, Inc. v. Rockefeller*, 357 F. Supp. 752, 764 (1975). Retrieved May 2, 2016 from http://openjurist.org/596/f2d/27/new-york-state-association-for-retarded-children-inc-v-l-carey.

[73] Ibid.

[74] *New York State Association for Retarded Children, Inc., et al. v. Hugh L. Carey*, 393 F. Supp. 715 (1975).

[75] 42 U.S.C. §§ 12101–12213 (2000).

people with disabilities. Congress's intention was to assure them equality of opportunity, full participation, independent living, and economic self-sufficiency.[76] It was
the first statute to explicitly identify institutionalization as a form of discrimination
against persons with disabilities. In the general provisions of the ADA, Congress
expressly found the following:

> [H]istorically, society has tended to isolate and segregate individuals with disabil-
> ities, and, despite some improvements, such forms of discrimination against
> individuals with disabilities continue to be a serious and pervasive social
> problem; ...
> [d]iscrimination against individuals with disabilities persists in such critical areas
> as ... housing, public accommodations, education, ... [and] institutionalization ...
> [i]ndividuals with disabilities continually encounter various forms of discrimina-
> tion, including outright intentional exclusion, ... overprotective rules and
> policies, ... [and] segregation ...[77]

At the heart of the legislation is Title II prohibiting discrimination on the basis of
disability in the provision of public services. It specifies that "no qualified individual with a disability shall, by reason of such disability, be excluded from participation in or be denied the benefits of the services, programs, or activities of a public
entity, or be subjected to discrimination by any such entity."[78] The regulations
require a public entity to "make reasonable modifications in policies, practices, or
procedures when the modifications are necessary to avoid discrimination on the
basis of disability ...."[79] However, these modifications are not absolute and can be
avoided if they "would fundamentally alter the nature of the service, program, or
activity."[80]

The "integration regulation" requires a public entity to "administer services,
programs, and activities in the most integrated setting appropriate to the needs of
qualified individuals with disabilities."[81] The preamble is very clear about the issues
of institutionalization and integration as "the most integrated setting appropriate" is
"a setting that enables individuals with disabilities to interact with nondisabled
persons to the fullest extent possible."[82]

The *Olmstead v. LC* Supreme Court decision[83] is probably the most important
interpretation of the ADA, and is therefore considered a milestone in the history of
persons with disabilities in the United States. On June 22, the United States
Supreme Court decided *Olmstead v. LC*, 1999 WL 407380 (1999), ruling that the
ADA makes a clear preference regarding placement of persons with mental illness
and intellectual disabilities in community settings rather than institutions if certain
conditions are met.

---

[76]   Ibid. § 12101(a)(8).   [77]   42 U.S.C. § 12101(a)(2), (3), (5). 54.   [78]   Ibid. § 12132.
[79]   28 C.F.R. § 35.130(b)(7) (2006).   [80]   Ibid.   [81]   28 C.F.R. § 35.130(d) (2006).
[82]   28 C.F.R. pt. 35, app. A, subpart B, § 35.130 (2006).   [83]   *Olmstead v. LC*, 527 U.S. 581 (1999).

THE BACKGROUND OF THE *OLMSTEAD* LAWSUIT

In May 1995, the Atlanta Legal Aid Society brought a lawsuit in the US District Court for the Northern District of Georgia on behalf of L.C. and E.W., two women with developmental disabilities and mental illness who had been voluntarily committed to the psychiatric unit of the state-run Georgia Regional Hospital. The professional staff at the hospital suggested that each woman was ready to move to a community-based program. Despite this decision, the women remained confined in the institution for several more years. The *Olmstead* plaintiffs alleged that they had failed to receive "minimally adequate care and freedom from undue restraint," in violation of the Due Process Clause of the Fourteenth Amendment, as well as discrimination under the ADA.[84] By the time the case came before the District Court, both women had been moved to community-based programs. Nevertheless, the courts determined that the case was not moot, since both women were subject to being returned to institutional placement.[85]

LOWER COURT RULINGS

The court granted the plaintiffs summary judgment on their ADA claim, holding that the plaintiffs were qualified individuals with disabilities who had been "excluded from participation in or denied the benefits of some public entity's services, programs, or activities, or . . . otherwise discriminated against" by reason of their disability.[86] The court found that "segregation" of the plaintiffs through institutionalization violated the regulations promulgated by the attorney general to implement Title II of the ADA, which clearly require public entities to administer services and programs "in the most integrated settings appropriate."[87] Because the defendants did offer community-based services to other people with disabilities, confining these plaintiffs to an institution was prohibited discrimination. The court found that it did not have to rule on the plaintiffs' Fourteenth Amendment claims, since it had found their continued institutionalization unlawfully discriminatory under the ADA. None of the later courts reviewing this decision addressed the Fourteenth Amendment arguments. The US Court of Appeals for the Eleventh Circuit affirmed the District Court, but remanded the case for determination of whether the further expenditure of state funds that would be required to treat the plaintiffs in a community setting "would be so unreasonable given the demands of the State's mental health budget that it would fundamentally alter the services it provides."[88]

---

[84]   *Olmstead v. LC ex rel. Zimring*, 527 U.S. 581, 597 (1999), 593.
[85]   *LC by Zimring v. Olmstead*, 138 F.3d 893, 895 (11th Cir. 1998).
[86]   Americans with Disabilities Act of 1990 as Amended, 41 U.S.C. § 12132.
[87]   28 C.F.R. § 35.130(d).   [88]   *LC by Zimring v. Olmstead*, 138 F.3d 893, 895 (11th Cir. 1998).

THE US SUPREME COURT'S *OLMSTEAD* DECISION

The *Olmstead* Supreme Court decision is based on the ADA of 1990. This anti-discrimination legislation "provide[s] a clear and comprehensive national mandate for the elimination of discrimination against individuals with disabilities."[89] *Olmstead* focuses on the essence of Title II of the ADA, which prohibits disability-based discrimination by state and local governments. In other words, Title II states that people with disabilities may not be excluded from participating in, or denied the benefits of, governmental services, programs, or activities.[90]

The implementing regulations are consonant with community integration, requiring state and local governments to "administer services, programs, and activities in the most integrated setting appropriate" to the needs of people with disabilities.[91] The regulations also require state and local governments to make reasonable modifications to policies, practices, and procedures to avoid disability-based discrimination, unless such modifications would fundamentally alter the nature of the service, program or activity.[92]

THE COURT'S DECISION

The Supreme Court was required to determine whether people with disabilities must receive services in the community rather than in institutions. Justice Ruth Bader Ginsburg, who wrote the majority opinion, thought that the ADA's prohibition of discrimination by a public entity required placement of persons with mental disabilities in community settings rather than in institutions.[93] The court found that community-based services must be offered if appropriate, if a person with a disability does not oppose moving from an institution to the community, and if the community placement can be reasonably accommodated considering the state's resources and the needs of other people with disabilities.[94]

The *Olmstead* Supreme Court decision concluded that the "[u[n]]justified institutional isolation of persons with disabilities is a form of discrimination."[95] The court based this statement on two judgments made by Congress in enacting the ADA. First, Congress recognized that the "institutional placement of persons who can handle and benefit from community settings perpetuates unwarranted assumptions that persons so isolated are incapable or unworthy of participating in community life."[96] Second, Congress found that "confinement in an institution severely diminishes the everyday life activities of individuals, including family relations, social contacts, work options, economic independence, educational advancement, and cultural enrichment."[97]

---

[89]   527 U.S. 581 3 (citing 42 U.S.C. §§ 12101(a)(2), (b)(1)).   [90]   Ibid. at 4 (citing 42 U.S.C. § 12132).

[91]   Ibid. at 6 (citing 28 C.F.R. § 35.130(d)).   [92]   Ibid. at 6–7 (citing 28 C.F.R. § 35.130(b)(7)).

[93]   Ibid. at 1.   [94]   Ibid.   [95]   Ibid. at 15.

[96]   Ibid. Also see http://kff.org/report-section/olmsteads-role-in-community-integration-for-people-with
       -disabilities-under-medicaid-issue-brief/ by Musmeci and Claypool.

[97]   Ibid.

The *Olmstead* decision also suggested a standard to determine whether state governments are avoiding disability-based discrimination and complying with the ADA's community integration mandate. The court also set the standards for the state if it

> demonstrat[ed] that it had a comprehensive, effectively working plan for placing qualified persons with mental disabilities in less restrictive settings, and a waiting list that moved at a reasonable pace not controlled by the State's endeavors to keep its institutions fully populated, the reasonable modifications standard would be met.[98]

IMPACT OF THE *OLMSTEAD* DECISION: CORE ISSUES

The *Olmstead* Supreme Court ruling is remarkable in that the court offers clarification of a few of the unresolved issues of the ADA[99] and its Integrated Regulations.[100] The *Olmstead* decision transfers the responsibility to the states to comply with Title II of the ADA, which says the states have a legal obligation to affirmatively remedy such discriminatory practices through reasonable modifications to their programs and services. This obligation is often referred to as the "integration mandate." Title II of the ADA applies to public entities and to the use of public funds.[101] The states are also responsible for using Medicaid funds to prevent institutionalization and to provide integrated community services.

Sara Rosenbaum and Joel Teitelbaum thought that the Supreme Court decision was a profound and ambitious rethinking of rights, remedies, and enforcement under federal law.[102] However, it made limited recommendations as to the nature of state compliance with the ADA in light of *Olmstead*. The court recognized the gaps between the anti-discrimination approach and current realities. It allowed that "the State generally may rely on the reasonable assessments of its own professionals in determining whether an individual is eligible for community-based services."[103] In addition, the court noted that there was no "federal requirement that community-based treatment be imposed on patients who do not desire it."[104] Finally, it remarked that a state can avoid liability if it can establish a "fundamental alteration" defense that, "in the allocation of available resources, immediate relief for the plaintiffs would be inequitable, given the responsibility the State has undertaken for the care and treatment of a large and diverse population of persons with mental disabilities."[105]

[98] Ibid. at 21.   [99] 42 U.S.C. §§ 12101–12213 (2000).   [100] 28 C.F.R. § 35.130(d) (2006).
[101] 42 U.S.C. § 12132.
[102] Sara Rosenbaum and Joel Teitelbaum, "Civil rights enforcement in the modern healthcare system: Reinvigorating the role of the federal government in the aftermath of *Alexander v. Sandoval,*" *Yale Journal of Health Policy, Law, and Ethics* 3 (2003), 2, Article 1; available at http://digitalcommons.law.yale.edu/yjhple/vol3/iss2/1.
[103] *Olmstead*, 527 U.S. at 602.   [104] Ibid.   [105] Ibid. at 604 (plurality opinion).

Amy Snyder-Hegener identified four issues that were left for interpretation after the *Olmstead* decision: reasonable modification vs. fundamental alteration, the cost, the slow response by the state, and the definition of community integration.[106] Most of these issues since *Olmstead* decision have been challenged in court or by community advocates.

REASONABLE MODIFICATION VS. FUNDAMENTAL ALTERATION

In developing an effectively working plan to address the *Olmstead* requirements, states were required to make "reasonable modifications," but not "fundamental alterations" to their state long-term care programs. States had difficulty distinguishing between the two, so the court offered the following approach: if, for example, the state were to demonstrate that it had a comprehensive, effectively working plan for placing qualified individuals with disabilities in less restrictive settings, and a waiting list that moved at a reasonable pace not controlled by the state's endeavors to keep its institutions fully populated, the reasonable-modifications standard would be met.[107]

MEDICAID COST

The Medicaid program has been geared toward institutional placement to eligible individuals as a mandatory benefit, while the provision of home and community-based services is considered an optional benefit. Although the center of the *Olmstead* decision was the expansion of community-based programs under Medicaid, the latter allowed the state to be flexible. Although the *Olmstead* decision emphasized placement in less restrictive settings and at a reasonable pace, the state may place a person in institutional care to avoid the waiting list and respond to the requirement of "reasonable pace."[108]

Slow Response by the States

States were mandated to comply with the *Olmstead* decision by demonstrating an effectively working plan to transition individuals from institutions to the community.

---

[106] Amy Snyder-Hegener, "Assessing the impact of Olmstead decision," *Social Work and Society* 12 (2012). Retrieved January 19, 2016 from www.socwork.net/sws/article/view/343/680.

[107] *Olmstead*, 527 U.S. at 605–06.

[108] Randy A. Desonia, "Is community care a civil right? The unfolding saga of the Olmstead decision," National Health Policy Forum Background Paper, Washington, DC, The George Washington University, March 12, 2003. The paper lays the groundwork for understanding the implications of the historic US Supreme Court decision in the case of *Olmstead v. LC*, which has far-reaching consequences for the long-term care of people with disabilities. One of the core conclusions is that regardless of future court decisions, there are still many issues impeding the expansion of home- and community-based long-term services that are not addressed by *Olmstead*. It does not increase the workforce needed to deliver more services, nor does it create an oversight system assuring that the community-based services delivered are of high quality.

However, states vary in their pace of implementation, primarily because of missing timeframes with regard to program implementation.[109] An additional ambiguous term used in the *Olmstead* decision was "reasonable pace."

DEVELOPMENT OF WORKING PLAN FOR COMMUNITY INTEGRATION

Each state was supposed to define what was to be considered as "community integration" and was then required to develop an effectively working plan. However, the final decision about community placement was dependent on professionals' determination that such a placement was appropriate. In order to determine appropriateness for community placement, these treatment professionals would be required to conduct a thorough assessment of the individual requesting such placement. According to Rosenbaum and Teitelbaum, professionals were required to assess "liberty" and "coverage."[110] Liberty assessments require the acknowledgement of basic due process. Moreover, these assessments tend to consider evidence that is more objective, such as observations by clinicians and reliable, valid assessment tools.

Coverage assessments require a process that involves fact-finding to determine what resources or benefits an individual would need to live in the community and whether or not the state either provides or has the capacity to provide such services. For example, there are situations where a particular individual may not want community placement, in which case states are not required to provide it.

IMPACT OF *OLMSTEAD*

Since the landmark *Olmstead* decision, many states have expanded their efforts to promote community integration and reduce reliance on institutional care for people with disabilities. In doing so, states face many challenges, including deep cuts in human services budgets, lack of affordable housing, lack of employment opportunities for people with disabilities, barriers to financing supportive services for people living in community-based settings, and stigma, bias, and discrimination.

One of the recent studies by Terence Ng, Alice Wong, and Charlene Harrington, examined the status of post-*Olmstead* litigations on deinstitutionalization and

[109] Jennifer Mathis, "Olmstead: Where are we after five years?" (Washington, DC: Bazelon Center for Mental Health Law, 2005). Retrieved from www.bazelon.org/LinkClick.aspx?fileticket=Z86S8xonTQs%3D&tabid=322. The report reflects little confidence in the *Olmstead* implementation planning by states and observers. A majority of states have not planned to identify or provide community placement to all institutionalized persons who do not oppose community placement. Few plans identify systemic barriers to community placement or state action steps to remove them and few plans contain timelines and targets for community placement. The greatest concern is the lack of funds to support *Olmstead*'s planning goals.

[110] See Sara Rosenbaum and Joel Teitelbaum, *Olmstead at five: Assessing the impact* (Washington, DC: US Government Printing Office, Liberty, 2004).

community living between 1999 and 2011.[111] There were a total of 131 *Olmstead* and related lawsuits filed in the courts. This averaged about ten cases a year in the thirteen years following the *Olmstead* decision, and almost half (sixty-four cases) were granted class action status. Most of the cases involved denial or lack of housing to prevent institutionalization. Interestingly, the majority of the *Olmstead* and related class action cases were settled before a verdict was handed down. Out of the 131 cases filed since 1999, most states had at least one *Olmstead* or related case. The authors reported that although the outcomes of these litigations have been successful, most of them took a few years (an average of three years) to complete and the implementation often took additional time.

However, it is quite difficult to determine the impact of these litigations, mainly because of the lack of time perspective and agreeable evaluation measures. In one study, the researchers contended that "Olmstead's legacy in the courts has been uneven" due to the subjectivity involved in deciding whether changes sought by plaintiffs to a state Medicaid program constituted a fundamental alteration.[112] However, Enbar and colleagues reviewed the use of litigation across the states, relating this to state efforts to increase deinstitutionalization and community integration of people with developmental disabilities and concluded that "litigation has been used as a catalyst" to stimulate such long-term care reforms.[113]

A recent report[114] provides an update on the progress made. The core findings reveal that in the years since the *Olmstead* decision, nationally there has been a fundamental rebalancing of spending on individuals with disabilities in institutions as compared to spending on HCBS (home and community-based services) that allows Americans with disability to be part of their communities. Between 1995 and 2010, states reduced the share of Medicaid spending on institutions, including nursing homes, mental hospitals, and institutions for people with IDD from 79 percent to 50 percent. The most striking finding is that there are still widespread inequities in access to HCBS across states. In 2009, the percentage of spending on HCBS Long-Term Services and Supports (LTSS)[115] varied from more than 80 percent to less than

---

[111]   Terence Ng, Alice Wong, and Charlene Harrington, "State Olmstead litigation and the Affordable Care Act," *Journal of Social Work in Disability & Rehabilitation* 13 (2014), 97–109.

[112]   See Sara Rosenbaum, Alexandra M. Stewart, and Joel Teitelbaum, "Defining 'reasonable pace' in the post-Olmstead environment," Center for Health Care Strategies, April 2002; Sara Rosenbaum, Joel Teitelbaum, and Alexandra M. Stewart, *An analysis of Olmstead complaints: Implications for policy and long-term planning*, Center for Health Care Strategies, December 2001.

[113]   E. G. Enbar et al., *A nationwide study of deinstitutionalization and community integration: A special report of the public policy and legal advocacy programs* (Chicago: Equip for Equality, 2004).

[114]   The July 18, 2013 report of United States Senate Health, Education, Labor, and Pensions Committee, "Separate and unequal: States fail to fulfill the community living promise of the Americans with Disabilities Act," is the result of requests for information sent by chairman Tom Harkin to all fifty states on the progress made to transition individuals out of institutions. Retrieved May 16, 2016 from www.help.senate.gov/imo/media/doc/Olmstead%20Report%20July%2020131.pdf.

[115]   Long-Term Services and Supports (LTSS) encompasses the broad range of paid and unpaid medical and personal care assistance that people may need – for several weeks, months, or years – when they experience difficulty completing self-care tasks as a result of aging, chronic illness, or disability.

20 percent, and thirty-eight states spent less than 50 percent of LTSS costs on HCBS. Hundreds of thousands of people with disabilities remain on waiting lists for community-based services.

Finally, perceived uncertainty about the potential total cost of providing HCBS to every eligible individual in the state may be preventing states from exercising new federal options for HCBS. Many states have focused more on enrolling people who are currently living in community settings into HCBS programs than on transitioning individuals living in institutional settings back into the community.

The committee's report calls on Congress to amend the ADA to clarify and strengthen the law's integration mandate in a manner that accelerates *Olmstead's* implementation and clarifies that every individual who is eligible for LTSS under Medicaid has a federally protected right to a real choice in how they receive services and supports. Congress is also encouraged to amend the Medicaid statute to end the institutional bias in the Medicaid program by requiring every state that participates in the Medicaid program to pay for HCBS. It calls on states to transition more individuals into community-based settings and shift away from waivers that allow states to set caps on the number of individuals served. Specifically, the reports calls for the federal government to ensure that states establish benchmarks designed to transition people with disabilities out of institutions and into the most integrated setting.

COMMUNITY-BASED SERVICES AND INSTITUTIONAL CLOSURE: VARIATIONS AMONG STATES

In the twenty-first century, there has been some progress in deinstitutionalization and community living policies and practices, regardless of the recession and economic restrains. A 2015 report by United Cerebral Palsy on inclusion demonstrated the variations among states with respect to institutional closures and the development of community-based services.[116] According to the report, the states of Arkansas, Illinois, Mississippi, and Texas were rated at the bottom primarily due to the small proportion of people and resources dedicated to those in small or home-like settings in these four states. There were thirty-two states, down from thirty-eight in 2007, that met the 80/80 Home and Community Standard, meaning that at least 80 percent of all individuals with ID/DD were served in the community and 80 percent of all resources spent on those with ID/DD were are for home (fewer than seven residents per setting) and community support. States that did not meet the 80/80 standard are Arkansas, Delaware, Florida, Illinois, Indiana, Iowa, Kentucky, Louisiana, Mississippi, New Jersey, North Carolina, North Dakota, Ohio, Oklahoma, South Carolina, South Dakota, Texas, Utah, and Virginia. As of 2013, fourteen states reported having no

[116] United Cerebral Palsy (UCP), "The case for inclusion 2015." Retrieved April 18, 2016 from http://cfi .ucp.org/wp-content/uploads/2015/07/UCP_2015_CaseforInclusion_FINAL.pdf.

state institutions to seclude those with ID/DD, including Alabama, Alaska, Hawaii, Indiana, Maine, Michigan, Minnesota, New Hampshire, New Mexico, Oregon, Rhode Island, Vermont, West Virginia, and Washington, DC. Another ten states had only one institution each (Arizona, Delaware, Idaho, Montana, Nebraska, Nevada, North Dakota, South Dakota, Utah, and Wyoming). Since 1960, 220 out of 354 state institutions have been closed (five more in the past year alone), according to the University of Minnesota's Research and Training Center on Community Living. Another thirteen were projected to close by 2016 in California, Massachusetts, New Jersey (3), New York (2), Oklahoma (2), Tennessee (2), and Virginia (2).

RESEARCH ON THE TRANSITION FROM INSTITUTIONS TO COMMUNITY LIVING

Most of the statistical reports from the United States show a steady increase in the number of people with intellectual disability live in community-based residences.[117] In fact, the number grew from 267,682 in 1988[118] to 460,597 in 2011.[119] Concurrently, there has been rapid growth in the number of small residential settings, most of them small (six or fewer people in an apartment). The shift toward smaller, more diverse residential settings is apparent in a national study of the residential settings of individuals with intellectual disability.[120] However, despite the *Olmstead* Supreme Court decision, there is still a substantial number of about 60,000 people with IDD who live in private or public residential institutions, and almost 30,000 living in nursing facilities.

There are a substantial number of studies that have examined the impact of the transition from institutional to community care. The research focuses on changes in adaptive behavior and primarily positive gains in basic skills of independent daily life, but also on a decrease in challenging behavior problems. One remarkable study, which examined US behavioral outcomes of deinstitutionalization between 1977 and 2010 for people with IDD, has been published by the University of Minnesota's Research and Training Center on Community Living, Institute on Community Integration, College of Education and Human Development.[121] In order to identify

---

[117] Ashley C. Woodman et al., "Residential transitions among adults with intellectual disability across 20 years," *American Journal of Intellectual and Developmental Disabilities* 119 (2014), 496–515.

[118] Charlie K. Lakin et al., "Change in residential placements for persons with intellectual and developmental disabilities in the USA in the last two decades," *Journal of Intellectual and Developmental Disability* 28 (2003), 205–10.

[119] Sheryl A. Larson et al., *Residential services for persons with intellectual or developmental disabilities: Status and trends through 2011* (Minneapolis: University of Minnesota, Institute on Community Integration, 2013).

[120] R. Tichá et al, "Correlates of everyday choice and support-related choice for 8,892 randomly sampled adults with intellectual and developmental disabilities in 19 states," *Intellectual and Developmental Disabilities* 50 (2012), 486–504.

[121] See Charlie K. Lakin, Sheryl A. Larson, and Shannon Kim, *Behavioral outcomes of deinstitutionalization for people with intellectual and/or developmental disabilities: Third decennial review of*

the changes, they differentiated between contrast groups and longitudinal studies. The group contrast studies compared the outcomes for people who moved from institutions to community residential settings with those of a "contrast" group of people who stayed in institutions. There were seven of eleven contrast group studies that showed significantly better outcomes in overall adaptive behavior associated with community placement. The findings regarding challenging behavior demonstrated that only one of five studies reported a difference between stayers and leavers. The remaining four studies were evenly divided (two each) in showing nonsignificant better outcomes for movers and stayers.

In terms of the longitudinal studies, fifteen out of twenty-five studies showed statistically significant improvements in overall adaptive behavior associated with moving to a community setting. It appears that the areas where there were consistent improvements were: academic skills, community living skills, language/communication skills, motor/physical skills, self-care/domestic skills, social skills, and vocational skills. The most gains were in self-care/domestic skills (thirteen out of sixteen studies), community living skills (nine out of ten studies) and social skills (ten out of eleven studies).

The findings attributed to challenging behavior showed the same variability that was reported for the contrast group studies. In four out of twenty-one studies, there were demonstrated improvements in challenging behavior after the move, including four studies in which these changes were statistically significant.

DEINSTITUTIONALIZATION AND NONDISCRIMINATION LEGAL POLICIES: A DISCUSSION

The chapter presents interesting historical changes in US policies toward community living of people with disabilities. The period of 1850–1950 marked the preference of institutional care, which began as a positive policy of improving care for people with disabilities during the societal transition from rural to urban living. However, the eugenics movement associated with economic and social changes changed the nature of these institutions from care to custodial in isolated and inhumane facilities. The policy changed gradually in the mid-1950s toward deinstitutionalization and anti-discrimination policies. The purpose of the discussion is to examine the deinstitutionalization and anti-discrimination policies with respect to processes and outcomes.

The failure or success of deinstitutionalization is under debate in the United States. The most critical criticism of deinstitutionalization is often expressed by mental health advocates and is tinged with the flavor of conspiracy. It is viewed as being supported by dedicated civil libertarians and conservative fiscal allies. Both

U.S. studies, 1977–2010, University of Minnesota, Institute on Community Integration, Policy Research Brief 11 (2), April 2011.

have been proven wrong in improving the life of people with mental illness. Paul S. Appelbaum maintains that the deinstitutionalization of people with mental illness was a tragedy.[122] They seemed particularly appropriate targets for a crusade against governmental power, for the state, they believed, was depriving them of liberty when they received treatment. Many of the mentally ill have drifted away entirely from any form of care. Given the freedom to choose, they have chosen to live on the streets; according to various estimates they comprise between 40 percent and 60 percent of homeless persons.

Michael L. Perlin believes that the failure of federal and state governments to invest in supports and services led to the disappointing results.[123] There are others who seem to be more ambivalent, such as David Rothman, who thinks that the policy was in the right direction but was disappointing in not providing adequate community support infrastructure and services.[124] Rothman criticized those who blamed deinstitutionalization for the growth of the homeless population, as the main reason was lack of sufficient funding for ex-patients that left them without housing and services.[125]

In one of the most interesting analyses about the impact of deinstitutionalization, Samuel R. Bagenstos estimated that the plan to move individuals with disabilities out of large institutions into community-based settings was much more positive and beneficial than several scholars and advocates believed. In his opinion, the legal strategy in the 1960s and 1970s was based primarily on the Due Process Clause of the Fourteenth Amendment.[126] The doctrine reflected procedural limitations on involuntary commitment and substantive guarantees of treatment for people confined to

---

[122]   Paul S. Appelbaum, "Crazy in the streets," *Commentary Magazine*, May 1987.

[123]   For a good example, see Michael L. Perlin, "Competency, deinstitutionalization, and homelessness: A story of marginalization," *Houston Law Review* 28 (1991), 92–93.

[124]   David J. Rothman, "The rehabilitation of the asylum," *The American Prospect* (Fall 1991), http://prospect.org/article/rehabilitation-asylum. Rothman believes that deinstitutionalization has generally failed to deliver appropriate services to ex-mental patients or other persons in need of them. It is not clear why the outcome of deinstitutionalization should have been so grim, and what should be done to remedy the situation.

[125]   See, for example, David Mechanic and David A. Rochefort, "Deinstitutionalization: An appraisal of reform," *Annual Review of Sociology* 16 (1990), 301–27. Mechanic and Rochefort refer to the decline of the number of inpatients in US public mental hospitals from 559,000 in 1955 to approximately 110,000 in 1990. They claim that the reductions resulted from release or transfer of long-term inpatients and from entrance barriers to new admissions. The timing and pace of deinstitutionalization substantially varied by state, but three-quarters of the national reduction followed the expansion of welfare programs in the middle 1960s. The establishment of community care alternatives was highly inadequate, leaving many severely and persistently mentally ill people without essential services. Problems of care were exacerbated by the contraction of welfare programs in the 1980s, which resulted in serious neglect and homelessness. Plagued by underfinancing and fragmentation of care, new strategies in developing mental health care systems include capitation, case-management approaches, and the development of strong local mental health authorities.

[126]   Samuel R. Bagenstos, "The past and future of deinstitutionalization litigation," *Cardozo Law Review* 34 (2012), 1–52.

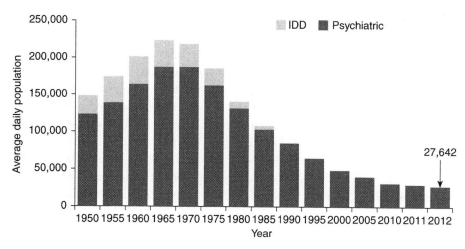

FIGURE 4.1. Average daily population in large public institutions for IDD
and psychiatric disabilities, 1950–2012.

state institutions.[127] Both espoused a mixed bag in terms of achieving completely satisfactory outcomes. The right against treatment doctrine could not change the quality of care because most of the treatment was custodial in nature. Although the right for treatment doctrine was much more relevant to deinstitutionalization because it was framed as an affirmative right to service, it was limited to availability of funding by the state.

There is no doubt that the number of people with developmental disabilities and psychiatric disabilities confined to state institutions in the United States decreased significantly. The Table above demonstrates the average daily population in large public institutions for IDD and psychiatric disabilities from 1950 to 2012.[128] Strangely, the number picked up in 1965 and reduced dramatically in the 1970s and 1980s.

The number of people with psychiatric disabilities hospitalized in psychiatric hospitals decreased even more dramatically than the IDD population, from 560,000 in 1955 to about 50,000 people in 2003, while data from eleven states showed increases in admissions and residents between 2002 and 2005. The number of admissions nationwide increased by 21.1 percent, and the number of residents increased by 1.0 percent. State mental health agency staff attributed the increases principally to the increase in the number of forensic admissions and residents. Staff also identified increases in the number of admissions with schizophrenia (increased

[127] These two due process theories did not exhaust the theories on which plaintiffs relied in early deinstitutionalization cases, but none of the others played as crucial a role.
[128] People with IDD in large public facilities. Adapted from Sheryl. A. Larson et al., *In-home and residential long-term supports and services for persons with intellectual or developmental disabilities: Status and trends through 2012* (Minneapolis: University of Minnesota, Institute on Community Integration, 2014).

by 23.2 percent) and affective disorders (increased by 16.3 percent) as a second factor, plus declines in the availability of housing and community-based care providers.[129]

Therefore, critics of deinstitutionalization of people with psychiatric disabilities blamed deinstitutionalization not only for homelessness but for the substantial number of those released from public mental hospitals who were jailed and placed in prisons.[130] In fact, the number of individuals with serious mental illness in prisons and jails in 2016 exceeded by tenfold the number in state psychiatric hospitals. Most of them would have been treated in the state psychiatric hospitals in the years before the deinstitutionalization movement led to the closing of the hospitals, a trend that continues even today. The treatment of mentally ill individuals in prisons and jails is critical, especially since such individuals are vulnerable and often abused while incarcerated.

Since the enactment of the ADA in 1990 and the *Olmstead* Supreme Court decision, constitutional due process has been replaced with the anti-discrimination approach. Under this doctrine, institutionalization is discrimination because it causes unnecessary segregation of people with disabilities. The question is whether this anti-discrimination decision was successful not only in closing and downsizing large institutions but in state resource-allocation toward community-based programs.

The Supreme Court *Olmstead* decision is definitely an important milestone in declaring institutionalization as discrimination. However, the Supreme Court limited its assessment to the statutory issue of the meaning of ADA Title II and declined to address the Fourteenth Amendment claims.[131] However, the court held that the fundamental alteration doctrine allows a state to show that allocating its available resources to provide immediate relief for plaintiffs would be inequitable because of the state's responsibility to provide care and treatment for a large, diverse class of people with mental disabilities.[132] The court recognized that for some individuals "no placement outside the institution may ever be appropriate" and expressed concern that phasing out state institutions would place some patients at risk.[133] In addition, the court just required states to provide a working plan for placing qualified persons in the least restrictive environment at a reasonable pace. By 2010 only half of the states had developed "Olmstead plans."[134]

---

[129] See Ronald W. Manderscheid, Joanne E. Atay, and Raquel A. Crider, "Changing trends in state psychiatric hospital use from 2002 to 2005," *Psychiatric Services* 29 (2009), 29–34.

[130] E. Fuller Torrey, et al., *More mentally ill persons are in jails and prisons than hospitals: A survey of the states* (Arlington, VA: Treatment Advocacy Center, 2010), pp. 9–11.

[131] *Olmstead v. LC ex rel. Zimring*, 527 U.S. 581, 594 n.6 (1999) note 588.   [132] Ibid. at 604.

[133] *Olmstead v. LC ex rel. Zimring*, 527 U.S. 581, 604–05 (1999).

[134] Among the barriers for implementation of *Olmstead* plans are financial constraints on Medicaid, the lack of affordable and accessible housing, labor shortage of home care workers, and political pressure of institutional staff concerned about losing their jobs. See: Terence Ng, Alice Wong, and Charlene Harrington, "Home and community-based services: Introduction to Olmstead lawsuits and Olmstead plans," (San Francisco: University of California, National Center for Personal Assistance Services, 2013) available at www.americanbar.org/content/dam/aba/events/homelessness_poverty/2013_Annual_Meeting_Medicaid/intro_to_olmstead_lawsuits_and_plans.authcheckdam.pdf.

The *Olmstead* Supreme Court decision is still debated among disability advocates. However, the federal government believes that the *Olmstead* decision is probably the most significant step to date in eliminating institutional isolation and discrimination under the ADA. They expect to be able to deal with the waiting lists for waiver services and the expanded access to community-based long-term services.[135] The skeptical advocates believe that the Supreme Court decision allows states to continue maintaining segregated institutions or changes in their Medicaid institutional funding, and limit access to community-based services. Unfortunately, most of those waiting for HCBS have to choose between two unattractive options: entering an institution to receive services or continuing to wait an unknown amount of time to receive HCBS.[136] In their opinion, these problems demonstrate the limitations of the anti-discrimination approach in ensuring the implementation of the community living option.[137] It appears that more than fifteen years after *Olmstead*, the debate is still ongoing.[138]

There is a distinctive difference between the *Olmstead* Supreme Court decision and the UNCRPD regarding deinstitutionalization and community-living policy.[139] While the *Olmstead* anti-discrimination decision allows states the freedom to determine the pace and cost of deinstitutionalization, the UNCRPD refers to the absolute right of persons with disabilities to choose where and with whom they prefer to live in the community. In this regard, the convention's human rights approach champions the needs and desires of the individual over financial or political concerns.

---

[135] Kaiser Commission on Medicaid and the Uninsured, "Olmstead v. L.C.: The interaction of the Americans with Disabilities Act and Medicaid," Kaiser Family Foundation, June 2004; available at https://kaiserfamilyfoundation.files.wordpress.com/2013/01/olmstead-v-l-c-the-interaction-of-the -americans-with-disabilities-act-and-medicaid.pdf.

[136] See, for example, two cases: in *Bryson v. Shumway*, the First Circuit Court of Appeals held that qualified individuals with disabilities are not "entitled to reasonable promptness" for community-based services unless they are on a wait list (308 F.3d 79, 1st Cir. 2002); in *Arc of Washington State, Inc. v. Braddock*, the Ninth Circuit Court of Appeals' decision allowed states to limit the size of their Medicaid waiver programs, permitting states to engage in practices that inhibit significant progress in integrating qualified individuals with disabilities into their communities (427 F.3d 615, 9th Cir. 2005).

[137] See Megan Flynn, "Olmstead plans revisited: Lessons learned from the U.N. Convention on the Rights of Persons with Disabilities," *Law and Inequality* 28 (2010), 407, 412.

[138] Melody Kubo, "Casenotes, Implementing Olmstead v. L.C.: Defining 'effectively working' plans for 'reasonably paced' wait lists for Medicaid home and community-based services waiver programs," *University of Hawai'i Law Review* 23 (2001), 731, 754.

[139] For a comprehensive analysis, see "Finding the gaps: A comparative analysis of disability laws in the United States to the United Nations Convention on the Rights of Persons with Disabilities (CRPD), National Council on Disabilities," May 12, 2008. Retrieved January 14, 2016 from www.ncd.gov /publications/2008/May122008; Arlene S. Kanter, "Finding the gaps: A comparative analysis of disability laws in the United States to the United Nations Convention on the Rights of Persons with Disabilities (CRPD)," *Drake Law Review* 63 (2015). Retrieved June 13, 2016 from apers.ssrn.com /sol3/papers.cfm?abstract_id=2633807; Robert D. Dinerstein, "Implementing legal capacity under Article 12 of the UN Convention on the Rights of Persons with Disabilities: The difficult road from guardianship to supported decision-making," *Human Rights Brief* 19 (2012), 8–12.

5

European Perspectives on the Right
to Community Living

Institutions for people with intellectual disabilities (ID) and mental illness emerged in European countries in the early nineteenth century.[1] Most of them were closed during the twentieth century, but there are still countries that have retained institutional care often side by side with community-based programs. The chapter reviews and analyzes institutionalization of people with mental illness and ID in selected European states, the efforts toward formulating deinstitutionalization,[2] and the development of community living in these countries. Special attention is given to legal, economic, and social development efforts by the Council of Europe and the European Union in promoting community living policy and to the importance of the UNCRPD in this regard.[3]

INSTITUTIONALIZATION OF PEOPLE WITH MENTAL ILLNESS IN EUROPE

Institutionalization of people with mental illness in Europe began in the early nineteenth century, although churches and nonmedical local organizations provided institutional care in earlier periods. Edward Shorter, who has reviewed the

[1] For a balanced historical view of humane attempts to help the insane as well as to exclude them, see Roy Porter, *Madness: A brief history* (Oxford: Oxford University Press, 2002); see also Ruth von Bernuth, "From marvels of nature to inmates of asylums: Imaginations of natural folly," *Disability Studies Quarterly* 26 (2006). Retrieved June 10, 2016 from http://dsq-sds.org/article/view/697/874.

[2] Deinstitutionalization has been defined by Leona L. Bachrach as "... the replacement of long-stay psychiatric hospitals with smaller, less isolated community-based service alternatives for the care of mentally individuals." This consists of three component processes: the release of patients from psychiatric hospitals to alternative facilities in the community, the diversion of potential new admissions to the alternative facilities, and the development of special community-based programs, combining psychiatric and support services, for the care of a non-institutionalized population; Leona L. Bachrach, "Deinstitutionalization: Promises, problems and prospects." In *Mental health service evaluation*. Edited by Helle C. Knudsen and Graham Thornicroft (Cambridge: Cambridge University Press, 1996), p. 4.

[3] Report on the implementation of the UNCRPD by the European Union. Brussels, June 5, 2014 SWD (2014) 182 final. Retrieved September 11, 2016, from http://ec.europa.eu/justice/discrimination/files/swd_2014_182_en.pdf.

history of mental health services in Europe, called the period from the early nine-teenth century to the mid-twentieth century, the era of the asylum.[4] It was quite common in rural Europe to offer custodial treatment and in rural areas to lock up and chain people with acute mental illness. Therefore, hospitalization was scarce and considered as a human and progressive intervention offered to select groups of patients.

The first facilities were formed at the end of the eighteenth century, followed by additional asylums.[5] The first effort to establish a district-level network of asylums began in England with the County Asylums Act of 1808, in France with the Law of 1838, and in other countries at later dates.[6] By the last third of the nineteenth century, there were hundreds of thousands of beds in district-level asylums across Western Europe. It is clear that there was no community infrastructure. Patients discharged from the asylums had to live on their own or in private family care facilities,[7] the latter being typical for Western Europe. Aside from those two examples there were also a few private psychiatric clinics that served as alternatives to large asylums[8] and charities offering support for those discharged from hospitalization.

After World War II, sentiments against institutionalization led policy-makers to opening up the use of general hospitals for treating psychiatric patients. A good example is Hungary, which, toward 1900 provided treatment in general hospitals rather than in state asylums. These years also witnessed a shift toward treatment for the well-to-do in spas and private sanatoriums, thus avoiding the stigmatization and exclusion experienced by the mentally ill.

The funding of hospitalization was covered in Germany by the health insurance law of 1833; however, the insurance was only valid for twenty-six weeks. Many of the psychiatrists worked privately and served mainly middle-class and upper-middle-class patients. After 1889, most of the funding came from the Reich Insurance

---

4   Edward Shorter, *A history of psychiatry from the era of the asylum to the age of prozac* (New York: Wile, 1997). Shorter introduces the scientific and cultural factors that shaped the development of psychiatry in Germany and the United States and the build-up of the asylums of the eighteenth and nineteenth centuries in Germany and the United States as the world capitals of psychoanalysis.

5   Ibid., pp. 8–21; Shorter reported that the first two hospitals were opened in Florence in the 1780s under the aegis of Vincenzo Chiarugi, and in Paris in the 1790s under Philippe Pinel.

6   See, for example, Pierre Pichot, *A century of psychiatry* (Paris: DaCosta, 1983), pp. 28–40; Kathleen Jones, *Asylums and after: A revised history of the mental health services: From the early 18th century to the 1990s* (London: Athlone, 1993). The book takes into account the seminal critiques of Goffman, Foucault, and Szasz, the historical revaluation of late twentieth-century perspectives, and assesses changes to mental health services.

7   Home care was initiated by the Engelken family in 1764 (Bremen, Germany). However, in other places similar services such as family care were offered in villages such as Dun-sur-Auron in France, Gheel in Belgium, and Uchtspringe in Germany, offering similar services as in family care. The Scottish Law of 1876 allowed facilities to admit patients directly to home care without passing through the asylum.

8   The first clinic was offered by Prof. Wilhelm Griesinger in 1868. This private facility and others of up to 100 beds provided short-stay care for acute cases, who would either recover or be transferred to a large asylum. Many university psychiatric hospitals also functioned as short-stay clinics in this sense.

Office.[9] Similar insurance was common in other countries in Europe, including Great Britain, the Netherlands, and Norway, and during the 1920s and 1930s in France and Sweden. The postwar years saw social insurance money being invested in mental health hospitals. In fact, most European countries demonstrated an increased number of mental health beds in 1970 as compared to the 1950s.[10] By 1971, a quarter of the mental hospitals in the WHO European Region had more than a thousand beds: "Impersonal custodial regimes, lack of privacy and of . . . stimuli leads to apathy and the aggravation of symptoms."[11] In fact, the number of patients hospitalized in public mental institutions in Europe stayed high until the early 1980s.

DEINSTITUTIONALIZATION

The postwar years saw more involvement of government in mental health systems across Western Europe and, in particular, an inclination to include mental health funding in social insurance. However, the 1950s and 1960s were an era of growth in hospital beds. Apart from the United Kingdom and Ireland, most countries had higher numbers of mental health beds in 1970 compared to the 1950s.[12] Sylvan Furman, who reflected practices in Western Europe in the mid-1960s, identified the following examples:[13] (1) mental hospitals dominated the European scene: Graylingwell and Littlemore Hospitals in England corresponded to this model, as did most of the asylums in Italy until 1978; (2) a partnership between mental hospitals and community health authorities existed in a few places, as in York, England;[14] (3) the psychiatric division in a general hospital looks after a catchment

9   Greg Eghigian, *Making security social: Disability, insurance, and the birth of the social entitlement state in Germany* (Ann Arbor, MI: University of Michigan, 2000). The book argues that the emergence of social insurance in Germany represented a paradigmatic shift in modern understandings of health, work, political participation, and government. By institutionalizing compensation, social insurance transformed it into a right that the employed population quickly came to take for granted. Social insurance is responsible for the conceptualization of "disability" and "rehabilitation" and the early twentieth-century development of political action groups for people with disabilities.

10 Mary A. Jansen, "Mental health policy: Observations from Europe," *American Psychologist* 41 (1986), 1273–78. Jansen reviews policies and practices in five European countries (Switzerland, England, Denmark, Sweden, and the Netherlands) with respect to deinstitutionalization and community support and rehabilitation services, health and social security benefits, financing mechanisms, and care for the homeless and young adult chronic populations. Compared to the United States, the system of care in these countries is based on a strong social welfare system allowing for community-based care administered by the mental health service system.

11 See World Health Organization (WHO), *Health Services in Europe* (Copenhagen: WHO Regional Office for Europe, 1975), p. 37.

12 Chris Breemer, Ter Stege, and Martin Gittleman, "The direction of change in western European mental health care," *International Journal of Mental Health* 16 (1987), 6–20.

13 Sylvan S. Furman, *Community mental health services in northern Europe: Great Britain, Netherlands, Denmark, and Sweden* (Bethesda: National Institute for Mental Health, PHS Pub. no. 1407, 1965), pp. 4–5.

14 Ibid., pp. 24–28.

area: a unique example is the Glostrup State Hospital in Denmark, a large psychiatric service adjacent to an 850-bed general hospital;[15] (4) community care controlled by a public health authority was practiced in the Netherlands in the 1960s, with the large public health departments of Amsterdam and Rotterdam integrating the mental health care of the local populations covered by national health insurance;[16] (5) transitional systems, from large mental hospitals to community care centered in general hospitals, existed only in Sweden.[17]

In sum, the postwar period saw increasing horizontal and vertical integration of mental health care and gradual absorption by social insurance programs.

In general, there are three patterns of countries in Europe: (1) countries where the asylum has never predominated, such as Hungary and some eastern European countries; (2) countries that have dramatically changed the asylum model and moved rapidly to community-based policy, such as Italy, Finland, and Denmark; (3) countries where the transition from public hospital to community care has been gradual. These include most western European countries, including the United Kingdom.

The difference in pace and direction of change appears to be related to domestic and historical circumstances. The impression is that most of the countries are still bound by their historical traditions and norms. For example, Austria, a former part of the Austro-Hungarian Empire, continues to have high rates of asylum care with little provision for community mental health. Hungary demonstrates the opposite pattern. Today, many eastern European countries have a large surplus of clinical beds, many of them unneeded and an inheritance of the Soviet era. On the other hand, countries with strong private and voluntary sectors, such as Britain and the Netherlands, have now gone over to statist national health and social insurance services in which non-state players have little to say about mental health.

An overall view of Western Europe demonstrates the thousands of individuals transitioning from long-term psychiatric hospitals to various forms of community-based living.[18]

The chart below presents the decline of psychiatric beds per 100,000 people in selected western European countries from 1975 to 2013. The trend is evident, with most of the countries except Belgium and Russia demonstrating a tremendous decline in psychiatric beds. Italy, Denmark, and Sweden demonstrate the lowest rates, and Belgium and France the highest rates. Interestingly, the United Kingdom and Israel have made great progress in the past ten years.

---

[15] Ibid., pp. 124–29.   [16] Ibid., pp. 104–16.

[17] See, for example, World Health Organization (WHO), *Mental health services in pilot study areas: Report on a European study* (Copenhagen: WHO Regional Office for Europe, 1987), p. 7.

[18] David McDaid and Graham Thornicroft, *Policy Brief. Mental health II: Balancing institutional and community care* (Copenhagen: WHO Regional Office for Europe, 2005), for European Observatory on Health Systems and Policies. Retrieved July 3, 2015 from www.euro.who.int/__data/assets/pdf_file /0007/108952/E85488.pdf.

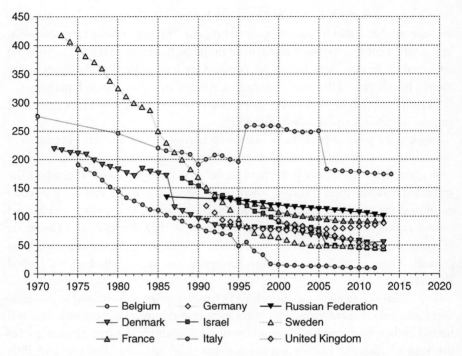

FIGURE 5.1. Psychiatric hospitalization beds per 100,000 in selected European
Countries and Israel, 1970–2015.
Adapted from European Health Database HFA-DB WHO, December 2015

In order to obtain a detailed and more insightful view of deinstitutionalization policy and legislation, the United Kingdom and Italy have been chosen,
basically because they present different approaches to change. The United
Kingdom presents a gradual and slower change toward community mental
health, whereas Italy demonstrates a faster transition but with growing concerns that the transition may cause inequalities in different regions of the
country.[19]

[19] Julia Jones, "Community-based mental health care in Italy: Are there lessons for Britain?" *Health &
Place* 2 (1996), 125–28; Julia Jones, "Mental health care reforms in Britain and Italy since 1950: A cross-
national comparative study," *Health & Place* 6 (2000), 171–87. Following her earlier article of 1996,
Jones discusses a cross-national comparative study which compares the implementation and geogra-
phical outcomes of mental health reforms in Britain and Italy since 1950. Working within a cross-
national framework, the research explores the social and spatial restructuring of mental health care
service provisions in two localities – Sheffield and Verona. She found huge diversity in the local
geographies of mental health services and facilities in both. Diversity exists despite the fact that both
Britain and Italy have introduced broadly similar mental health care reforms: closing psychiatric
hospitals and introducing community-based mental health care provisions. In addition to international variations, she found intra-regional and intra-city differences which were particularly pro-
nounced in Italy.

THE UNITED KINGDOM

The first indication of change from asylums to community health systems is marked by the Royal Commission on Lunacy and Mental Disorder in 1926.[20] The 1930 Mental Treatment Act was based on this approach, and can be viewed as a first step toward the empowerment of patients. One of its major reforms concerned patient status. Although patients were not yet able to act as full consumers, they were no longer mere passive recipients of treatments whose nature other people had decided. Regardless of their financial status, patients could now enter mental hospitals of their own volition, providing they were capable of signing the admission form.[21]

After World War II, most of the asylums were largely incorporated into the National Health Service (NHS), which was established in 1948. The number of patients in asylums peaked in the mid-1950s. The 1959 Mental Health Act abolished the distinction between psychiatric and other hospitals and encouraged the development of community care.[22] However, asylum-based care was the main model of psychiatric care for people with mental illness until the 1960s. The core reasons for the transition to community-based treatment were advances in psychiatry and drug treatment, in particular the introduction of phenothiazine, while the social and political climates of the time were the driving forces behind the closure of Victorian-era institutions.[23]

Two remarkable developments had an impact on the human rights of people with mental illness. The 1957 Royal Commission on the Law Relating to Mental Illness and Mental Deficiency recommended that patients who were ready to return home

---

[20] "Report of the Royal Commission on Lunacy and Mental Disorders" (Cmd. 2700) (London: HMSO, 1926). In 1922, the Royal Commission on Lunacy and Mental Disorders was established to review the existing legislation. In its 1926 report, it concluded that "the keynote of the past has been detention. The keynote of the future should be prevention and treatment." Recognizing that treatment is at its most effective when it is consensual, the commission suggested that "certification should be the last resort in treatment, not the prerequisite of treatment."

[21] The Mental Treatment Act 1930 is presented in the *British Medical Journal* 1930; 2 doi: http://dx.doi .org/10.1136/bmj.2.3648.978 (Published December 6, 1930). Cited as: Br Med J 1930; 2:978.

[22] Mental Health Act, 1959 7 & 8 ELIZ. 2 CH. 72. Retrieved January 23, 2016 from www.legislation.gov .uk/ukpga/1959/72/pdfs/ukpga_19590072_en.pdf. The 1959 Act was based almost entirely on the recommendations of the Royal Commission on the law relating to mental illness and mental deficiency chaired by Lord Percy ("The Percy Commission") which gave its report in 1957 (Royal Commission, 1957). Sweeping away much of the legalistic framework of the old acts of 1890 and 1930, the 1959 Act was guided by the philosophy that, whenever possible, care should be provided without the use of compulsion. However, in terms of treatment, it was assumed that detained patients admitted for treatment could be treated against their will.

[23] For further reading on the changes in five European countries, See J. van Weeghel et al., "The components of good community care for people with severe mental illnesses: Views of stakeholders in five European countries," *Psychiatric Rehabilitation Journal* 28 (2005), 274–81. Researchers and practitioners collaborated in a project across five European countries aimed at defining the characteristics of good community care for people with severe mental illnesses and to explore the values of stakeholders in this debate (clients, families, professionals, policy-makers, other citizens). In a concept mapping procedure, all stakeholders afforded highest priority to a trusting and stimulating relationship between clients and professionals. Secondly, good care was seen as effective treatment tailored to individual needs. Accessibility of services came in at third place.

would not be left in the hospital.[24] The 1959 Mental Health Act[25] was the first mental health legislation to clarify the reasons an individual might need to be admitted to hospital and treated against their will.

During the 1970s, more detailed and explicit mental health policies began to emerge dealing with the establishment of acute psychiatric units in general hospitals and the beginnings of community care. In 1971, a government paper on Hospital Services for the Mentally Ill[26] proposed the complete abolition of the mental hospital system with all services being delivered by district general hospitals with close liaison with general practitioners and social services. Outpatient clinics, therefore, became an integral part of psychiatric service provision and moved from having a triage function to becoming a resource for both assessment and follow-up.

It is evident that the 1980s demonstrated a shift toward community-based services for people with mental illness.[27] However, as in the United States, the policy was criticized for lacking adequate infrastructure and resources, which led to increased homelessness.[28] In 1983, a forward-looking Mental Health Act was introduced which consisted essentially of a substantial update of the landmark 1959 Act. Reforms included the creation of a Mental Health Act Commission to defend the rights of detained patients One of the most visible cases, that of Christopher Clunis, a man with a diagnosis of schizophrenia, who murdered Jonathan Zito in an unprovoked attack at Finsbury Park station in London,[29] highlighted the concern about the ability of community services to contain and handle problems. One of the responses was the Care Program Approach (CPA) which was introduced in 1990 to improve continuity of care for people with severe mental health problems.[30] In 2011, the government published a new mental

---

[24]　Department of Health and Social Security, "Royal Commission on the law relating to mental illness and mental deficiency" (London: HMSO, 1957).

[25]　See the full text at www.legislation.gov.uk/ukpga/Eliz2/7–8/72/contents.

[26]　Department of Health and Social Security, *Hospital services for the mentally ill* (London: HMSO, 1971).

[27]　See, for example, two publications of the time: Department of Health and Social Security, "Better services for the mentally ill" (London: HMSO, 1975); Department of Health and Social Security, "Care in the community" (London: HMSO, 1981).

[28]　Jeremy Coid, "Failure in community care: Psychiatry's dilemma," *British Medical Journal* 308 (1994), 805–06. Coid is concerned about the lack of adequate community care, abandoning mentally ill people on the streets, and imprisoning them. In his opinion, there is still a debate between professionals who claim that all seriously mentally ill people can be conveniently and easily managed in the community if resources are available and those who doubt the suitability of community care for a substantial minority of patients. The unresolved debate contributes to the current problem.

[29]　See Jean H. Ritchie, Donald Dick, and Richard Lingham, "The report of the inquiry into the care and treatment of Christopher Clunis," Norwich, HMSO, February 24, 1994. Retrieved February 17, 2016 from www.hundredfamilies.org/wp/wp-content/uploads/2013/12/CLUNIS_LON_1994.pdf.

[30]　The CPA model was reviewed in 1999 with the publication of the Mental Health National Service Framework and incorporated lessons learned about its use since its introduction. Great Britain Department of Health, Social Services Inspectorate, *Effective care co-ordination in mental health services: Modernising the care programme approach: A policy booklet* (London: Department of Health, Social Services Inspectorate, 1999) sets out current policy on the role and purpose of the CPA. In March 2008, Department of Health, *Refocusing the care programme approach: Policy and positive*

health strategy – "No Health without Mental Health"[31] – setting out their plans to improve people's mental health and well-being in the United Kingdom, and the services and support they were able to access.

Overall, the impression is that the United Kingdom is progressing gradually to a community-care policy, particularly in the twenty-first century. The early efforts included using the old psychiatric hospitals to supplement community care.[32] Then in the 1970s there was a decline in beds in psychiatric hospitals. They were replaced with acute psychiatric units in district general hospitals. The Mental Health Act of 1983, which was described earlier, was pivotal to the change in policy. The adoption of the CPA in the 1990s, together with the National Service Framework for Mental Health (NSF) of 1999, definitely changed the scene for persons with mental illness.[33]

An overall review of deinstitutionalization policy reveals that community mental health services were developed gradually in the 1990s in a climate of stringent resources. These services are provided by regionally organized "statutory" mental health care trusts which are part of the NHS, a publicly financed health care system under the direct control of the Department of Health. Although the government covers psychiatric costs, the supplementary areas such as housing, education, and work are offered by voluntary organizations that draw their income from a broad range of sources. In the past decade, the development of these nonstatutory social services has been stimulated by central government policy.

Also, during the past fifteen years national policy regarding mental health care has evolved from the prescriptive approach to the desired community mental health care structure, to a broader promotion of social inclusion and recovery objectives.

ITALY

Italy is probably one of the most revolutionary countries in Europe in transition-ing from institutional to community-based policy. In 1978, the Italian

practice guidance (London: Department of Health, 2008) was published to update policy and set out positive practice guidance.

31   "No health without mental health: A cross-government mental health outcomes strategy for people of all ages," London, Department of Health, Mental Health and Disability, February 2, 2011. This strategy sets out six shared objectives – more people will have good mental health; more people with mental health problems will recover; more people with mental health problems will have good physical health; more people will have a positive experience of care and support; fewer people will suffer avoidable harm; fewer people will experience stigma and discrimination – to improve the mental health and well-being of the nation and to improve outcomes for people with mental health problems through high quality services. It supports the government's aim of achieving parity of esteem between physical and mental health, stressing the connections between mental health, housing, employment, and the criminal justice system. Retrieved January 12, 2016 from www.gov.uk/govern ment/uploads/system/uploads/attachment_data/file/213761/dh_124058.pdf.

32   Andrew McCulloch, Matt Muijen, and H. Harper, "New developments in mental health policy in the United Kingdom," *International Journal of Law and Psychiatry* 23 (2000), 261–76.

33   Department of Health, *National service framework for mental health* (London: Department of Health, 1999).

parliament passed a radical mental health reform act known as the Basaglia Law[34] (Law 180),[35] abolishing psychiatric hospitals entirely and replacing them with community-based mental health services. Prior to this progressive legislation, the Italian mental health system relied on asylums and earlier legislation of 1904 and 1909, which defined admission procedures and types of psychiatric treatment.[36]

The 1978 psychiatric reform called for prohibition of all admissions to state mental hospitals, including readmissions. Existing mental hospital patients were not forcibly discharged to the community; the focus was on prevention of institutionalization rather than deinstitutionalization. The second principle was the establishment and expansion of community-based services responsible for the full range of psychiatric interventions. The intention was to order voluntary and involuntary hospitalizations only in emergency situations when community alternatives had already been tried and failed. In addition, hospitalization was only took place in general hospitals and in small units (no more than fifteen beds).[37]

While the reform law in Italy set out general principles and guidelines. it failed to provide detailed standards for service and staff provision, as well as an adequate budget to support the new community-based services. Each region was expected to define proper norms and methods according to the existing local situation. Although the number of patients residing in mental hospitals continued to decline over time, residential facilities, day hospitals, and day centers were unevenly distributed across Italy, with 56.5 percent of them located in the north and only 19.4 percent in the south. Overall, they were still lacking in 78.5 percent of local health districts.[38] The inequalities have been reduced over time, but the quality of care is still a matter of

[34] Franco Basaglia was among the prominent leaders of the deinstitutionalization movement. In 1961, he and his colleagues took over the state hospital of Gorizia, a small city in northeastern Italy, and were able to transform it completely in the course of the next few years. All wards were gradually opened and patients were allowed to move freely within the hospital and in the town. The Gorizia model was replicated in other cities and became the model for the 1978 Italian psychiatric reform and community mental health system.

[35] Basaglia Law or "Law 180" (Italian: *Legge Basaglia, Legge* 180) is the Italian Mental Health Act of 1978 which is known as the most significant reform of the psychiatric system in Italy, calling for the closure of all psychiatric hospitals and replacing them gradually with a whole range of community-based services, including settings for acute in-patient care. More than three decades later, "Law 180," reflects significant change toward mental illness in Italy. It appears that the closure of psychiatric hospitals and social acceptance of mental illness have been its main achievements. See Carlo A. Altamura and Guy M. Goodwin, "How Law 180 in Italy has reshaped psychiatry after 30 years: Past attitudes, current trends and unmet needs," *The British Journal of Psychiatry* 197 (2010), 261–62.

[36] The 1904 law implied that people affected by mental derangement had to be kept in custody and treated in mental hospitals when they are dangerous to themselves or to others. The 1909 regulations set the foundation for mental hospital organization. For further reading, see Mario Maj, "Brief history of Italian legislation from 1904 to 1978 reform," *Acta Psychiatrica Scandinavica* 71 (1985), 15–25.

[37] Giovanni de Girolamo et al., "The current state of mental health care in Italy: Problems, perspectives and lessons to learn," *European Archives of Psychiatry and Clinical Neuroscience* 257 (2007), p. 83; Lorenzo Burti, "Italian psychiatric reform 20 plus years after," *Acta Psychiatrica Scandinavica* 104 (2001), Issue Supplement s410, 41–46.

[38] Marco Piccinelli, Pierluigi Politi, and Francesco Barale, "Focus on psychiatry in Italy," *The British Journal of Psychiatry* 181 (2002), 638.

debate, in particular in terms of drug and rehabilitation treatments. These services are not readily available for most severe illnesses, leading to high readmission rates.

In order to improve the reform, in 1994 Parliament passed a national mental health plan. The plan prescribed the integration of all local mental health and human services under one administrative organization. This was a difficult responsibility for the Department of Mental Health (DMH) to provide services in Community Mental Health Centers (CMHC) and to standardize residential services. The plan was passed between 1998 and 2000, based on managed care and strict regulations in terms of spending.[39]

The unique Italian case provides interesting lessons for deinstitutionalization and the transition to community based-policy.[40] First, it appears that the process cannot be accomplished simply by closing mental health hospitals. Appropriate alternative facilities must be provided and this requires adequate time for planning and implementation. Second, deinstitutionalization requires political and administrative support, and in particular must take into account the growing cost of community-based options. Third, deinstitutionalization and any transition from asylums to community-based services have to be monitored and evaluated to pinpoint problems that need to be resolved.

SUMMARY OF CORE EUROPEAN STUDIES ON DEINSTITUTIONALIZATION

There are several studies on the impact of deinstitutionalization on people with mental illness, focusing on the reforms in Italy and England, whose policies and reforms were reviewed earlier in the chapter. Most of the follow-up studies on deinstitutionalization deliver favorable results about their reforms in the area of mental health.

Kemali and Maj[41] predicted outcomes for people with schizophrenia in six Italian cities (Trieste, Verona, Arezzo, Naples, Cetraro, and Cagliari) and found favorable outcomes in particular for those who used social and/or vocational skills training services. However the number of days hospitalized was not considered a predictor of success in community-based programs.

Balestrieri, Micciolo, and Tansella studied long-stay patients with mental illness in South Verona.[42] The two cohorts from the hospital and the community were similar in terms of basic socio-demographic variables and consisted of a similar proportion of psychotic patients. Findings indicated that while 88 percent of the long-stay inpatients were still long-stay after two years, only 45 percent of the

[39] Burti, "Italian psychiatric reform," 43.
[40] See de Girolamo et al., "The current state of mental health care in Italy," 90–91.
[41] Dargut Kemali and Mario Maj, "Attuazione della legge di riforma e valutazione dei servizi psichiatrici in Italia," *Rivista Sperimentale di Freniatria* (Suppl III) (1988).
[42] Matteo Balestrieri, Rocco Micciolo, and Michele Tansella, "Long-stay and long-term psychiatric patients in an area with a community-based system of care. A register follow-up study," *International Journal of Social Psychiatry* 33 (1987), 251–62.

long-term patients in the community remained in long-term treatment over the same period. Mosher and Burti, who compared them to people treated in other outpatient settings found that they had the greatest number of met needs.[43] Finally, Mignolli, Faccincani, and Platt carried out a seven-year follow-up study that compared patients with schizophrenia in hospital versus community-based programs and found improved symptomatology for half of those participating in community settings; the symptoms for hospitalized patients were either unchanged or had deteriorated.[44]

The most important study in England was carried out by the Team for the Assessment of Psychiatric Services (TAPS), which was established in 1985. It provided one of the few detailed evaluations of the national policy focusing on the planned closure of two of six large psychiatric hospitals in North London and their replacement with community-based services. The decision taken in 1983 by the regional health authority (North East Thames Health Authority) to close these hospitals was based on the relatively high cost of patient care and a large backlog of repairs.[45] After a ten-year re-provision program, one of the hospitals, Friern Hospital, closed in March 1993 on schedule. By contrast, financial constraints delayed the closure of the second hospital, Claybury, until January 1997.

Mental hospital/psychiatric hospital patients discharged to the community were followed up extensively. A one-year follow-up of 737 patients discharged from Friern and a proportion from Claybury revealed very little change in psychiatric symptoms and social behavior.[46] Almost half of the discharged patients had been hospitalized for more than twenty years; and 78 percent were moved to staffed homes in the community. Patients generally appreciated their less restrictive environments and 80 percent wished to remain in their community homes. Social friendships increased, but contacts with relatives decreased significantly. There were twenty-four recorded deaths, two of which were suicides; seven patients were lost to follow-up, presumed to have become homeless, and two received prison sentences.

At a five-year follow-up, 18.8 percent (126 of the 670 mental hospital/psychiatric hospital patients discharged) had died and twelve were untraceable.[47] Data were thus available for 523 (or 97 percent) of the discharged patients who were assessed at

43　Loren R. Mosher and Lorenzo Burti, Community mental health: Principles and practice (New York: Norton, 1989).

44　Giancarlo Mignolli, Cristina Faccincani, and Stephen Platt, "Psychopathology and social performance in a cohort of patients with schizophrenic psychoses: A 7-year follow-up study." In Community-based psychiatry: Long-term patterns of care in South Verona. Edited by Michele Tansella (Psychological Medicine Monograph Supplement; Cambridge: Cambridge University Press, 1991).

45　Julian Leff, Noam Trieman, and Cristopher Gooch, "The TAPS Project 33: A prospective follow-up study of long-stay patients discharged from two psychiatric hospitals," American Journal of Psychiatry 153 (1966), 1318–24.

46　Ibid.

47　Julian Leff and Noam Trieman, "Long-stay patients discharged from psychiatric hospitals. Social and clinical outcomes after five years in the community – The TAPS Project 46," British Journal of Psychiatry 176 (2000), 217–23.

three time points (baseline, one year, and five years). There were no significant changes in symptoms over time and about 40 percent of patients assessed, using the Present State Examination, experienced active delusions and/or hallucinations during the follow-up period. Similar findings were also found for social outcomes, in which community skills had improved significantly by one-year follow-up and maintained by five years. Domestic skills increased significantly at one year, but then decreased at five years. Social networks and the numbers of friends made in the first year were maintained over the five years, while the number of confidants had increased at each stage of follow-up.

THE CHALLENGES OF COMMUNITY MENTAL HEALTH IN EUROPE

Reviews of deinstitutionalization efforts in the United Kingdom and Italy reveal that both countries experienced the process of deinstitutionalization of psychiatric care in the second half of the twentieth century; however, the speed and methods by which it was implemented varied, notably due to differences in social and political contexts.

The driving force in both countries was government. In the United Kingdom, the creation of the NHS in 1948 and a favorable social and political climate led to the progressive closure of old psychiatric hospitals. The change in Italy began with the Mariotti Law of 1968 and the Basaglia Law of 1978, with tremendous changes in legislation, of climate, and the impact of civic society, particularly Franco Basaglia's impact. The change in Italy has been more radical, prohibiting all new admissions into psychiatric hospitals and denouncing hospitalization as a violation of human rights.

The political system clearly plays a major role in supporting community care policies. The United Kingdom is an excellent example of a country with incremental change, whereas Italy presents a rapid change, reflected by disparities in implementation.

Overall, in most European countries, the development of community services is a complex process that faces several important barriers. Some of these barriers are related to policy and may occur where there is a lack of adequate mental health policies and legislation, budgets are insufficient, or where there is procedural discrimination in terms of limited or lack of health insurance.

Other barriers are associated with difficulties the health systems face in reallocating resources from the large institutions to community-based services, lack of integration of mental health services into the general health system, and poor coordination with housing, welfare, and employment services. Therefore, the World Health Report of WHO of 2001[48] suggested that European countries promote new knowledge,

---

[48] See World Health Report 2001, *Mental health: New understanding, new hope* (Geneva: World Health Organization, 2001).

understanding, and the concomitant solutions, including a range of policy options, at the service of governments and policy-makers. The report assumed that there were no simple solutions; thus governments were encouraged to make strategic decisions and choices that would bring positive changes in the acceptance and treatment of mental and behavioral disorders. They would need to develop policy and to establish norms and standards that protect public health. This would include defining the respective roles of the public and private sectors in financing and provision of services and identifying policy instruments and organizational arrangements required in the public and private sectors to meet mental health objectives.

These human rights and mental health care problems challenge the European Human Rights System, which has played a key role in driving the process of deinstitutionalization across Europe.

INSTITUTIONALIZATION OF PEOPLE WITH INTELLECTUAL DISABILITIES IN EUROPE

A historical review of the status of people with intellectual disabilities in western European countries reveals that the state was hardly involved in their destiny. The English Elizabethan Poor Law of 1601 required each parish to select two overseers of the poor, whose job was to determine how much money it would take to care for the poor in his or her parish. The overseer was then to set a poor tax and collect the money from each landowner. For the poor, there were two types of relief available. First, there was outdoor relief, the more common type, in which the poor would be left in their own homes and either given money to buy the items they needed or given clothes and food. Then there was indoor relief, which provided shelter. For instance, orphans were taken to orphanages, the ill were admitted to hospitals, the deserving poor were taken to local almshouses, and the idle poor were taken to poorhouses or workhouses where they had to work. In other words, it transferred their care to parishes. In the eighteenth century, most of those categorized as idiots were left to the care of their families. The increase in institutionalization of people with intellectual disabilities in Europe is related to major migration from rural to urban regions. In England, the 1834 Poor Law Act 350 offered some assistance to the destitute disabled as well as social services for local parishes. Soon many of the parishes were not housing the able-bodied poor, who avoided them if they could, but only the disabled and the mentally ill.[49] At the beginning of the nineteenth century, a few hundred people lived in nine small charitable asylums. By 1900 more than 100,000 "idiots and lunatics" were

---

[49] The Poor Law Amendment Act 1834 (PLAA), known widely as the New Poor Law, was an Act of the Parliament of the United Kingdom passed by the Whig government of Earl Grey. It completely replaced earlier legislation based on the Poor Law of 1601 and attempted to fundamentally change the poverty relief system in England and Wales.

living in 120 county pauper asylums, with an average intake of almost 1,000. A further 10,000 were in workhouses.[50]

However, the eighteenth century was also marked by scientific attempts to educate children with intellectual disabilities by Jean-Marc-Gaspard Itard and Edouard Séguin.[51] This contribution resulted in the establishment of training institutions by Johann Jakob Guggenbühl in Switzerland and Berlin (1942) and in Leipzig (1846). In reality, these asylums separated people with intellectual disabilities from their communities, but this fact was secondary in the minds of the early workers. The asylums were founded on the theory that with training and education these people could gain sufficient skills to survive in society.

The same development took place in England in terms of legislation and planning of institutional care. The Idiots Act of 1886 encouraged the prospects for training and education,[52] leading local authorities to make a distinction between lunatics on the one hand and "idiots" and "imbeciles" on the other. The authorities built asylums and provided care, education, and training for the "idiots" and "imbeciles," who were distinct from "lunatics," who had simply become mentally ill, and could possibly recover. The 1890 Lunacy Act, however, did not make that distinction.[53]

The first decade of the twentieth century saw the rise of the eugenics movements in Europe. The earliest eugenics movements were founded in Germany in 1904 and in Britain in 1907. Other eugenics movements appeared subsequently in France, Norway, Sweden, Denmark, and Russia.

Interestingly, each country was concerned with a different population. British eugenicists were particularly concerned with the high fecundity and inherited mental degeneracy of the urban working class. Germany focused on the mentally

---

[50]   For a comprehensive and rigorous review of Victorian England and Earlswood Asylum (formerly the National Asylum for Idiots), see David Wright, *Mental disability in Victorian England: The Earlswood Asylum 1847–1901* (Oxford: Oxford University Press, 2001).

[51]   Edward Seguin (1812–1880), a French doctor who studied medicine and surgery under Itard (who wrote *Victor, the wild boy of Aveyron*), and psychiatry under Esquirol. Seguin is considered "the first great teacher" in the field of developmental disabilities. Although Seguin was a "free thinker," Pope Pious IX recognized his contributions by calling him "the apostle to the idiots." Working as director at the school for "idiots" in the Salpetriere asylum, Seguin improved upon Itard's method of sensory training. In studying Itard's work, Seguin saw the potential benefits of a physiological method in treating mental retardation. Seguin believed that mental deficiency was caused by a weakness of the nervous system, and could be cured through a process of motor and sensory training. By developing the muscles and senses, Seguin believed his pupils – regardless of their level of mental retardation – would obtain more control over their central nervous systems, thus allowing them to have more control over their wills.

[52]   Idiots Act, 1886 is presented in *The British Journal of Psychiatry* 33 (1887), 103–108.

[53]   The Lunacy Act of 1890 set the parameters for admission, providing a legal system in which a patient had to be certified as insane in order to be admitted to the asylum. Under the Act, asylums became the last resort. No psychiatric opinion was sought prior to admission. The parish doctor declared patients insane and they were then placed on a compulsory reception order by a local magistrate and taken to the asylum. The main components of the law can be retrieved from http://studymore.org.uk/1890s.htm.

ill, psychotic, psychopathic, and psychiatric patients along with the congenitally deaf, blind, and feebleminded. Great Britain's policy leaned toward institutionalization by enacting the Mental Deficiency Act of 1913[54] which legalized the detention of individuals with varying degrees of mental defect. It identified four categories of mental defects that provided the necessary diagnostic criteria for the certification of this group: *idiots* – persons so deeply affected in mind from birth or from an early age as to be unable to guard themselves against common dangers; *imbeciles* – persons who, whilst not being as defective as "idiots," were still incapable of managing their own affairs; *feebleminded persons* – persons who, whilst not being as defective as imbeciles, still required care, supervision, and control for their own protection or for the protection of others, and *moral defectives*, persons who, from an early age, displayed some permanent mental defect coupled with vicious or criminal propensities on which punishment had little or no effect.

Germany implemented mass genocide, and between 1939 and 1945 the Nazis systematically murdered as many as 200,000 mentally ill or physically disabled people who they stigmatized as "life unworthy of life." This complex and covert series of operations was known as the "euthanasia" program. It recruited and developed much of the personnel and the technical expertise later deployed in the "Final Solution."[55] Nordic countries adopted the sterilization of the feebleminded policy, while Sweden practiced compulsory sterilization between 1935 and 1975.[56]

Sterilization laws were enacted in the Nordic states against institutionalized women with intellectual disabilities. The prevailing eugenics ideas in these welfare states seem contradictory to current practices. However, most of the scientists then thought that involuntary sterilization was acceptable to prevent this genetic heritage from being passed on.[57] In Sweden, approximately 63,000 people were sterilized under Sweden's policy of eugenics which began in 1935 and came to a quiet close in 1976, when the law was silently dropped from the books.[58]

In Great Britain, the Wood Committee (1929)[59] called to accelerate institutionalization of 100,000 individuals with mental deficiency by construction of self-sufficient "colonies" that would cater to all groups of mental defectives, regardless of age or level

54 The Mental Deficiency Act 1913; available at http://hansard.millbanksystems.com/acts/mental-defi ciency-act-1913.

55 See Michael Burleigh, *Death and deliverance: Euthanasia in Germany 1900–1945* (Cambridge: Cambridge University Press, 1995).

56 Torbjörn Tännsjö, "Compulsory sterilization in Sweden," *Bioethics* 12 (1998), 236–49.

57 For extensive reading, see Gunnar Broberg and Nils Roll-Hansen, *Eugenics and the welfare states: Sterilization policy in Denmark, Sweden, Norway and Finland* (East Lansing, MI: Michigan State University Press, 2004).

58 Robert Fox, "Sweden promises full inquiry into forced sterilization," London *Daily Telegraph*, August 27, 1997.

59 *The Wood Report (1929)*. Report of the Mental Deficiency Committee. A Joint Committee of the Board of Education and Board of Control (London: HMSO, 1929); available at www.educationeng land.org.uk/documents/wood/wood1929.html.

of disability. A quote from the summary of the report provides an insight into the thinking of the time:

> In an institution school it is easy to find "worthwhile" work. For instance, comparatively low grade girls can each have their own locker in school for their underclothes, and repair them and make them tidy when they come back from the laundry, and they make the simpler garments they will wear, such as pinafores and vests. One or two school sessions are given up each week to definite instruction in housework and laundry work as actual school subjects and as preparatory to future work in the institution. Boys also learn to do simple repairs with a needle. As the boy approaches fourteen years of age it is usually found that he has learned as much as he can at school, including school manual work, and he is then drafted first for half a day and later for the whole day to the real trade shops of the institution or to the gardens. There he works under a skilled tradesman actually making things for sale or for the institution use. When a boy is thus transferred does not depend on his age, on whether he is sixteen or not, but only on his actual mental capacity and his progress.[60]

The term "colony" was to be eventually replaced with the term "hospital" with the implementation of the NHS Act 1946, under which control of colonies was transferred from local councils to Regional Hospital Boards.

According to Michael Burleigh, German eugenics scholars were in favor of involuntary euthanasia of the sick and those with disabilities, mainly because the country could not afford their funding and institutionalization.[61] The path to sterilization and the passing of the Law for the Prevention of Hereditary Diseased Progeny on July 14, 1933 was clear;[62] involuntary sterilization became legal. In the coming years, as the Nazi Party took control over the nation, the idea of killing them would be discussed by senior officials responsible for the administration of Germany's asylums.[63] According to postwar testimony by Dr. Karl Brandt, Hitler advised Gerhard Wagner, the Reich's chief doctor, that in the event of war he would need to practice euthanasia to "solve the problem of asylums in a radical way."[64] This was a preview to the planning of "Aktion T4."[65] The latter ran officially from September 1939 to August 1941, during which time a recorded 70,273 people were killed at various extermination centers located in Germany and Austria.[66]

DEINSTITUTIONALIZATION AND COMMUNITY LIVING

The post–World War II era brought tremendous changes to Europe, and to the quality of life of people with disabilities. The period is characterized by the

---

[60] Ibid., p. 66.   [61] Burleigh, *Death and deliverance*, pp. 20–25.   [62] Ibid., p. 42.   [63] Ibid., p. 47.

[64] Jeremy Noakes and Geoffrey Pridham, *Nazism 1919–1945 Volume 1: The rise to power: A documentary reader* (Exeter: University of Exeter Press, 1998).

[65] Ibid., p. 112.

[66] For further reading, see Michael S. Bryant, *Confronting the "good death": Nazi euthanasia on trial, 1945–1953* (Boulder: University Press of Colorado, 2005).

abandonment of eugenics ideas of sterilization and euthanasia and the recognition that people with intellectual disabilities had the right to live in the community. These gradual changes were based on changes in political and economic systems, values and ideology, and the leaning toward the welfare state model. Valerie Bradley listed the two major forces for change toward deinstitutionalization policies in Western Europe and the United States as the concept of normalization and the rejection of segregation of people with intellectual disabilities from the rest of society.[67] She differentiated between the first generation of deinstitutionalization policy focusing primarily on successful transition from institutions to community-based residences and the second aimed at their actual inclusion.

There was also growing research evidence that community-based services were preferable. In the 1950s, Jack Tizard and colleagues found that sixteen children with intellectual disabilities who moved from a long-stay hospital to "Brooklands," a community-based property, gained social skills that were not seen in the children who remained at the hospital setting.[68] A review of seventy-one studies published between 1980 and 1993, examining the effect of moving from institutional to community services in the United Kingdom and Ireland, found positive gains in five areas – competence and personal growth, observed challenging behavior, community participation, engagement in meaningful activity, and contact from staff.[69]

There was a growing recognition that deinstitutionalization could not end with institutional closure and downsizing but with building community-based services, social participation, and choices and control by people with disabilities.[70] However, there are differences in deinstitutionalization policies among European countries. Nordic states adopted earlier the normalization principle that led them to deinstitutionalization and community living legislation and policy. The United Kingdom adopted deinstitutionalization and community living policies but at a slower pace. Other countries are still caught in a mixed model of institutions and community care, particularly eastern European countries that have a substantial number of institutional care facilities.

DEINSTITUTIONALIZATION IN NORDIC STATES

Institutionalization for people with intellectual disabilities was the prevailing model of care in Sweden, as in most of the Nordic countries. However, in parallel and

---

[67] Jim Mansell and Kent Ericsson, *Deinstitutionalization and community living: Intellectual disability services in Scandinavia, Britain and the USA* (London: Chapman and Hall, 1995). See Foreword written by Valerie Bradley, vice-chair and presiding officer of the U.S. President's Committee on Mental Retardation.

[68] Jack Tizard, "Residential care of mentally handicapped children," *British Medical Journal* 1 (1960), 1041–46.

[69] Eric Emerson and Chris Hatton, *Moving out: Relocation from hospital to community* (London: HMSO, 1994).

[70] Valerie J. Bradley and James Knoll, *Shifting paradigms in services to people with disabilities* (Cambridge, MA: Human Services Research institute, 1991).

gradually, the Nordic countries adopted a new socio-political approach with the introduction of the normalization principle in Sweden in 1946.[71] In brief, the policy embraces three core concepts: the welfare state, democratic rights, and normalization principles. In other words, participation of people with disabilities in the welfare society is seen as a democratic right, which granted and confirmed their role as citizens. As such, they made up part of the general public whose welfare was to be guaranteed by the new services which were to be established. Therefore, it is societal responsibility to offer them services according to the normalization principle in the least restrictive environment.

In the 1960s, normalization became the core ideological approach, advocating for using least restrictive practices. In the first phase, which occurred during the 1970s and early 1980s, the effort focused on normalizing institutional facilities, whereas the second phase marked a rapid deinstitutionalization, interpreted as institutional closure and building up community-based services.[72]

The first phase of normalization called for improving rather than replacing institutions. By the late 1960s, across Nordic states the investment was in modern and small facilities, including convergence. In Denmark, the average number of residents per institution went down to sixty-five by 1969.[73] Sweden downsized institutional care more rapidly, and moved to the congregate care model, which Norway adopted a few years later,[74] although the change was pushed to the 1980s in Norway, Finland, and Iceland.

It is evident that deinstitutionalization was practiced in all Nordic states but at a different pace. By 2000, Norway and Sweden had closed all of its institutions for people with ID.

[71] A government committee stated that people with disabilities have the right to live, socialize, and work in less restricted environments. See SOU 1946:24. Förslag till effektiviserad kurators-och arbetsförmedlingsverksamhet för partiellt arbetsföra m.m. A quotation from the report of the committee reflects the message: ... the agreed upon principle that the partially able-bodied to as great an extent as "possible be included in the ordinary system of social services which are being developed in our country.... It is hardly necessary to emphasize that this, even for the partially able-bodied themselves, must be seen as a basic right as a citizen; it is entirely in keeping with the very essence of democracy that equal human value and equal rights are put in the foreground.... Psychologically this 'normalization' of conditions of life, education, employment exchange etc. of the partially able-bodied must be a great achievement" (SOU 1946:24, p. 28).

[72] See Jan Tøssebro et al., "Normalization fifty years beyond—current trends in the Nordic countries," *Journal of Policy and Practice in Intellectual Disabilities* 9 (2012), 134–46. A comprehensive analysis of developments in services for people with intellectual disabilities in the Nordic countries. The authors highlight the important progress toward deinstitutionalization and decentralization in the 1990s. They note that the main goal of the twenty-first century is to promote civic rights and reduce inequality across municipalities.

[73] See J. Smith, "Oversigt over udviklingen i Statens Åndssvageforsorgs byggeri i årene 1959–1969 [State care services for people with intellectual disabilities 1959–1969]." In *Ti års åndssvageforsorg. 1.* Edited by Statens Åndssvageforsorg (Copenhagen: Statens Åndssvageforsorg, 1969), pp. 11–16.

[74] K. Grunewald, *Från idiot till medborgare. De utvecklingsstördas historia. [From idiot to citizen: The history of intellectual disability]* (Stockholm: Gothia, 2010). Grunewald was one of the advocates of decentralization of services and supported local solutions rather than national ones.

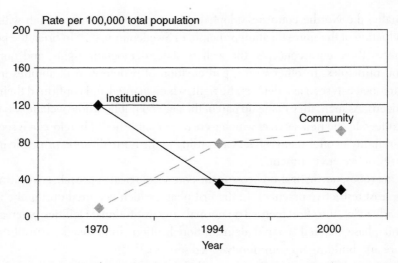

FIGURE 5.2. Deinstitutionalization and community living in Sweden, 1970–2000.
The graph was taken from Karl Grunewald, "Close the institutions for the intellectually
disabled: Everyone can live in the open society," former head of Division for Care
of People with Disability, National Board of Health and Welfare, Stockholm, 2003.

Figure 5.2 illustrates the change in Sweden between 1970 and 2000. In the other
three Nordic countries, the pace has been slower. The Finnish government set an
ambitious goal to reduce the number of people in institutions to 500 by 2015.[75] In
Norway and Iceland, deinstitutionalization meant transforming institutions into
group homes. The process was associated with changes in legislation and regulations. Denmark abolished the old specific legislation in 1976 and Norway did so in
1991. Iceland, on the other hand, retained special legislation for people with disabilities, supplementing the special legislation with general legislation in 1982, and
in 1994 introduced rights-based legislation for people with severe disabilities. The
latter is a significant change because it shifted the focus to personalized services
rather than normalizing institutions.

The change in Nordic states was also in shifting service delivery from central to
local governments. Most of the 1990s reforms were carried out by central governments, whereas the service delivery was transferred to local governments. Finland,
Norway, and Sweden cancelled earmarking of central government funding for
services to people with ID, whereas Denmark made local authorities fully responsible for funding in 2007.[76]

[75] Ympäristöministeriö (Ministry of Environment in Finland) (2009), Asuntoja kehitysvammaisille ja
vaikeavammaisille. Ehdotus kehitysvammaisten ja muiden vaikeavammaisten asunto-hjelmaksi vuo-
sille, 2010–2015.
[76] For further information on the service delivery system, see M. Tideman, *Normalisering och kategorisering.
Om handikappideologi och välfärdspolitik i teori och praktik för personer med utvecklingsstörning*

DEINSTITUTIONALIZATION IN UNITED KINGDOM

The 1950s and particularly the 1960s saw increased public awareness of the terrible conditions in institutional care facilities and their violation of human and civil rights. There was also growing professional recognition that people with intellectual disabilities would benefit more from community-based programs. The Report of the Royal Commission on the Law Relating to Mental Illness and Mental Deficiency of 1957, known as the Percy Commission, recommended fundamental changes commensurate with the huge changes that had occurred in psychiatric thinking and practice. The report concluding that the default treatment conditions should be "informal" was revolutionary, as was the reliance on medical judgment in determining involuntary admission in the first instance and the expansion of residential care.[77] It paved the way for the 1959 Mental Health Act, and the discharge of many people with intellectual disabilities from long-stay institutions – which became hospitals with the advent of the NHS – into community settings. However, the most notable inquiry about the damage to people with intellectual disabilities was released in 1969 known as the *Report of the Committee of Enquiry into Ely Hospital*[78] (a.k.a. the Howe Report).[79] The committee, under the chairmanship of Mr. Geoffrey Howe, QC, accepted allegations against the staff including ill treatment, using food supplied for patients, and abuse. The committee also criticized the procedures for dealing with complaints in the hospital service as a whole and recommended inspection of all institutions in the United Kingdom.

In 1971, the White Paper "Better Services for the Mentally Handicapped" was introduced and recommended a 50 percent reduction in hospital places by 1991 with increased local authority residential and day care. It also recommended the retraining of hospital staff. One of the earliest indications that the principle of normalization[80]

[*Normalization and categorization. On ideology and welfare policy in theory and practice for people with intellectual disabilities*]. Lund: studentlitteratur, 2000.

[77] The Percy Commission, *Report of the Royal Commission on the law relating to mental illness and mental deficiency 1954–1957* (London: HMSO, 1957).

[78] When the scandal broke at Ely Hospital, in Cardiff, in August 1967, the building was already more than one hundred years old. It had just marked its centenary, having been opened in 1862 as a Poor Law Industrial School for Orphaned Children. In 1903, it had become a workhouse and remained so until it was made part of the NHS in July 1948.

[79] See *Report of the Committee of Inquiry into allegations of ill-treatment of patients at the Ely hospital* (Cardiff: HMSO, 1969). Retrieved February 28, 2016 from www.sochealth.co.uk/national-health-service/democracy-involvement-and-accountability-in-health/complaints-regulation-and-enquries/report-of-the-committee-of-inquiry-into-allegations-of-ill-treatment-of-patients-and-other-irregularities-at-the-ely-hospital-cardiff-1969/.

[80] Normalization of the time was based on O'Brien and Tyne's five service accomplishments, which include the right to take part in community life and to live and spend leisure time with other members of the community, the right to experience valued relationships with nondisabled people, and the right to make choices, both large and small, in one's life. These include choices about where to live and with whom to live; the right to learn new skills and to participate in meaningful activities with whatever assistance is required; and the right to be valued and not treated as a second-class citizen. See John O'Brien and Alan Tyne, *The principle of normalization: A foundation for effective services* (London: Campaign for People with Mental Handicaps, 1985).

was beginning to influence social policy discourse, even at central government level, came with the publication of the *Report of the Committee of Enquiry into Mental Handicap Nursing and Care*.[81] This report, among other things, called for a review of nurse training and proposed a new model of training in line with the philosophy of ordinary life. The main focus of the report emphasized the individual's right to a normal life. The report, known also as the Jay Report, after the name of the chair Peggy Jay, was critical of large institutional forms of care in the community, such as large hostels, on the grounds that housing people in purpose-built units on the outskirts of towns and cities did not promote participation in the community.

Caring for People of 1989[82] and the NHS and Community Care Act 1990[83] announced and instigated some of the government's plans for the development of community-based services. The White Paper, *Caring for people*, proposed measures to end the confused and fragmented nature of service provision (from social security, health, local authorities, and private and voluntary agencies). An increase in consumer choice and making service providers more accountable was also called for but not earmarked. Responsibility for planning, coordinating, and paying for services was to be handed to local authorities, yet no ring "fencing" of funds was put forward in the Paper, nor was there any suggestion of an increase in funds. Funding was a major issue in the formulation of the NHS Community Care Act itself.

The overarching aim of the NHS Community Care Act was to help people live safely in the community. Social Services were assigned to assess the needs of individuals and arrange for the provision of social care services to meet those needs. Other responsibilities included the creation of procedures for receiving comments and complaints, organizing registration and inspection procedures and, crucially (given the concerns over cost), the assessment of an individual's ability to contribute.

The Community Care (Direct Payments) Act (1996)[84] gave disabled people the legal right to receive payment of community care funds to purchase their own assistance. Disabled people can receive Direct Payments if they are sixteen or over and have been assessed by Social Services as needing a service. In agreement with the social worker assigned to the disabled person, Direct Payments can be used to purchase personal help with, for example, dressing, washing, or eating meals.

Indication that the policy in the twenty-first century is geared toward supporting people with intellectual disabilities in the community appears in two white

[81] *Report of the committee of enquiry into mental handicap nursing and care* (Chairman: Peggy Jay) (London: HMSO, 1979).

[82] Department of Health, *Caring for people: Community care in the next decade and beyond* (London: HMSO, 1989).

[83] National Health Service and Community Care Act, 1990. Retrieved February 28, 2016 from www .legislation.gov.uk/ukpga/1990/19/content.

[84] Community Care (Direct Payments) Act, 1996. Retrieved January 16, 2016 from www.Legislation.gov .uk/ukpga/1996/30/section.

papers, *Valuing people,* 2001[85] and *Valuing people now,* 2009.[86] In *Valuing people,* one of the core government objectives was to enable people with learning disabilities and their families to have greater choice and control over where and how they live. An additional commitment was to complete the re-provision of the remaining long-stay hospitals to enable people still living there to move to more appropriate accommodations in the community by 2004. *Valuing people now* is seen as an effort to personalize their community living services and supports, in particular for people with the most complex needs that had been forgotten in the past.

Two additional pieces of legislation, the Disability Discrimination Act (1995)[87] and the Equality Act (2010)[88] present a new generation of disability rights approaches, primarily because they aimed to protect disabled people and prevent disability discrimination. The 1995 Disability Discrimination Act was introduced by the Conservative government to protect and promote the rights of disabled people and to make it unlawful to discriminate against them. The DDA enshrines the rights of those in society who have disabilities in areas such as disability employment opportunities, education and training, transport, and access to buildings, among others. It also encourages the public sector to promote equality of opportunity and inclusion for disabled people. It made it unlawful to discriminate against disabled people in connection with employment, the provision of goods, services or facilities, or the disposal or management of premises. It introduced a duty for service providers to make "reasonable adjustments" to allow disabled people to take advantage of their services. This might include provision of equivalent services.

From October 1, 2010 the Equality Act replaced most of the Disability Discrimination Act but most of the Disability Equality Duty in the original act remains. Such legislation has meant that disabled people have the right to goods, services, facilities, and premises. It is illegal for people with disabilities to be discriminated against or harassed in accessing everyday goods and services in shops, cafes, banks, and cinemas, to name but a few.

The graph below demonstrates the major decline in the rate of people with intellectual disabilities institutionalized in England from 1970 to 2000, and the parallel increase in rate of people placed in community-based accommodation.

---

[85] *Valuing people: A new strategy for learning disability for the 21st century.* White paper presented to parliament by the secretary of state for health by command of Her Majesty, March 2001. Retrieved January 23, 2016 from www.gov.uk/government/uploads/system/uploads/attachment_data/file/250877/5086.pdf.

[86] *Valuing people now: A new three-year strategy for people with learning disabilities,* Department of Health, January 19, 2009. Retrieved January 23, 2016 from http://base-uk.org/sites/base-uk.org/files/[user-raw]/11–06/valuing_people_now_strategy_.pdf.

[87] Disability Discrimination Act 1995. Retrieved January 27, 2016 from www.Legislation.gov.uk/ukpga/1995/50/contents.

[88] Equality Act 2010. Retrieved January 29, 2016 from www.Legislation.gov.uk/ukpga/ 2010/15/contents.

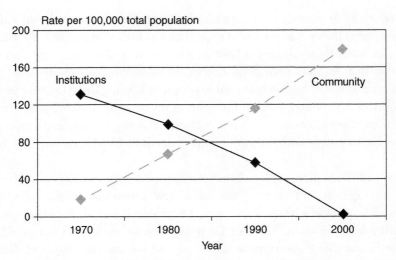

FIGURE 5.3. Deinstitutionalization and community living in England, 1970–2000.[89]

In terms of outcome of deinstitutionalization, in England institutional beds have decreased from more than 51,000 in 1976 to fewer than 4,000 in 2002.[90] However, the closure of hospitals has not led to a large number of people living in their own homes.

A report shows that two-thirds of people with intellectual disabilities who were receiving statutory support were living in congregated settings. Community Care[91] statistics in 2004 show that of those people who were receiving financial assistance for residential support, 96 percent were living in staffed homes or nursing homes. The most recent data on the current housing situation is based on Cordis Bright's detailed report to Mencap (The Royal Mencap Society, a charity that works with people with learning disability), which revealed that the last long-stay hospital in England was closed in 2009.[92] Local authorities arranged housing with support or care homes for an estimated 63,000 people in 2011. According to the report, three out of four people with intellectual disabilities lived with their families, with the rest in registered care homes and supported accommodations. However, the report marked the core challenges for years to come: the growing demand for housing and support services, the lack of future planning to meet these needs, and the fact that there were

[89]   Adapted from *Health and personal social services statistics for England* (London: Department of Health, HMSO, 2004); and Jim Mansell, "Better services 25 years on," *Tizard Learning Disability Review* 2 (1997), 45–46.
[90]   Eric Emerson, "Deinstitutionalization in England," *Journal of Intellectual and Developmental Disability* 29 (2004), 79–84; doi:10.1080/13668250410001662838
[91]   *Facing the facts: Services for people with learning disabilities: A policy impact study of social care and health services* (London: Department of Health, 1999).
[92]   Mencap, *Housing for people with learning disability*, 2012. Retrieved March 1, 2016 from www.men cap.org.uk/sites/default/files/documents/2012.108%20House.

not enough supplies available. The Welfare Reform Act,[93] enacted in 2012, was supposed to provide the budget for housing benefits on April 1, 2013.

DEINSTITUTIONALIZATION IN OTHER EUROPEAN COUNTRIES

Deinstitutionalization policies and practices vary in other western European countries. Germany, which adopted a eugenics policy at the beginning of the first half of the twentieth century and euthanasia during the Nazi regime, is definitely a unique case. After World War II, developments in East and West Germany followed different patterns. In the German Democratic Republic, disability concepts and policies followed the Soviet concept of "defectology." Services for children and adults with more severe intellectual disabilities were either run as a part of the statutory health sector, led by medical doctors, usually psychiatrists, or by Protestant institutions that had existed before the war. The conditions in these institutions were similar to those in other Communist countries of the time, and materially very poor.[94]

The change in institutional practices was the result of Lebenshilfe für geistig Behinderte (a strong parents association) lobbying for finding alternatives to institutional care facilities, culminating in the Social Assistance Act of 1962 known as the Bundessozialhilfegesetz (BSHG). At the time of initial implementation, poverty was in sharp decline compared to high postwar poverty in West Germany and was expected to decline even further. The political decision-makers who drafted the BSHG explicitly stated that the most important part of the new social assistance (SA) system would be the benefits for special living conditions (HbL).[95]

Although the largest group of long-term recipients of regular SA were older women, mostly widows who had lost their husbands in World War II and were otherwise receiving no or inadequate old age pensions, it provides a financial basis for the development of community living services, including residential homes.

The ongoing criticism of institutional care and increasing cost pressures in the funding system led to the creation of a mandatory, universal social assistance program for long-term care in unified Germany in 1994.[96] The program shifted the financial burden of long-term care from the states and municipalities to the federal level, and expanded HCBS. However, Germany is moving at a slower pace toward individualized, person-centered approaches, with thousands of people still residing in institutional and congregate care.

---

[93] Information about Welfare Reform 2012 available at services.parliament.uk/bills/2010–11/welfarere form.html.

[94] Mansell et al., *Deinstitutionalisation and community living*, pp. 36–37.

[95] The Federal Social Assistance Act of 1962 can be retrieved in German from www.gesetze-im-internet .de/bundesrecht/bshg/gesamt.pdf.

[96] Mansell et al., *Deinstitutionalisation and community living*, p. 35.

Ireland, which had a substantial number of people with intellectual disabilities in institutional care[97] in 2011, adopted the proposals in the report *Time to move on from congregated settings: A strategy for community inclusion.*[98] The report called for a new policy for residential support in the mainstream community, where people with disabilities were supported to live ordinary lives in ordinary places. In line with the report's recommendations, it was proposed that over the seven-year time frame, 2013–2019, residents – living in congregated type setting defined as living arrangements where ten or more people share a single living unit or where the living arrangements are campus based – would be provided with alternative housing in mainstream communities and the remaining institutions and residential campuses serving ten or more people would close progressively. Countries like Belgium, France, the Netherlands, and Spain, which used to have large institutional care systems, began the process of deinstitutionalization more than ten years ago.[99] In most of the former Soviet bloc countries (Hungary, Poland, Romania, Czech Republic), the number of people with intellectual disabilities living in institutions is substantially high. These countries in the twenty-first century shared similar characteristics with other European bodies – poor conditions and the need to adopt a deinstitutionalization policy.

In the first research project that explores institutions for people with disabilities in twenty-five European countries, there has been confirmation of the diversified picture of almost 2,500 institutions.[100] There are discouraging in-depth findings from France, Hungary, Poland, and Romania showing substantial numbers of large residential institutions. Residents in these large institutions have increased numbers of hours of inactivity, boredom, and isolation; staff numbers are frequently too low to provide habilitation and therapy; the physical environment is relatively impersonal and does not provide any kind of privacy and homeliness; and contact with family, friends and community is limited.

The overall impression that emerges from this explorative research is that, on average, community-based services offer better outcomes in terms of quality of life for disabled people than do institutions. Replacement of institutions by community-based

97   See Roy McConkey, Fiona Mulvany, and Steve Barron, "Adult persons with intellectual disabilities on the island of Ireland," *Journal of Intellectual Disability Research* 50 (2006), 227–36; Fiona Mulvany, Steve Barron, and Roy McConkey, "Residential provision for adult persons with intellectual disabilities in Ireland," *Journal of Applied Research in Intellectual Disability* 20 (2007), 70–76.

98   *Time to move on from congregated settings: A strategy for community inclusion.* Report of the Working Group on Congregated Settings Health Service Executive June 2011; available at www.hse.ie/eng/services/list/4/disability/congregatedsettings/congregatedsettingsreportfinal.pdf.

99   European Intellectual Disability Research Network, *Intellectual disability in Europe: Working papers* (Canterbury: Tizard Centre, University of Kent at Canterbury, 2003). Can be retrieved from www.enil.eu/wp-content/uploads/2012/07/Intellectual-Disability-in-Europe.pdf.

100 See Jim Mansell, Julie Beadle-Brown, and S. Clegg, "The situation of large residential institutions in Europe." In *Included in society: Results and recommendations of the European research initiative on community-based residential alternatives for disabled people.* Edited by Geert Freyhoff et al. (Brussels: Inclusion Europe, 2004), pp. 28–56.

alternatives therefore provides opportunities, but does not of itself guarantee better outcomes – it is a necessary but not sufficient condition. The study of the legal and financial framework of large residential institutions has revealed some problems for service providers in the process of moving to community-based residential services.

SUMMARY OF EUROPEAN STUDIES ON DEINSTITUTIONALIZATION

If most of the American studies on the impact of deinstitutionalization on people with ID/DD focus on changes in adaptive behavior, most of the European research uses quality of life as a primary outcome measure.[101] Jim Mansell, a leading international authority in deinstitutionalization studies, found that most of the studies have consistently shown that community-based services are better than institutions.[102] Specifically, people with ID/DD experience many benefits when moving from institutions to the community. Their personal skills increase and they are more engaged in activities. They have more contact with friends, wider social networks, and more community presence. They experience greater choice, satisfaction, and quality of life.

Although the transition to the community increases well-being,[103] the gains plateau over time,[104] suggesting they may be due to greater opportunities in community settings, rather than development of personal skills. There is strong evidence that living in community-based accommodation results in greater community presence, participation, and integration.[105] However, active participation is often not achieved, particularly for those with high support needs.[106]

Despite many gains experienced by people with intellectual disabilities in the community, there are some areas where there is no improvement, or indeed poorer outcomes. A population-based confidential Inquiry in southwest England reviewing deaths in 2010–2012 found that 37 percent of deaths of individuals with intellectual disabilities were due to factors associated with poorer access to health care (compared to 13 percent for the general population).[107]

---

[101] Jan Šiška and Julie Beadle-Brown, "Developments in deinstitutionalization and community living in the Czech Republic," *Journal of Policy and Practice in Intellectual Disabilities* 8 (2011), 125–33; Patricia Noonan Walsh et al., "Supported accommodation for people with intellectual disabilities and quality of life: An overview," *Journal of Policy and Practice in Intellectual Disabilities* 7 (2010), 137–42.

[102] Jim Mansell, "Deinstitutionalization and community living: An international perspective," *Tizard Learning Disability Review* 10 (2005), 22–29.

[103] Walsh et al., "Supported accommodation," 137–42.

[104] Eric Emerson and Chris Hatton, "Deinstitutionalization in the UK and Ireland: Outcomes for service users," *Journal of Intellectual and Developmental Disability* 21 (1996), 17–37.

[105] Ibid., p. 28.

[106] Peter A. Baker, "Individual and service factors affecting deinstitutionalization and community use of people with intellectual disabilities," *Journal of Applied Research in Intellectual Disabilities* 20 (2007), 105–09.

[107] Pauline Heslop et al., *Confidential inquiry into premature deaths of people with learning disabilities (CIPOLD): Final report* (Bristol: Norah Fry Research Centre, 2013).

Contributory factors suggested by the inquiry included inappropriate accommodation, problems with advanced care planning, not adjusting supports as needs changed, health care workers not feeling listened to, problems following the Mental Capacity Act, lifestyle choices, and delays in treating health problems. Community living is associated with poorer health behaviors (smoking, diet, activity), leading to poorer physical health, including obesity.[108] Some researchers have suggested that these are inevitable outcomes of increased choice, and may indeed be interpreted as people with intellectual disabilities experiencing the "dignity of risk."[109]

In the case of challenging behaviors, moving to community living has been associated with a decrease in such behaviors, but, as has been found in the United States, no change or an increase.[110] The differences depended on reporting methods, as staff typically reported no change, whereas observation studies reported fewer behaviors that challenge.[111]

COUNCIL OF EUROPE DEINSTITUTIONALIZATION AND COMMUNITY LIVING POLICY

The Council of Europe's role in the disability area is to promote the human rights of all citizens, including people with disabilities. The council's activity is channeled through the Commission of Human Rights which has been very dominant in advocating for deinstitutionalization and community living policies in Europe; the European Court of Human Rights, which has been pivotal in protecting the human rights of people with disabilities; and the European Social Charter treaty which guarantees fundamental social and economic rights as a counterpart to the ECHR (European Court of Human Rights), which refers to civil and political rights. It guarantees a broad range of everyday human rights (including people with disabilities) related to employment, housing, health, education, social protection, and welfare.

There is no doubt that the most important instrument in recent years in the disability area was the Council of Europe Disability Action Plan 2006–2015 (DAP),[112] which was adopted in April 2006 and launched at the European conference "Improving the quality of life of people with disabilities in Europe: Participation

[108] Walsh et al., "Supported accommodation," pp. 137–42.
[109] David Felce et al., "Outcomes and costs of community living: Semi-independent living and fully staffed group homes," *American Journal on Mental Retardation* 113 (2008), 87–101.
[110] Shannon Kim, Sheryl A. Larson, and Charlie K. Lakin, "Behavioral outcomes of deinstitutionalization for people with intellectual disability: A review of US studies conducted between 1980 and 1999," *Journal of Intellectual and Developmental Disability* 26 (2001), 35–50.
[111] Emerson and Hatton, "Deinstitutionalization in the UK and Ireland."
[112] See *Council of Europe action plan to promote the rights and full participation of people with disabilities in society: Improving the quality of life of people with disabilities in Europe 2006–2015*, Council of Europe, 2006. Retrieved June 5, 2015 from www.coe.int/t/e/social_cohesion/soc-sp/Rec_2006_5%20Disability%20Action%20Plan.pdf.

for all, innovation, effectiveness," in St. Petersburg in September 2006. The promotion, implementation, and follow-up of the plan was overseen by the European Coordination Forum for the Council of Europe Disability Action Plan 2006–2015.

The plan was viewed as a practical tool to guide member states in developing strategies to bring about full participation of people with disabilities in society and ultimately mainstreaming disability throughout all policy areas and programs. It consisted of fifteen action lines that set out key objectives and specific actions to be implemented by member states.

These action lines focused on: (i) participation in political and public life; (ii) participation in cultural life; (iii) information and communication; (iv) education; (v) employment, vocational guidance, and training; (vi) the built environment, with specific attention to ensure the safety of people with disabilities when designing emergency and evacuation procedures; (vii) transport; (viii) community living; (ix) health care; (x) rehabilitation; (xi) social protection; (xii) legal protection; (xiii) protection against violence and abuse; (xiv) research and development; and (xv) awareness raising. "Community living" (viii), calls for building a strategy for transitioning people with disabilities from institutional care to community-based settings, ranging from independent living arrangements to small group homes.

DAP has come to an end. A recent report underlined its added value for the European region and its contribution to the new plan for 2016–2020. The section that examined the impact of "community living" demonstrated the variations among states in deinstitutionalization policy and practice.[113] The report claims that many persons with disabilities still live in large segregated institutions, with detrimental consequences for the individual's life and personal development. They remain exposed to high risk of abuse and violations of their human rights and dignity. Person-centered and individualized services such as personal assistance, social housing, among others, remain underdeveloped due to the consequences of the economic and financial crisis. In fact there are signs of reinstitutionalization instead of developing new infrastructure for community-based programs.

The impression from the report is that the European Association of Service Providers for Persons with Disabilities (EASPD) has been very active in contributing to implementation by organizing numerous meetings in Skopje, Bulgaria, and in launching a road map on deinstitutionalization and the transition to community-based services.[114] The report compiled by EASPD suggested that community-based services can become a reality when people with disabilities themselves, their families, and their providers of support services were involved in every stage of the

[113] See Committee of Experts on the Rights of People with Disabilities (DECS-RPD), Report by the European Association of Service Providers for Persons with Disabilities (EASPD) "Enjoyment of rights in practice: towards the new CoE Disability Action Plan," submitted at Strasbourg Council of Europe, April 22–24, 2015, pp. 10–11.

[114] EASPD – Service Foundation for People with Intellectual Disability, "Making community-based services a reality: Roadmap on deinstitutionalization," December 4, 2013. Retrieved April 16, 2016 from www.easpd.eu/sites/default/files/sites/default/files/Policy/easpd_di_roadmap_final.pdf.

planning, design, and delivery of services. It recommended the UNCRPD as a road map for transforming the way they provide care and support to children and adults by replacing long-stay institutional services with family- and community-based services. The European Association of Service Providers for Persons with Disabilities (EASPD) also took part in a number of European projects on deinstitutionalization and community-based services. The recommendation for 2016–2020 is to continue these efforts based on the principle of the UNCRPD and to focus on knowledge base, best practices collection, and policy recommendation.

Additional steps of the Council of Europe include the 2008 second resolution of the Parliamentary Assembly of the Council of Europe portraying the damage of institutionalization to people with disabilities, in particular to their well-being and human rights. The declaration, which consists of nineteen statements, calls for the adoption of deinstitutionalization policy as a prerequisite to enabling people with disabilities to become as independent as possible and to take their places as full citizens.[115]

In 2009, the Parliamentary Assembly called for "Access to rights for people with disabilities and their full and active participation in society."[116] This resolution reflects the commitment to change, supporting the preparation by the DAP to promote the rights and participation of people with disabilities in society for 2006–2015, but more importantly it reminds states of the importance of the UNCRPD and the need to adopt the language and the guidance of the UNCRPD. In statement 7.1, there is guidance to guarantee that people with disabilities retain and exercise legal capacity on an equal basis (similar to Article 12 of the UNCRPD). Statement 8.1 is a reminder to the states to commit themselves to the process of deinstitutionalization by reorganizing services and reallocating resources from specialized institutions to community-based services.

If the action plan and Council of Europe declarations intended to advocate and promote progressive policies and practices, then the ECHR represents protection against individual or state alleging violations of the civil and political rights set out by the ECHR. Persons with disabilities held in institutions are among the most excluded groups in European society, routinely suffering from multiple violations of their rights.

There are two illustrations demonstrating the ECHR's rulings and approach in cases of legal capacity. In *Mihailovs v. Latvia*,[117] the ECHR found that Mr. Mihailovs'

---

[115]   "Access to rights for people with disabilities and their full and active participation in society," Council of Europe, Parliamentary Assembly, August 8, 2008, paragraph 44. Retrieved May 3, 2016 from http://assembly.coe.int/Main.asp?link=/Documents/WorkingDocs/Doc08/EDOC11694.htm.

[116]   Parliamentary Assembly, assembly debate on January 26, 2009 (2nd Sitting) (see Doc. 11694, report of the Social, Health and Family Affairs Committee, rapporteur: Mr. Marquet). Text adopted by the Assembly on January 26, 2009 (2nd Sitting). See also Recommendation 1854 (2009). Resolution 1642 (2009) paragraph 2; available at embly.coe.int/nw/xml/XRef/Xref-XML2HTML-en.asp?fileid=17697&lang=en.

[117]   The case is available at www.mentalhealthlaw.co.uk/Mihailovs_v_Latvia_35939/10_(2013)_ECHR_65,_(2013)_MHLO_15.

placement in an institution was unlawful, in particular as there had been no objective medical opinion to justify his detention, and that under Latvian law there was no possibility for a person in such a situation to have their detention reviewed by the courts. In the decision given by the ECHR on January 22, 2013, there is a clear recognition that Mr. Mihailovs' institutionalization for years against his will without any review was a violation of Article 5 §1 (right to liberty and security) of the European Convention on Human Rights.[118] This applied to the period between January 2002 and April 2010. In addition, the court decided that there was a violation of Article 5 §4 (right to liberty and security). The court was also concerned about his legal capacity and that he had been held against his will in a social care institution for more than ten years without possibility of release.

The decision is based on European law but was also sending a clear message to European countries that ratified the UNCRPD. The mechanisms and practices conducted by the state that permit forced institutionalization, forced treatment, deprivation of legal capacity, and discrimination against persons with psychosocial disabilities represent serious violations of fundamental human rights. The latest developments in international law demonstrate the need for states to eliminate these practices and the legal constructions which support them in order to ensure, in principle and in practice, the enjoyment and exercise of rights by persons with disabilities on an equal basis with others.

The second case, *Stanev v. Bulgaria,*[119] which reached the Grand Chamber decision on January 17, 2012, presents similar violations of human rights. In 2000, at the request of two of the applicant's relatives, a court declared him to be partially lacking legal capacity on the grounds that he was suffering from schizophrenia. In 2002, the applicant was placed under partial guardianship against his will and admitted to a social care home for people with mental disorders near a village in a remote mountain location. Under Article 5 (right to liberty and security) of the UNCRPD, the applicant alleged in particular that he had been deprived of his liberty unlawfully and arbitrarily as a result of his placement in an institution against his will and that it had been impossible under Bulgarian law to have the lawfulness of his deprivation of liberty examined or to seek compensation in court.

The court held that there had been a violation of Article 5 §1 (right to liberty and security) of the UNCRPD, in that the applicant had been illegally detained in the institution in question. It observed in particular that the decision to place the applicant had not been lawful within the meaning of Article 5 §1 of the UNCRPD since none of the exceptions provided for in that article were applicable, including Article 5 §1(e) – deprivation of liberty of a "person of unsound mind."

The period that had elapsed between the expert psychiatric assessment relied on by the authorities and the applicant's placement in the home, during which time his

---

[118] Retrieved January 28, 2016 from www.echr.coe.int/Documents/Convention_ENG.pdf.
[119] Accessed February 1, 2016 at www.bailii.org/cgi-bin/markup.cgi?doc=/eu/cases/ECHR/2010/1182.

guardian had not checked whether there had been any change in his condition and had not met with or consulted him, had furthermore been excessive and a medical opinion issued in 2000 could not be regarded as a reliable reflection of the state of the applicant's mental health at the time of his placement in the home (in 2002). The court further held that there had been a violation of Article 5 §4 (right to have lawfulness of detention decided speedily by a court) of the UNCRPD, concerning the impossibility for the applicant to bring proceedings to have the lawfulness of his detention decided by a court, and a violation of Article 5 §5 (right to compensation). concerning the impossibility for him to apply for compensation for his illegal detention and the lack of review by a court of the lawfulness of his detention.

The European Union ratified the UNCRPD on December 23, 2010, the first time in its history that the EU has become a party to an international human rights treaty.[120] The impression is that the ratification has already begun to shape the jurisprudence of the, ECHR, and in many areas it is proving to be a key instrument for promoting law reform and requiring states to reexamine how persons with disabilities are perceived.[121] Often, it has asked fundamental questions regarding paternalistic welfare policy, and particularly, the legal capacity and institutionalization of people with disabilities.

THE EUROPEAN UNION

The EU institutions, including the European Commission, are required to comply with the EU Charter on Fundamental Freedoms ("the EU Charter"),[122] which is legally binding on member states when implementing EU law. There is a considerable overlap between the rights set out in the EU Charter and those contained in the ECHR,[123] and while the EU is not yet party to the ECHR,[124] the ECHR has a special position in EU law.[125] Much of the case law of the Court of Justice of the European Union (CJEU) refers expressly to the ECHR and in practice it seeks, if at all possible, to make its judgments consistent with those of the ECHR in Strasbourg.

Reflecting socio-legal change during the second half of the twentieth century, the EU Charter, unlike the ECHR, is explicit in its protection of the rights of

---

[120] Official website of the European Commission, "The European Commission (EU) ratifies UN Convention on disability rights," press release, Brussels, January 5, 2010; available at http://europa.eu/rapid/pressReleasesAction.do?reference=IP/11/4&format=HTML&aged=0&language=EN&guiLanguage=en.

[121] For studying the possible impact of the UNCRPD on European Law, see Jarlath Clifford, "The UN Disability Convention and its impact on European equality law," *The Equal Rights Review* 6 (2011), 11–25.

[122] Retrieved March 3, 2016 from www.europarl.europa.eu/charter/pdf/text_en.pdf.

[123] Retrieved March 3, 2016 from www.echr.coe.int/Documents/Convention_ENG.pdf.

[124] Article 6(2) of the Treaty on European Union provides that the "Union shall accede to the European Convention for the Protection of Human Rights and Fundamental Freedoms."

[125] See, for example, Opinion 2/94 Accession of the European Community to the European Convention for the Safeguard of Human Rights and Fundamental Freedoms, 1996.

persons with disabilities. Article 21 specifically lists disability as one of the grounds on which discrimination must be prohibited, and Article 26 recognizes the right of people with disabilities to "benefit from measures designed to ensure their independence, social and occupational integration and participation in the life of the community."

The DAP was developed as the result of the European Year of People with Disabilities in 2013.[126] The DAP's main focus was independent living of people with disabilities. The strategy focused on the activities carried out by the commission at the EU level. It aimed to bring coherence to and coordination of the activities of the various commission services. The strategy was based on three pillars: mainstreaming, accessibility, and legislation against discrimination in employment. A mid-term evaluation of the DAP (VT/2007/008) recommended aligning the activities to the full implementation of the UNCRPD.

The UN Convention on the Rights of Persons with Disabilities (UNCRPD)

Since March 2007, all EU member states have signed the UNCRPD and a majority has also signed its Optional Protocol. The ratification by the member states is underway. The European Union has also signed the UNCRPD and the council adopted the decision for conclusion of the UNCRPD in November 2009.[127] Furthermore, the commission has issued a proposal for a council decision to accede to its Optional Protocol.[128] The UNCRPD is based on the human rights approach to disability, and its conclusion entails an obligation to bring disability policy in line with this approach and to align current practices with the social model of disability. It addresses many areas where the commission has active policies, from employment to transport, education, and information society.

The new strategy was adopted on November 15, 2010 with the overall objective of breaking down the barriers that prevent people with disabilities from participating in society on an equal basis. The 2010–2020 Strategy[129] placed emphasis on the respect of the rights of people with disabilities and, more specifically, on the implementation of the UNCRPD. Consequently, most of the actions described in the Strategy are geared to the national level and the main role of the European Commission will shift from implementer to coordinator.

---

[126] Communication from the Commission to the Council, the European Parliament, the European Economic and Social Committee, and the Committee of the Regions – Equal opportunities for people with disabilities: A European Action Plan /* COM/2003/0650 final */.

[127] Retrieved April 12, 2016 from http://eur-lex.europa.eu/LexUriServ/LexUriServ.do?uri=OJ: L:2010:023:0035:0061:EN:PDF.

[128] Retrieved April 12, 2016 from http://eur-lex.europa.eu/LexUriServ/LexUriServ.do? uri=SPLIT_COM:2008:0530(02),FIN:EN:PDF.

[129] The comprehensive analysis of the 2010–2020 Disability Strategy is available at www.epr.eu/images/ EPR/documents/policy_documents/The%20EU%20Disability%20Strategy%20Analysis% 20paper.pdf.

One of the important goals of the strategy is participation, calling to promote the transition from institutional to community-based care by using the Structural Funds and the Rural Development Fund to support the development of community-based services.[130] The aim is also to develop and disseminate a quality framework for community-based services which will be based upon the European quality for Social Services of General Interest which was launched by the Social Protection Committee in October 2010. Finally, it aims to promote the exchange of good practices among member states in the Disability High level group on the personal assistance funding scheme.

THE STRUCTURAL FUNDS: SUPPORTING INSTITUTIONAL VS. COMMUNITY LIVING

The Structural Funds is a core instrument in the European Union's strategy to support social inclusion and anti-poverty policies and reducing economic and social disparities. In many member states, in particular in Eastern Europe, the EU Structural and Investment Funds aim at investing in economic and social development in countries suffering from the impact of the financial and economic downturn.

In the financing period of 2007–2013, the Structural Funds promoted sustainable development by strengthening growth, competitiveness, employment, and social inclusion, and by protecting and improving the quality of the environment. The Structural Funds budget was large – €347.410 billion (around €50 billion per annum and a third of the EU budget).[131] The impact on eastern European countries is significant and probably more so in the 2014–2020 period as the budget has been increased by 8 percent.[132]

The Structural Funds provide the opportunity to assist governments in planning and implementing their deinstitutionalization strategies and in developing the community living alternatives according to the UNCRPD and other international and European human rights standards. However, in some cases the Structural Funds have been used to support institutional care instead of community-based programs.

[130]   Ibid, pp. 6–7. Goal 3.24 states the importance of participation: "There are still many obstacles preventing people with disabilities from fully exercising their fundamental rights and limiting their participation in society on an equal basis with others. To cope with this issue, the Commission will notably: Promote the transition from institutional to community-based care by using the Structural Funds and the Rural Development Fund to support the development of community-based services; Develop and disseminate a quality framework for community-based services which will be based upon the European quality for Social Services of General Interest which was launched by the Social Protection Committee on October 2010; Promote the exchange of good practices among Member States in the Disability High level group on the personal assistance funding scheme."

[131]   See European Union, "The control system for cohesion policy: How it works in the 2007–2013 budget period (Luxembourg: Office for Official Publications of the European Union, 2009), p. 5.

[132]   This figure was referred to in the briefing "EU structural and cohesion funds." Retrieved May 10, 2016 from www.publications.parliament.uk/pa/cm201012/cmselect/cmeuleg/428-xli/42803.htm.

In one of the reports published in 2010,[133] the ECCL explained why there was such concern about the inappropriate use of the Structural Funds among the EU Member States of Central and Eastern Europe (CEE).[134] The Structural Funds was used to renovate institutions for people with disabilities or to build new residential institutions rather than to develop community-based alternatives, contrary to EU policy objectives, EU law, and European and international human rights standards. One of the most frustrating findings was that in some states it was impossible to change the rules and build up alternatives to institutional care.

There are a few reasons for the difficulties in using the Structural Funds for deinstitutionalization and community living reform. One of the evident difficulties is related to the operation of the Structural Funds in the European Union. In some cases there is lack of clarity in the European Union regarding the scope and purpose of the programs being financed. This has been observed in Hungary, which submitted an operational program to close its large institutions; however, the action plan did not reflect that with the large institutions being downsized to fifty-bed units.

Another problem is the lack of monitoring or evaluation of the use of the Structural Funds, with some problems arising from the way member states use the Structural Funds. The report, *Wasted time, wasted money*, outlines two key aspects of this concern.[135] The first is the construction of new institutions because of the lack of community-based services, as in the case of Romania which offer to build up modern infrastructure. In some cases, the provision of the Structural Funds regulations has been misinterpreted by a member state. For example, under the current Structural Funds regulations there are strict eligibility criteria for housing.[136]

It is clear that the Structural Funds is a powerful instrument to facilitate transition from institutions to community-based services. The purpose of the Structural Funds is to support the goals of Europe 2020 by providing member states with the financial and technical support they need to replace their institutional care system with

[133] European Coalition for Community Living (EECL), *Wasted time, wasted money, wasted lives ... A wasted opportunity?* 2010. A focus report on how the current use of the Structural Funds perpetuates the social exclusion of disabled people in Central and Eastern Europe by failing to support the transition from institutional care to community-based services. This report is a publication of the European Coalition for Community Living. It was produced as part of a project, supported by the Open Society Mental Health Initiative, looking at the use of the Structural Funds in relation to services for people with disabilities in Central and Eastern Europe. The project was implemented in cooperation with the Institute for Public Policy in Romania, the Soteria Foundation and the Eötvös Loránd University (ELTE) in Hungary. Retrieved April 23, 2016 from Project Nr. 2005/9/VPD1/ERAF/CFLA/GS/1.4.6.2./0001/0008.
[134] Retrieved May 18, 2016 from www.enil.eu/wp-content/uploads/2012/07/Focus-Report-on-how-the-current-use-of-Structural-Funds-perpetues-social-exclusion-of-PWD-in-CEE-by-failing-support-the-transition-from-institutional-to-community-based-care.pdf.
[135] EECL, *Wasted time, wasted money*, pp. 25–26.
[136] Regulation (EC) No. 1080/2006 of the European Parliament and of the Council of 5 July 2006 on the European Development Fund and repealing Regulation (EC) No. 1783/1999 (referred to in this report as "the ERDF regulations").

community living programs. It is essential that the problems with the Structural Funds have to be addressed so that they can be avoided in the future.

CONCLUSION

Institutionalization in Europe was expanded at the beginning of the twentieth century up to the beginning of World War II. Although there are differences and variations among countries, most western European countries were influenced by the eugenics movement. This period is overshadowed by sterilization and segregation policies to the extreme of killing of the "unfit" in Germany.

The review of institutional care and deinstitutionalization policies and practices in mental health and intellectual disabilities reveals different patterns. In mental health, the chapter introduces two case examples, Italy and the United Kingdom, demonstrating different commitment to transitioning from segregated hospitals to community living programs. The overall impression is that the difference between Italy and the United Kingdom is related to domestic circumstances. There is no doubt that deinstitutionalization in the United Kingdom has taken place at slower pace, and is more regulated by central government.

The deinstitutionalization of people with disabilities was quite influenced by the normalization principle led by Scandinavian scholars who called for less restrictive policies and practices. Therefore, Scandinavian countries are considered the frontrunners in deinstitutionalization and community living policies. It appears that Anglo-Saxon countries reduced the number of institutions but spent less public money to expand community-based services. The least progressive in Western Europe in terms of transitioning from institutional to community-based services are conservative countries such as France and Germany, which provide both institutional and community care and are less committed to moving forward to close or downsize their congregate care services for people with disabilities. The former eastern European bloc countries have the highest rate of institutionalization and lag behind in transitioning from institutional to community living policies, primarily because they experience tremendous economic hardships and difficulties in changing their social systems and values.

The challenge of the Council of Europe and the European Union is how to narrow the disparities between Western and Eastern Europe, in particular with respect to institutionalization and the lack of sufficient community living programs. The core bodies of the Council of Europe are the European Convention on Human Rights, which has been very dominant in advocating for deinstitutionalization and community living policies in Europe, and particularly the European Court of Human Rights, which has been pivotal in protecting the human rights of people with disabilities. The latter has achieved growing visibility in the twenty-first century and particularly since 2006 in ruling against human rights violations of people with disabilities in eastern European countries who have been institutionalized against their will.

The EU road map is the 2010–2020 strategy plan committed to the implementation of the UNCRPD. It appears that the core instrument is the Structural Funds supporting social inclusion and anti-poverty policies and reducing economic and social disparities. However, earlier practices have shown that the money was used instead to renovate institutions for people with disabilities or to build new residential institutions rather than develop community-based alternatives. This concern, which is contrary to EU policy objectives, EU law and European and international human rights standards, is definitely a challenge for the European Union in years to come.

6

Comparing Community Living Policies

United States vs. Europe

The policies of the United States and European countries toward people with disabilities are considered as different in nature and scope. On the surface, the two present different social welfare and legal systems, but a comparative analysis demonstrates common historical processes in respect to institutionalization, deinstitutionalization, and community living policies. The challenge is the provision of current comparative analysis based on ideological and conceptual perspectives, policy and legislation, and implementation in light of the UNCRPD.

THE DARK HISTORY: EUGENICS IN THE UNITED STATES AND EUROPE

The history of exclusion of people with disabilities from communal life in the first half of the twentieth century is rooted in eugenics values and policies on both sides of the Atlantic. Interestingly, the eugenics movement started in the United States and later spread to Europe. In 1914, more than half of the states changed their marriage laws. Many voided marriages of people with intellectual and mental disabilities, others restricted marriage among people they saw as "unfit" for reasons such as feeblemindedness and people with venereal diseases. Indiana enacted the first law allowing sterilization on eugenics grounds in 1907, with Connecticut following soon after. Connecticut sterilization legislation called for imprisoning people for three years if they violated it. This law did not allow the marriage of "the eugenically unfit."[1] Between 1907 and 1917, more than fifteen states adopted sterilization laws.[2] California, for example, was responsible for a third of forced sterilizations in the United States.[3] Oregon had sterilizations laws until the 1980s.[4] Even

[1] Available at http://edwardmcphail.com/eugenics/assignments/kelves_reading2.pdf.

[2] Reflecting the practice of the time was (www.encyclopediavirginia.org/buck_v_bell_1927), a court case in which Carrie Buck was deemed genetically unfit and the court wished to order her sterilization.

[3] For further reading, see Jon Gottshall, "The cutting edge: Sterilization and eugenics in California, 1909–1945," *The Welebaethan*, 1995; available at www.gottshall.com/thesis/article.htm.

[4] O. Larsell, "History of care of insane in the state of Oregon," *Oregon Historical Quarterly* 46 (2000), 295–326.

the United States Supreme Court endorsed eugenics as national policy. In an infamous 1927 decision,[5] Supreme Court Justice Oliver Wendell Holmes wrote, "It is better for all the world, if . . . society can prevent those who are manifestly unfit from continuing their kind . . . Three generations of imbeciles are enough." This decision opened the floodgates for thousands to be coercively sterilized or otherwise persecuted as subhuman.

Eugenics was not only adopted in Germany, which transmogrified the mass sterilization program to the killing of all children and people with disabilities, but also by northern European countries, including the Nordic states.[6] All four main Nordic countries – Denmark, Finland, Norway, and Sweden – passed eugenics laws in the 1930s. More remarkably, some of those laws existed until the mid-1970s, though apparently they were not latterly used very often. The fact that these Scandinavian countries, known as welfare states, have adopted such regressive policies, is ambiguous and confusing. Part of the efforts to explain this puzzling approach is related to their eagerness to create a "better society" by sterilizing a large number of institutionalized intellectually and mentally disabled people. This progressed into a policy of sterilizing disadvantaged young women who were seen as at risk of producing illegitimate children and then a more extensive and largely voluntary use of sterilization for contraceptive purposes. The truth is that sterilization was viewed as a cheap and simple means for reducing the numbers of the socially undesirable and marginalized and reducing welfare spending at a time of global economic depression.[7]

The fact that liberal and welfare states are failing in protecting the rights of people with disabilities, primarily women, is a lesson that has to be learned in the twenty-first century, i.e., that persons with disabilities have legal capacity and cannot be denied the right to make choices wherever they live in the community. This is particularly relevant today in light of the New Eugenics ideas that prevail in most Western countries.

THE ESSENCE OF EUROPEAN DISABILITY POLICY

Historically, European disability policy is based on the social welfare model that views disability as a defect in an individual that renders him or her unable to work or function in society in a conventional way.[8] In this approach, there is some

---

[5] *Buck v. Bell.* See n. 463.
[6] For further reading on Germany's Eugenics and T4 Program, see Götz Aly, Peter Chroust, and Christian Pross, *Cleansing the fatherland: Nazi medicine and racial hygiene* (Baltimore: The Johns Hopkins University Press, 1994).
[7] For comprehensive reading, see Gunnar Bromberg and Nils Roll-Hansen, *Eugenics and the welfare states: Norway, Sweden, Denmark, and Finland* (East Lansing, MI: Michigan State University Press, 2005).
[8] Lisa B. Waddington and Matthew Diller, "Tensions and coherence in disability policy: The uneasy relationship between social welfare and civil rights models of disability in American, European and international employment law." In Breslin and Yee, *Disability rights law and policy*, pp. 241–80.

commitment to accommodate people with disabilities, but in a separate parallel track to the nondisabled majority. The model is rooted in traditional central European policies allowing society to establish protection services and social institutions without regard for people with disabilities, based on their medical limitations.

The emergence of the social model of disability in Western Europe is in response to the criticism of medicalization and the social welfare approach. A thorough look at the development of disability policy at the European level from the mid-1970s reveals significant changes of thinking about disability that are also evident in global policy debates driven by activism from the international disabled people's movement.

Early policy was based on social welfare and medical rehabilitation compensating people with disabilities for their limitations. In the 1980s and the beginning of the 1990s, there was more responsiveness to human rights, citizenship, full participation issues, and removal of structural barriers to inclusion. Europe has been influenced by Europeanization and the need of the European Union to interface with national and global policies. Europeanization reflects high levels of national subsidiarity in relevant policy domains and the emergence of new global regimes of governance (including the UNCRPD in 2007).

However, it seems that the European Union is caught between globalization and the need to transfer policies at the national level.[9] The latter, which focuses on responding to the individual's medical and social welfare needs, has been replaced by the social approach, indicating that people with disabilities are socially excluded and lack opportunities in society.[10] It is important to note that the adoption of the social model occurred at the same time as growing recognition for rights in law and policy.[11] The progress toward a European rights perspective is considered insufficient by European policy-makers because it does not address the underlying structural causes of disabled people's exclusion. This is evident in examining the positive gains in the life of people with intellectual disabilities, most of which have been attributed to advances in negative rights.[12] For example, legal action is probably more successful in dealing with abuse and neglect rather than providing more choices of access and options for care. In addition, negative rights are often handled after the fact without the ability to prevent or handle the reasons for violation of rights.

9   Mark Priestley, "In search of European disability policy: Between national and global," *ALTER: European Journal of Disability Research/Revue européenne de recherche sur le handicap* 1 (2007), 61–74.
10 See Michael Oliver, *Understanding disability: From theory to practice* (London: Palgrave Macmillan, 1996).
11 Doris Zames Fleischer and Frieda Zames, *The disability rights movement: From charity to confrontation* (Philadelphia: Temple University Press, 2001). This is particularly evident in the United States. Fleischer and Zames conducted close to 100 interviews to compile the research for this study on the disability rights movement in the United States. They provide a historical look at the social context of the rights of the vast number of Americans who are disabled and the ever-evolving attitude toward them from the time of Franklin D. Roosevelt to today.
12 Damon A. Young and Ruth Quibell, "Why rights are never enough," *Disability & Society* 15 (2000), 747–64.

An insightful look reveals that European disability policy include four core conceptual themes: the interface between the social model and rights-based policy claims; the emergence of "Europeanization" policies, institutions, and citizenship identities; the development of mechanisms of policy transfer implicated in that process; and the emergence of globalization and new forms of global governance that transcend the European system.

Europeanization is definitely a second influence, a bottom-up effort to become more "European" in character.[13] Interestingly, the founding Treaty of the European Economic Community of 1957 was an economic one and focused on monetary and political integration rather than social or human rights. It was not until the Single European Treaty of 1987 that citizenship rights were introduced more explicitly.

The European disability policy is rooted in an economic political approach, but was also influenced by the shift toward a rights-based approach during the 1990s, which can be interpreted both as a European response to internal citizenship and nondiscrimination claims and external international developments (such as the ADA [Americans with Disabilities Act] or the 1993 Standard Rules on the Equalization of Opportunities for Persons with Disabilities).

Specifically, disability policy in the mid-1980s was associated with a recommendation to offer fair employment opportunities and adequate social security protection. The transition from compensatory to rights-based policy in Europe was gradually influenced by the development of rights-based approaches elsewhere in the world, including the UN International Year of Disabled People in 1981, the 1990 ADA in the United States, and the adoption of the 1993 UN Rules on the Equalization of Opportunities for Persons with Disabilities.

The legal basis for EU action is provided in Article 13 of the European Treaty[14] dating from 1999, which permits the European Council to take appropriate action to fight against discrimination based on sex, racial or ethnic origin, religion, disability, age, and sex orientation. It has been expressed in a variety of forms, including the Charter of Fundamental Rights and the European Commission's effort, "Toward a barrier free Europe for people with disabilities."[15] In principle, existing member states had to follow the anti-discrimination laws from December 2003, but in practice their compliance was postponed until December, 2006. However, there is no doubt that the adoption and ratification of the UNCRPD by the European Union and the Council of Europe marked the final change in European disability policy. European Disability Strategy 2010–2020 is committed to implement the UNCRPD by the European Union and support member states in their implementation.

[13]   For examining Europeanization, see Robert Harmsen and Thomas M. Wilson, *Europeanization: Institution, identities and citizenship* (Atlanta: Rodopi, 2000).

[14]   For further reading, see Ian Bryan, "Equality and freedom from discrimination: Article 13 EU Treaty," *Journal of Social Welfare and Family Law* 24 (2002), 223–38. Retrieved May 16, 2016 from http://papers .ssrn.com/sol3/papers.cfm?abstract_id=1423842.

[15]   European Commission, "Towards a barrier-free Europe for people with disabilities." A communication from the commission, May 12, 2000 (COM [2000] 284 final).

Regardless of the remarkable changes in European disability policy, the impression is that Europe is still caught in the tension between the social welfare and the civil rights/anti-discrimination models. Can the two models coexist? The fact is that many nations have policies and programs based on both of these models, and in some instances, on a mixture of the two. Most of the benefits provided to people with disabilities, including social security and housing, are based on medical- and means testing procedures, which makes it very difficult to reconcile the two divergent models of disability in Europe. For this reason it is not surprising to find that there has largely been no attempt to develop a logical and coherent policy. Newer policy instruments, such as anti-discrimination laws that are based on the civil rights model of disability, have been added to existing policy instruments inspired by the social welfare model. In this way, numerous layers are developed in an ad hoc approach to policy development. Rarely do policy-makers have the time or the inclination to take a step back and consider the coherence and logic of disability policy.[16]

US DISABILITY CORE APPROACH

US disability policy is based on two major pieces of legislation related to employment. The Rehab Act of 1973 prohibits discrimination in federally funded programs and activities.[17] In 1990, the ADA (American with Disabilities Act) prohibited discrimination against individuals with disabilities in both the public and private sector in a broad range of activities, including employment.[18] Legislation was passed in 2008, with the ADA Amendments Act (ADAAA), which attempts to reform the ADA and redefine the word "disability" to conform to the original intent of Congress when it first passed the act.[19]

Although US disability policy is identified with the human rights and an anti-discrimination approach, it is criticized for being associated with a welfare disability law.[20] There is an impression that it is embedded in the complex systems of Social Security and Medicaid. Progressive scholars such as Rachel Heather Hinckley believe that the answer to creating progressive legislation may be found in the first

[16] See online paper by Lisa Waddington and Matthew Diller, "Tensions and coherence in disability policy: The uneasy relationship between social welfare and civil rights models of disability in American, European and international employment law." Retrieved April 29, 2016 from http://dredf .org/news/publications/disability-rights-law-and-policy/tensions-and-coherence-in-disability-policy/.

[17] ADA, 42 U.S.C. §§ 12101–12213 (2006).

[18] See Samuel R. Bagenstos's argument that anti-discrimination law cannot eliminate structural inequalities that operate before an individual is in a position to seek a job: "The future of disability law," *Yale Law Journal* 114 (2004); available at http://works.bepress.com/samuel_bagenstos/7/.

[19] ADA Amendments Act of 2008, Pub. L. No. 110–325, 122 Stat. 3553, sec. 2 (2008). Known as the ADAAA.

[20] Rachel Heather Hinckley, "Evading promises: The promise of equality under U.S. Law and how the United Nations Convention on the Rights of Persons with Disabilities can help," *Georgia Journal of International and Comparative Law* 39 (2010), 185–214; available at http://digitalcommons.law.uga .edu/gjicl/vol39/iss1/5.

comprehensive human rights convention of the twenty-first century – the UNCRPD (UN Convention on the Rights of Persons with Disabilities). In her opinion, the United States has to ratify the UNCRPD and demonstrate more comprehensive and dedicated commitment to the participation and their inclusion into society of people with disabilities.

However, this criticism does not reflect the general view of legislators that the United States already has a wide range of federal laws that protect the rights of Americans with disabilities, such as the Rehab Act, the ADA, the Individuals with Disabilities Education Act and the Fair Housing Act. Plus, there are executive and judicial mechanisms available that meet or exceed the treaty's provisions. The criticism of the UNCRPD is that it is too ambiguous and that the current legislation is a firm foundation that can be modified or expanded as necessary through the legislative or regulatory process.

COMPARATIVE ANALYSIS OF EUROPEAN VS. US DISABILITY POLICIES

The difference between European and US disability policies is not distinctive, probably because of global and mutual influences. The traces of the medical model are still visible on both sides of the Atlantic. The social model that is so prominent in the United Kingdom has been translated into anti-discrimination in the US Rehab Act and, more particularly, in writing the 1990 ADA.[21] It is of note that the role of social movements in the United States was much more influential than translating the social model to a rights-centered version at the community level.[22]

It is important to note that European disability policy was dominated until 1996 by the medical model, and the effort to establish unified European policy has been marginal. The only organization that has contributed to a unified approach has been the European Disability Forum (EDF), an umbrella organization at the community level of the national disability rights movements.[23] The EDF, influenced by the disability

---

[21] See discussion of alternative ways of periodization of disability rights in the European Union in Anne Waldschmidt, "Disability policy of the European Union: The supranational level, 3 EUR," *Journal of Disability Research* 8 (2009), 16–18.

[22] See Council Directive 2000/78/EC, 2000 O.J. (L 303) 16.

[23] See Christine Quittkat and Barbara Finke, "The EU Commission consultation regime." In *Opening EU-governance to civil society: Gains and challenges*. Edited by Beate Kohler-Koch, Dirk de Bièvre, and William Maloney (CONNEX Report Series, 5; Mannheim: University of Mannheim, Centre for European Social Research), pp. 183–222. The consultation regime of the European Commission is marked by the role the commission assigns to nongovernmental actors or civil society organizations. The commission's documents on its policy of consultation and cooperation with external nongovernmental actors reveal that a reflective approach has emerged during the 1980s, referring to a more elaborate concept of "good governance." The gradual extension is most noticeable in the change of terminology, from "consultation" (1960/1970s) to "partnership" (1980/1990s) and "participation" (1990s/2000s). This trend was fostered by the recognition of "civil society" as the addressee of the commission's consultation policy and potential source of democratic legitimacy.

movement's role in shaping the ADA, played a crucial role in advocating for anti-discrimination policy. There is no doubt that the EDF's unified approach produced the platform for the future European Community disability policy in the late 1990s.[24] In parallel, US disability policy was shaped earlier and was more advanced because of the crucial role played by the disability movement in promoting social integration and anti-discrimination in the early 1960s. If European disability policy did not exist in the early 1970s, the Rehab Act marked the beginning of change in the United States. Although Section 504 was not a response to societal pressure, it recognized persons with disabilities as a minority group engaged in a struggle for recognition similar to that of the civil rights and the women's movements. The sociologist John Skrentny has explained the development of Section 504 as lack of interest in what the statute would mean and what limits there might be to the potential remedies for exclusion. No one paid any attention to what would become a revolutionary new policy, and there was never even any discussion of Section 504.[25] Compared to Section 504 of the Rehab Act, the ADA of 1990 is considered a landmark of anti-discrimination policy.

The European Community Strategy 1996 marked the shift of EU policy from accommodation to the social integration and mainstreaming that are pivotal in the social model. Unlike the ADA, the strategy lacked a legal basis for anti-discrimination measures and still relied in the late 1990s on previous legislation.[26] Although European policy at this stage had been influenced by processes on the other side of the Atlantic, the European community lacked the tradition to use the courts for social change through rights adjudication.

It is evident that while the European policy is different, it has been partially influenced by the American approach. The European rights strategy embraces the principle of equality, which entails the concept of equal opportunity (which itself subsumes the principle of nondiscrimination). Unlike the US approach, the European anti-discrimination measure is broader. Furthermore, the European model is rooted also in earlier social welfare policy in terms of provisions and is highly regulated by the state. The current European Disability Strategy (2010–2020) builds upon the UNCRPD.

COMMUNITY LIVING POLICIES ON BOTH SIDES OF THE ATLANTIC

Deinstitutionalization policies of people with disabilities were initiated in the second half of the twentieth century. Most of the efforts on both sides of the

---

[24] See "Commission communication on equality of opportunity for people with disabilities: A new European Community disability strategy," COM (1996) 406 final (July 30, 1996).

[25] For sociological comprehensive analysis, see John D. Skrentny, *The minority rights revolution* (Boston: Harvard University Press, 2003).

[26] See Deborah Mabbett, "The development of rights-based social policy in the European Union: The example of disability rights," *Journal of Common Market Studies* 43 (2005), 97–120.

Atlantic were aimed at downsizing, closing institutions, and transitioning people with intellectual and psychiatric disabilities to community care.

US and European deinstitutionalization policies are conceptually different in nature and scope. Deinstitutionalization is attributed in the United States to the civil rights era and the call to improve the terrible conditions in institutions by promoting human rights. The early 1970s saw many class action suits challenging poor institutional conditions. The key legislative impetus behind this movement was the Rehab Act.[27] Section 504 of the Rehab Act was the first broad civil rights–oriented federal statute to address discrimination against people with physical and mental disabilities.[28] The 1980s brought new evidence about the merit of community-based services. Probably the most important evident impact was the seminal 1984 Pennhurst case used by states in their arguments against deinstitutionalization.[29]

European deinstitutionalization in the beginning of the 1960s is less associated with human rights than with the normalization principle, an ideology developed and articulated by Bengt Nirje in the 1960s calling to provide less restrictive services to people with disabilities.[30] In Nordic countries, deinstitutionalization efforts were regulated and supported by the welfare state. The social model of disability was another influence, particularly evident in the United Kingdom, deriving from dissatisfaction and criticism of the medical model and the institutional model as one of its most visible expressions.

The twenty-first century marks the importance of the human rights model and personalization on both sides of the Atlantic. However, United States policy was influenced greatly by the ADA of 1990 and particularly the *Olmstead* Supreme Court anti-discrimination decision regarding institutionalization. At the same time, European policy leans more toward the UNCRPD regarding human rights and the EU social policy of reducing gaps in community living care among states by using the Structural Funds as an incentive to bring about change.

DEINSTITUTIONALIZATION POLICIES IN TWENTIETH-CENTURY MENTAL HEALTH

There are similarities and differences in deinstitutionalization policy and practice between Europe and the United States. The deinstitutionalization movement and policy in the United States has changed dramatically over a very short period and has been controversial in terms of processes and outcomes. The European scene is more scattered, with differences between the Nordic countries and Italy, which leads

---

[27]   29 U.S.C. Ch. 16 (2000).

[28]   Sandra L. Yue, "A return of institutionalization despite Olmstead v. L.C.? The inadequacy of Medicaid provider reimbursement in Minnesota and the failure to deliver home- and community-based waiver services," *Law and Inequality* 19 (2001), 307, 312.

[29]   *Pennhurst State School v. Halderman* 465 U.S. 89 (1984).

[30]   Bennet Nirje, "The basis and logic of the normalization principle," *Australian and New Zealand Journal of Developmental Disabilities* 11 (1985), 65–68.

progressive and early deinstitutionalization policies, and more conservative countries (such as Germany and France) offering mixed institutional and community care processes, while eastern European countries lag in adopting community-based policy. The US deinstitutionalization process was mobilized by the growing concern of civil rights advocates about the abusive conditions found in most state psychiatric hospitals and the negative effects of long-term institutionalization. This created a response from conservative governments concerned about the enormous expense of caring for patients in large institutions. If the core indicator of success is reduction of patients in state and county psychiatric hospitals, the deinstitutionalization efforts were quite successful in reducing the number from 559,000 in 1955 to less than 200,000 in 1978,[31] and to 125,000 in the mid-1980s.[32] The second goal, of developing community-based programs, which was supposed to be responded to by the Community Support Program initiated in 1977 by the NIMH, was accomplished partially due to cuts by the Reagan administration and shifting of responsibilities to local government. An examination of the history of mental illness and its treatment reveals that the mentally ill have few advocates except each other and that their treatment has consisted of confinement and neglect.[33]

Critics of deinstitutionalization policy claim that 100,000 formerly institutionalized mental patients were placed in nursing homes[34] and that many of the mentally ill have been incarcerated in jails and prisons. Studies of jail and prison inmates in California, Colorado, and Oklahoma indicated that 6.7, 5.0, and 5.2 percent respectively were psychotic.[35] When the average of these percentages is used (5.6 percent), an estimated 26,000 seriously mentally ill persons are confined in jails and prisons.

In Europe, deinstitutionalization of people with psychiatric disabilities has been uneven, sometimes leading to a gap between closure of institutions and the availability of community-based services. In fact, only Italy and some Nordic countries finalized institutional closure and transitioning during the twentieth century, while countries including the United Kingdom adopted a gradual policy of transitioning from public hospital to community care. France, for instance, began the transition in 1990 and was successful in decreasing the number of beds from 81,225 beds to 44,311 by 2004. In Germany, the number fell from 45,000 to 33,033 beds between 1990 and 2000. Countries like the Czech Republic decreased the number of

[31] "President's Commission on Mental Health: Report to the President" (Vol. I; Washington, DC: US Government Printing Office, 1978).

[32] David Mechanic, *From advocacy to allocation: The evolving American health care system* (New York: Free Press, 1986).

[33] Albert R. Roberts and Linda Farms Kurtz, "Historical perspectives on the care and treatment of the mentally ill," *The Journal of Sociology & Social Welfare* 14 (2015); available at http://scholarworks .wmich.edu/jssw/vol14/iss4/5.

[34] Department of Health and Human Services, *Toward a national plan for the chronically mentally ill* (Washington, DC: Public Health Service DHHS publication no. ADM-1-1077, 1980).

[35] Richard H. Lamb and Robert W. Grant, "The mentally ill in an urban county jail," *Archives of General Psychiatry* 39 (1982), 17–34.

TABLE 6.1 *Community Care Policy in Selected Western European Countries*

Country	Mental Health Policy	Community Care Policy	Availability of Community Care Services	Injection of Additional Resources to Community Care
England	Present	Yes	Widely	Yes
France	Present	No	Limited	No
Germany	Present	Yes	Limited	Yes
Poland	Yes	No	Very Limited	Yes
Norway	Present	Yes	Widely	Yes
Italy	Present	Yes	Widely	No
Spain	Absent	Yes	Limited	Limited

Adapted from Helena Medeiros, David McDaid, and Martin Knapp, "Shifting care from hospital to the community in Europe: Economic challenges and opportunities," *MHEEN II Policy Briefing* 4 (2008), 11.

psychiatric beds from 15,000 to 11,591 between 1990 and 2004, and in Poland the number decreased from 31,558 in 1990 to 19,966 in 2003.[36]

In terms of the development of community-based policy, there are still variations. Table 6.1 presents the existence of community-based policies and availability of services and the injection of additional resources to community care. It demonstrates the differences between progressive countries (for example, England, Italy, and Norway) and others. France and Spain lag behind other western European countries. Italy, which is the most progressive in respect to policy, spent only 5 percent of its health budget on mental health as compared to Germany, which spent 10.14 percent, and France, 8 percent.

INTELLECTUAL AND DEVELOPMENTAL DISABILITY (IDD)

Deinstitutionalization and the transitioning to community-based facilities were probably the most important goals in intellectual and developmental disability policy in the second half of the twentieth century.[37] Similar to deinstitutionalization in mental health, the most significant progress in ID/DD with respect to institutional closure and the development of community-based programs was made in the United States, Scandinavian states, and the United Kingdom. However, other European countries, such as Belgium, the Netherlands, Germany, Spain, and Greece, lag behind in areas of deinstitutionalization and community-based services. The majority of these conservative states have a mixed model of institutional and community care. Their

[36] Helena Medeiros, David McDaid, and Martin Knapp, "Shifting care from hospital to the community in Europe: Economic challenges and opportunities," *MHEEN Group II Policy Briefing* 4 (2008), p. 8.
[37] Jim Mansell, "Issues in community services in Britain." In *Deinstitutionalization and community living: Intellectual disability services in Britain, Scandinavia and the USA*. Edited by Jim Mansell and Kent Ericsson (London: Chapman and Hall, 1996), pp. 49–63.

process of deinstitutionalization began in the 1990s.[38] Deinstitutionalization has only just been initiated in the former Soviet bloc countries, and the majority of people with IDD live in large facilities with poor quality standards of human care.

In a very comprehensive paper, Jim Mansell summarized deinstitutionalization and community living in the context of different welfare state models in disability and public administration.[39] There is no doubt that Norway and Sweden are the leaders in closing institutions and offering community-based programs. England is slightly behind as in 2004 there were about 750 places left in the old long-stay institutions for people with intellectual disabilities.[40] This figure does not include several thousand places in congregate care and new private institutions.[41]

By the end of the twentieth century, the United States had the same pattern as Sweden but institutional closure has not been fully completed.[42]

The deinstitutionalization process in the United States is very impressive, regardless of the differences among states, with a decrease from 194,650 in 1967 (the peak year) to 41,653 in 2004.[43] The number of individuals in private facilities for sixteen or more people and the number of people with ID/DD living in nursing facilities has also been declining. In 1990, 44,903 people with ID/DD lived in nursing homes, while 32,926 lived in large private intermediate care facilities for persons with mental retardation (ICF/MRs). By 2002, these numbers had declined to 30,308 and 24,708 respectively.[44] In terms of institutional closure, eight state institutions specifically for persons with ID/DD closed between 1960 and 1976, and 174 state institutions or special units of sixteen or more persons with these disabilities closed between 1960 and 2004.[45] As with the differences among European countries, there are differences with respect to states. Until 2000, most of the states reduced the number of people with ID/DD significantly. States that still continue to support an "extensive network of public institutions" are Arkansas, Louisiana, Mississippi, North Carolina, and Virginia.[46]

[38] European Intellectual Disability Research Network, *Intellectual disability in Europe: Working papers* (Canterbury: Tizard Centre, University of Kent at Canterbury, 2003).

[39] Jim Mansell, "Deinstitutionalization and community living: Progress, problems and priorities," *Journal of Intellectual and Developmental Disability* 31 (2006), 65–76.

[40] Speech by Stephen Ladyman, MP, Parliamentary Undersecretary of State for Community, to conference "Learning disability today," November 26, 2003, Department of Health.

[41] Health and personal social services statistics for England (London: Department of Health, HMSO, 2004).

[42] David Braddock, Richard Hemp, and Mary C. Rizzolo, "State of the states in developmental disabilities: 2004," *Mental Retardation* 42 (2004), 356–70.

[43] Robert W. Prouty, Gary Smith, and Charlie K. Lakin, *Residential services for persons with developmental disabilities: Status and trends through 2004* (Minneapolis: University of Minnesota, Institute on Community Integration, 2005).

[44] Mary K. Rizzolo et al., *The state of the states in developmental disabilities* (Washington, DC: American Association on Mental Retardation, 2004).

[45] Prouty, Smith, and Lakin, "Residential services for persons with developmental disabilities."

[46] David Braddock, *Disability at the dawn of the 21st century and the state of the states* (Washington, DC: American Association on Mental Retardation, 2002).

If the core reason for differences in deinstitutionalization has been economic-political, the challenge in the United States was also the economic burden on states' budgets and growing resistance from public employee unions to cutting jobs.[47]

COMMUNITY LIVING POLICIES IN THE UNITED STATES AND EUROPE: CHALLENGES OF THE TWENTY-FIRST CENTURY

In terms of outcome, the beginning of the twenty-first century found a significant decrease in the number of people with disabilities living in institutional care on both sides of the Atlantic. The United States' *Olmstead* Supreme Court decision is considered a road map in examining the impact of anti-discrimination policy on community living of people with ID/DD, particularly fifteen years after this landmark ruling.[48] European deinstitutionalization community living policies are more diverse because of core differences between Nordic, central, and eastern countries. On the one hand, the European Union has ratified the UNCRPD and recognized the legal obligation of implementing its Article 19 of the UNCRPD. On the other hand, there are significant gaps in current infrastructures and community living policies among member states.[49] If the core aim of United States community living policy is aligned with implementation of the *Olmstead* decision, the European challenge seems more demanding, in particular in governing the Structural Funds in the 2014–2020 strategy and responding to Article 19 of the UNCRPD.

US CHALLENGES

The *Olmstead* Supreme Court decision calls for a community living policy and makes clear that community-based services must be offered if appropriate when a person with a disability does not oppose moving from an institution to the community. However, the court decision considers the difficulties in achieving the goal – the community placement has to be reasonably accommodated and it considers the state's resources and the needs of other people with disabilities.[50]

In terms of funding, there has been a significant shift from institutional to HCBS. Figure 6.1 demonstrates that in 2013, HCBS exceeded 50 percent of total LTSS spending. The percentage rising from 49.3 in FY 2012 to 51.3 in FY 2013 continues

---

[47] Charlie K. Lakin and Robert W. Prouty, "Trends in institution closure," *Impact: Feature Issue on Institution Closures* 9 (1995–1996), 4–5 (Minneapolis: University of Minnesota, Institute on Community Integration).

[48] Mary Beth Musumeci and Henry Claypool, "*Olmstead*'s role in community integration for people with disabilities under Medicaid: 15 years after the Supreme Court's *Olmstead* decision," The Kaiser Commission on Medicaid and the Uninsured, June 2014.

[49] "The Report of the ad hoc expert group on the transition from institutional to community-based care," European Commission, Directorate-General for Employment, Social Affairs and Equal Opportunities, September 2009.

[50] 527 U.S. 581 (1999); available at www.law.cornell.edu/supct/html/98-536.ZS.html.

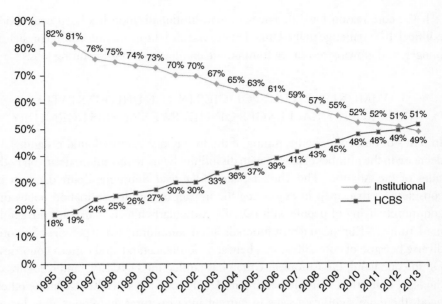

FIGURE 6.1. Medicaid HCBS expenditures as a percentage of total Medicaid LTSS expenditures for fiscal years 1995–2013.
Source: Steve Eiken, Kate Sredl, Brian Burwell, and Paul Saucier, *Medicaid expenditures for Long-Term Services and Supports (LTSS) in FY 2013: Home- and community-based services were a majority of LTSS spending,* June 30, 2015. Truven Health Analytics, p. 7.

a pattern of one to three percentage point increases nearly every year since FY 1995. This trend is attributable to a combination of increased HCBS spending and decreased institutional spending as state and federal efforts to promote LTSS system balance continue

Among the core obstacles to the funding of HCBS is the interpretation of finance by Medicaid. While *Olmstead* did not change federal Medicaid law, Medicaid has been required to change its interpretation of community integration as the major payer of LTSS, including HCBS on which people with disabilities rely to live independently in the community. Therefore, most of the *Olmstead* cases submitted to courts that tested the role of Medicaid in provision of community-based services (instead of institutional care) examined funding of integrated settings and difficulties in providing integrated services that enable people with disabilities to interact with nondisabled peers.

A good case example demonstrating the need to provide community care instead of institutional care was demonstrated in 2012 in *Amanda D. v. Hassan; U.S. v. N.H.* A federal court approved a settlement on behalf of a class of thousands of people with mental illness living in a state-operated psychiatric hospital and nursing facility in New Hampshire. Under the settlement terms, the state agreed to provide expanded community mental health, mobile crisis units, supported employment services, and additional scattered-site supported housing units. The Department of Justice (DOJ) investigated and then intervened in support of the plaintiffs in this case.[51]

Another *Olmstead* case (2013) demonstrating the ADA's requirement that people with disabilities receive services in the most integrated setting is *U.S. v. N.Y.*, as the DOJ reached a settlement in a New York case on behalf of people with mental illness seeking scattered-site supportive housing in apartments instead of large adult care homes with more than 120 residents. The settlement requires that within five years, the state will assess current adult care home residents and transition them to supported housing if appropriate. The state will also provide supported employment and community mental health services such as care coordination, psychiatric rehabilitation, assistance with medications, home health and personal assistance services, assertive community treatment, and crisis stabilization. The terms of the settlement presume that supported housing is the most appropriate setting for beneficiaries unless certain exceptions are met.[52]

However, the purpose of the ADA is also to prevent unnecessary institutionalization due to lack of community-based services. In a 2014 case, *Smith v. Department of Public Welfare of the Commonwealth of Pennsylvania*, the plaintiffs alleged that the Commonwealth of Pennsylvania put them at serious risk of institutionalization by reducing funding for Act 150, a state-funded program providing attendant care services in the community.[53] The statement of interest highlights the legal principles governing ADA claims, including the fact that individuals who are at risk of entering an institution because of a state policy need not wait until they enter the institution in order to assert an ADA integration claim. The statement of interest also addressed what constitutes a request for a reasonable accommodation for the purposes of bringing an ADA integration claim. An earlier case, *Pitts v. Greenstein*, challenged Louisiana's reduction of the maximum number of personal care services per week that beneficiaries could receive was settled, with the state agreeing to increase its number of Medicaid HCBS waiver slots to expand capacity. The DOJ filed a statement of interest supporting the beneficiaries' claim that the reduction in service hours placed them at risk of institutionalization in violation of *Olmstead.44.*[54]

Finally, a serious obstacle that was challenged in the early years after the *Olmstead* decision was old Medicaid rules, such as service hours and/or cost caps, to reasonably accommodate the needs of people with significant disabilities pursuant to the

[51]   *Amanda D. v. Hassan; U.S. v. N.H.*, 1:12-cv-53 (D.N.H. 2012); available at www.ada.gov/olmstead/ olmstead_cases_list2.htm#fla; see also NDRN docket at pp. 26–27.

[52]   *U.S. v. N.Y.*, 13-cv-4165 (E.D.N.Y. 2013); available at www.ada.gov/olmstead/olmstead_cases_list2.htm #fla; see also *Disability Advocates v. Paterson* at idem; NDRN docket at pp. 41–42.

[53]   *Smith v. Department of Public Welfare of the Commonwealth of Pennsylvania* – 2:13-cv-05670; available at www.ada.gov/olmstead/documents/smith-soi.pdf.

[54]   *Pitts v. Greenstein*, 10-cv-635 (M.D.La. 2010); available at www.ada.gov/olmstead/olmstead_cases_list2 .htm#fla.

ADA. An interesting illustration of this issue was presented in the case of *Knowles v. Traylor*. In 2004, the Seventh Circuit Court of Appeals held that the ADA required Illinois to waive its cap on private duty nursing hours for adults. In that case, the Medicaid beneficiary seeking services had received sixteen hours per day under EPSDT, but qualified for only five hours per day as an adult, which was insufficient for him to remain safely at home. The court applied *Olmstead* and concluded that waiving the service hour cap would not fundamentally alter the state's Medicaid program because so few people had such extensive care needs.[55]

Regardless of litigating *Olmstead* cases, it appears that there is a long way to go in challenging Medicaid funding of community-based programs. One of the most debated problems is related to the 200,000 people placed through deinstitutionalization efforts in nursing homes.[56] One of the important goals is to develop no wrong door/single entry-point systems and core standardized assessments to achieve greater equity among different populations receiving Medicaid HCBS.

Another problem is the unevenness of state plans to comply with ADA obligations. Since 1996 and particularly from 2007, important incentives carried out by Medicaid afford states additional options and flexibility to rebalance their LTSS spending and ensure sufficient community-based programs in all states.[57]

EUROPEAN CHALLENGES

The long-term goal of the European Commission (EU) strategy (2003–2010) was "Independent Living of People with Disabilities."[58] The core instrument to narrow the gap in community living between western and eastern Europe was money in the form of the Structural Funds. The latter was part of its regional policy to promote economic and social cohesion in the European Union. The funds are earmarked for development purposes, and they are very substantial: the Structural Funds budget package for 2007–2013 was 347.410 billion EUR, which is a third of the total European Union budget.[59] Given that the European Union has allocated the Structural Funds to improve the lives of Europeans, it is important to inquire whether central and eastern European countries have used them to promote closure of institutions and the development of community care alternatives.

---

[55] *Knowles v. Traylor*, 10–10246 (N.D. Tex. 2008; 5th Cir. 2010), NDRN docket at 10, 70.

[56] See, for example, Chairman Tom Harkin, US Senate Health, Education, Labor, and Pensions Committee, *Separate and unequal: States fail to fulfill the community living promise of the Americans with Disabilities Act* at 18, 44, 46 (July 18, 2013); available at www.harkin.senate.gov /documents/pdf/OlmsteadReport.pdf. The report is based on a request to states for information about HCBS, to which thirty-one states provided substantive responses.

[57] Such as MFP, Community First Choice, § 1915(i), and the Balancing Incentive Program.

[58] Commission Communication COM (2003) 650 of 30.10.2003, "Equal opportunities for people with disabilities: A European action plan."

[59] European Union, *The control system for cohesion policy*, p. 5.

The overall impression is that there were significant problems in implementing them in most central and eastern European countries. An interesting briefing of the use of the Structural Funds in Bulgaria, Hungary, Latvia, Lithuania, Romania, and the Slovak Republic during 2007–2013 demonstrated the key problems of the European Union's strategy.[60]

The most significant problem with Structural Funds investments during the current financing period is that in some countries they have been used to renovate or build new, long-stay residential institutions. The ECCL and the Open Society Mental Health Initiative (MHI) report that the Structural Funds have been invested in such projects in Hungary, Latvia, Lithuania, Slovakia, Bulgaria, and Romania. Other organizations have expressed similar concerns in the Czech Republic. In some cases, the projects clearly stated that they are for renovation and expansion of such institutions, whereas other projects that appear to be for the development of community-based alternatives create replicas of institutions in smaller settings. A particular concern is Bulgaria, which has failed to develop community-based services. The ECCL claimed that the inappropriate use of the Structural Funds was contrary to EU policy objectives, EU law and European and international human rights standards. For example, in Hungary no EU funds were used to close the large institutions and develop community-based alternatives to institutionalization. This was because at that time, EU regulations did not specifically cover social services, and therefore the documents outlining Hungary's social policy on its accession to the EU in 2004 did not include such plans. Despite the existence of domestic legislation requiring the closure of large institutions, all funds until 2010 were used to support existing residential institutions rather than to develop alternatives. Similarly, in Latvia, the government renovated an institution of 168 people in Talsi district by using 1,433,985 EUR of ERDF funds (from the programming period 2004–2006) instead of offering alternative community care projects.[61]

The two examples, among many that can be introduced here, are not only to show the inappropriate use of the Structural Funds to promote deinstitutionalization policy but also to demonstrate the lack of obligations to protect human rights. First, institutional care leads to serious human rights abuses. Contrary to states' obligations to challenge discrimination and promote equality of opportunity, the unjustified segregation of disabled people in institutions is a serious infringement of individuals' rights and freedoms, often for life, and runs counter to states' obligations to challenge discrimination and promote equality of opportunity. Finally, the rebuilding of existing institutions diverts resources away from the development of

---

[60] Camilla Parker (Open Society Foundations—Mental Health Initiative) and Ines Bulic (coordinator of the European Coalition for Community Living at the European Network on Independent Living), *Briefing on structural funds investments for people with disabilities: Achieving the transition from institutional care to community living* (Budapest: European Network on Independent Living, European Coalition for Community Living, 2013).

[61] EECL, *Wasted Time, Wasted Money.*

community-based services that are needed to ensure that disabled people are able to live in the community and participate fully in society.

However, there is concern that the problems will persist in the next financing period of 2014–2020. The purpose of the Structural Funds is to support the goals of Europe 2020 by providing member states with the financial and technical support they need to replace their infrastructure with systems equipped to facilitate smart, sustainable, and inclusive growth. In order to prevent the inappropriate use of the Structural Funds, the underlying rule is Article 19 of the UNCRPD, meaning that the ultimate goal is not only closing institutions but developing individualized services based in the community, including those aimed at preventing institutionalization.

COMPARING COMMUNITY LIVING POLICIES ON BOTH SIDES OF THE ATLANTIC

Overall, the second half of the twentieth century marks remarkable changes in the lives of people with psychiatric and intellectual disabilities on both sides of the Atlantic. The change has been overwhelming in Italy, Scandinavia, the United Kingdom, and at a slower pace in other western European countries. Thousands of individuals were transferred from long-term psychiatric hospitals to various forms of community-based living. Unfortunately, these changes were either absent from former Communist former bloc countries or only began sporadically toward the end of the twentieth century.[62]

At the same time, the United States experienced a dramatic reduction in the number of people with psychiatric disabilities in institutions and hospitals. However, compared to the deinstitutionalization in Western Europe, the deinstitutionalization process has been portrayed as problematic if not a failure in offering sufficient community-based services. The result was increased numbers of people who became homeless or were placed in jails and prisons.[63] In fact, the number of individuals with serious mental illness in prisons and jails in 2016 exceeded tenfold the number in state psychiatric hospitals.

The deinstitutionalization policy of people with intellectual disabilities in Europe varies from country to country. Nordic states were quicker in adopting the normalization principle that led them to deinstitutionalization and community living legislation and policy. The United Kingdom adopted deinstitutionalization and community living policies but at a slower pace. Other countries are still caught in a mixed model of institutions and community care, particularly eastern European countries that have substantial numbers of institutional care facilities.

The picture in the United States is much more complex and the process more gradual than in Europe. The major catalyst for institutional closure was a series of

---

[62]   McDaid and Thornicroft, *Policy brief*, pp. 2–4.
[63]   Torrey et al., *More mentally ill persons are in jails and prisons than hospitals*.

class action lawsuits and increasingly growing protests against the inhuman conditions and practices and the poor treatment of patients in these institutions. These important and significant developments increased awareness of alternative care options, in particular for those residents who were capable of living in the community. The 1970s brought an additional challenge: to eliminate the unnecessary institutionalization of people with developmental disabilities who were capable of living in their own communities. The most important development came later, in 1991, as entities such as New Hampshire, District of Columbia, Alaska, Maine, New Mexico, Rhode Island, and Vermont developed community-based services instead of institutional care.[64] It appears that the reasons for the differences between the United States and the Europe are conceptual with different political views of human rights and social policy. Even as there are many different conceptions of welfare in Europe, there is more inclination among members to lean toward greater responsibility of the state in providing and promoting human and social welfare of their peoples. By comparison, the US Constitution focuses on the idea of individual freedom and views the state's primary role as that of providing the conditions for the individual's pursuit of freedom rather than promoting or supporting any particular conception of welfare or equality. It is clear that the two differ in their disability policy: the European path reflects welfare policy first and anti-discrimination law second,[65] while the United States' relies solely on anti-discrimination legislation. The European system is also different in terms of its political system; it is fairly diffuse, highly technocratic, regulated, and leans toward the consensual mode and integration rather than being disputed politically.[66] Therefore, anti-discrimination legislation is considered to be less relevant in solving human rights and social issues.

These differences are reflected also in European and American policies toward disability. European disability policy is collective, based on the social model and the responsibility of the social and political systems to correct evils and solve problems. The belief is that any disability policy has to eliminate environmental and societal barriers including the responsibility to close institutions and build community-based services. The US perspective is based on a "minority group approach," claiming that the rights-based approach implies that the "legitimate demands" of disabled people for legal protection might be pursued within an existing political system, without overtly challenging the system itself. This is evident in the ADA, the *Olmstead* decision and, in particular, in using anti-discrimination litigation as a core

---

[64] Braddock et al., "The state of the states," pp. 23–54.

[65] It seems that EU anti-discrimination law was a development in the beginning of the twenty-first century, influenced by ECHR case law on discrimination.

[66] The European Court of Justice has been notably more reluctant to invalidate EU legislative and other measures as compared with measures taken by member state, and has been accused of double-standards in fashioning more aggressive and effective procedures for judicial review of member state acts than of EU acts. See, for example, Ewa Biernat, "The locus standi of private applicants under article 230 (4) EC and the principle of judicial protection in the European Community," Jean Monnet Working Paper 12/03, New York University School of Law, 2003.

instrument to achieve progress. Although the call for institutional closure and building community living infrastructure was an earlier development in the United States, the ADA marked the path to fundamental change.

Although US disability policy is different in nature from the European, the EU ratification of the UNCRPD marks the bridging of the US civil rights model and the EU social welfare/anti-discrimination approach. This new international instrument, in turn, seems likely to put fresh pressure on the European Union – and on the United States, especially if it ratifies the convention – to broaden and intensify reform in the field of disability discrimination.

Current EU and US policies demonstrate the different approaches to deinstitutionalization and community living policies. The European Union 2010–2020 Strategy is consonant with the UNCRPD. Interestingly, the core instrument is the Structural Funds, a social welfare effort to support social inclusion and antipoverty policies. There is growing evidence that the money was used to renovate institutions for people with disabilities or build new residential institutions rather than to develop community-based alternatives. The supplementary measure to promote community living policy is demonstrative and includes the role of the European Court of Human Rights which, in the twenty-first century, has ruled against enforcing institutionalization and violation of human rights in eastern European countries.

US deinstitutionalization and community living policy is guided by anti-discrimination legislation (the ADA and the *Olmstead* Supreme Court decision). Institutionalization is considered to be discrimination and as segregating people with disabilities. The landmark *Olmstead* Supreme Court decision transferred the implementation of policy to the states, expecting that they would provide plans and reasonable accommodation. If the main obstacle in Europe is EU inability to enforce adequate implementation of the Structural Funds, the United States obstacle seems related to the *Olmstead* Supreme Court decision. The decision was limited only to Title II of the ADA and declined to address the Fourteenth Amendment claims.[67] The court understood that the process of transitioning people from institutional to community care imposed a serious financial burden on the states and justified a slower pace of transition. The decision did not rule out institutionalization of people with disabilities who could be at risk in the community.[68] The court showed some understanding that the planning and implementation had to be undertaken at a reasonable pace. Therefore, there is differentiation between the importance of the *Olmstead* decision and the fact that it allows states to continue maintaining segregated institutions or changes in their Medicaid institutional funding and limit access to community-based services.

Another fundamental difference between European Union and United States community living policies is related to their approach toward the UNCRPD.

[67] *Olmstead v. LC ex rel. Zimring*, 527 U.S. 581, 594 n. 6 (1999) note 588.   [68] Ibid., pp. 604–05.

The European Union ratified the UNCRPD in 2011,[69] and in fact used it as a road map to the European Disability Strategy of 2014–2020. However, there is growing concern that Article 19, which is central to promoting community living policy, will not be implemented and the current misuse of the Structural Funds will continue and hamper the transition from institutional to community-based care for disabled people. The United States has not ratified the UNCRPD and based its community living policy on the *Olmstead* anti-discrimination interpretation of ADA Title II. While the *Olmstead* anti-discrimination decision allows states the freedom to determine the pace and cost of transitioning, the UNCRPD refers to the absolute right of persons with disabilities to choose where and with whom they prefer to live in the community. In this regard, the UNCRPD's human rights focus is viewed as superior to any financial, political, or administrative concerns or considerations.

The second half of the twentieth century marks the transition from institutions to community-based living on both sides of the Atlantic. Most of the efforts have been on closing institutions and hospitals, offering people with psychiatric and intellectual disabilities adequate housing in the community (including supporting them at home). The focus was for them to live in the least restrictive environment, but not necessarily respect preferences and choices where and with whom to live. For example, the *Olmstead* decision transfers the responsibility to the state and professionals to offer reasonable community accommodation, although it cannot be determined against the person's will. However, it cannot stand against the person's preference. The EU Structural Funds do not imply personal desires and choices, because the primary focus is on decreasing institutional care.

If the second half of the twentieth century reflected transition from institutions to community care, the twenty-first century brings the idea of personhood to disability policy. Personhood means personal choice and legal capacity ideas that are reflected in Article 12 and specifically in Article 19 of the UNCRPD, the right of person with a disability to choose with whom and where he or she prefers to live. The idea of personal planning and budgeting is supported in earlier policies in the United States and the United Kingdom.

Person-centered services are common in the United States and the United Kingdom in serving people with intellectual disabilities.[70] The term "personalization" dominates current policy and practice for people with ID/DD in the United Kingdom. Although personalization of care and support can manifest itself in many different ways, personalization generally means that the person, thought of as an individual with strengths, preferences, and aspirations, is put at the center of the process of identifying his or her needs and making choices about how, where, and when he or she is supported to live their lives. Personalized services are also practiced in the United States primarily for individualized planning. Professionals

[69] "EU ratifies UN Convention on disability rights," European Commission press release, January 5, 2011; available at http://europa.eu/rapid/pressReleasesAction.do?reference=IP/11/4.
[70] Mansell and Beadle-Brown, "A response to the commentaries," pp. 31–35.

are required to attend to what matters to the service user rather than impose their own goals upon him or her. This means that the person chooses who is involved in the process, the timing and surroundings of the meetings, family members and friends are partners in planning, and the plan reflects what is important to the person, his or her capacities and what support he or she require.

The challenge in the United States and Europe is to provide a complete person-centered service, which implies that funding of services follows the person and not the service provider, and consumers are free to choose their preferred degree of personal control over service delivery according to their needs, capabilities, current life circumstances, preferences, and aspirations. Their range of options includes the right to custom-design their own services, which requires that the user decides who is to work, with which tasks, at which times, and where and how.

7

Promoting Change in Community Living of People with Intellectual Disabilities

The Case of Israel

Israel's legislation concerning persons with Intellectual Disabilities (ID) was enacted in the late 1960s[1] and has never been substantially amended. The legislation was influenced by the misconception of the time that people with ID caused burden of care and therefore the main policy effort was geared toward relieving the family by proposing institutional care.[2] This approach is evident in the Ministry of Ministry of Social Affairs and Social Services (MOLSA)'s policy and budget allocation, as about 84 percent is dedicated toward out-of-home placement.[3] While the legislation has remained unchanged, Israel's services have in fact departed from the original pro-institutionalization approach. In the 1980s, MOLSA was influenced by international legislation and particularly by the normalization principle, and thereafter by the rights-based approach of the 1990s.[4] The 1980s and 1990s saw the development of smaller-scale residential facilities such as group homes and supported apartments, which had not originally been contemplated by the Israeli legislator. Thus, the current state of affairs in Israel reflects a gap between the original legislation and contemporary policies and practices. The result is a patchwork quilt that is out of step with the original legislation and which is situated halfway toward best international practice. It is therefore recommended to change the existing legislation so that it would build on positive trends already present in Israel and more visibly reflect best practice internationally.[5]

---

[1]   The Welfare Law (Care for Mentally Retarded), 5730–1969.

[2]   See, for example, Simon Olshansky, "Chronic sorrow: A response to having a mentally defective child," *Social Casework* 43 (1962), 190–93; Lynn M. Wikler, Mona Wasow, and Elaine Hatfield, "Chronic sorrow revisited: Parents vs. professional depiction of the adjustment of parents of mentally retarded children," *American Journal of Orthopsychiatry* 51 (1981), 63–70.

[3]   The Ministry of Social Affairs and Social Services (MOLSA) was established in 1990. It is responsible for social policy (e.g., people with disabilities, social services, social benefits, family policy), and social security (e.g., pensions, sickness insurance).

[4]   Arie Rimmerman et al., "Mapping the terrain of disability legislation: The case of Israel," *Society & Disability* 30 (2015), 46–58.

[5]   Arie Rimmerman, "The changes and developments that took place in the State of Israel in the area of developmental disabilities, and the role of Beit Issie Shapiro." Paper presented at "Closing circles:

In 2011, then minister of Labor and Social Affairs Isaac Herzog invited an international panel of experts[6] to examine the status of community living of people with ID in Israel and to propose future policy. Such ad hoc advisory expert panels are widely used by governments in the United States and Europe to analyze current policy or propose alternative ones.[7] Unlike a standing or permanent committee, ad hoc committees are generally tentative and therefore their impact is limited to initial phase and not implementation. An expert panel is usually composed of independent policy or program specific specialists. The panel is mostly employed as an instrument for synthesizing information from a range of sources and drawing on a range of viewpoints in order to arrive at overall conclusions.

The main advantage of working with panels of experts is that they offer policy-makers diversity of ideas and innovative directions. These panels are often used in Israel, but they have been little studied. It is also unknown whether their recommendations are fully or partially adopted by policy-makers. In this chapter, we introduce, review, and analyze the international committee of experts' report on Community Living of People with Intellectual Disabilities, which based its work and recommendations on Articles 12 and 19 of the UNCRPD.[8] Specifically, the panel of international experts demonstrated how the UNCRPD could be used as an effective instrument at the national level, examined the current Israeli system, and offered progressive changes toward future community living policy.

The members of the panel learned that there were various and, at times, contradictory opinions and views on community living programs of people with ID. For example, AKIM (the National Association for the Habilitation of Children and Adults with Intellectual Disabilities), believed that institutional care had to be downsized to facilities of no more than thirty to forty individuals. On the other hand, Bizchut (Israel Human Rights Center for People with Disabilities), called for

---

30 years of social change," in honor of the retirement of Ms. Naomi Shtuziner from Beit Issie Shapiro. January 26, 2011 (Hebrew).

6   The panel consisted of the author, Prof. Arie Rimmerman, University of Haifa; Prof. Gerard Quinn of the University of Ireland (Galway School of Law); Dr. Joel Levy, former CEO of YAI Network, New York; Prof. Peter Blanck of Syracuse University, New York; and Prof. Meindert Haveman of TU Dortmund University, Germany. The committee's coordinator was Dr. Michal Soffer, University of Haifa.

7   See a special issue by Åse Gornitzka and Cathrine Holst, "The role of expert knowledge in EU executive institutions," *Politics and Governance Open Access Journal* 3 (2015), which was devoted to the role of expertise of EU executives since the establishment of the European Union. It explores the role and use of expert knowledge in decision-making in and by EU executive institutions. Developments in the EU are decisive for executive organization and politics in Europe, in particular due to the position of the European Commission as the EU's executive center, but also because of the growing number of EU-level agencies; Yehuda Figura, "Ad hoc public committees in Israel," *Studies in the State's Audit* 62 (2011) (Hebrew); available at www.mevaker.gov.il/serve/contentTree.asp?bookid=589&id=156&contentid =&parentcid=undefined&sw=1024&hw=530.

8   The panel report is reviewed in a forthcoming chapter by Arie Rimmerman and Michal Soffer. "The making of disability policy in Israel: ad hoc advisory expert panels". In Gila Menahem and Amos Zahavi (eds.), *Policy Analysis in Israel*, Policy Press, University of Bristol, UK (2016) pp. 109–120.

the complete closure of all institutions and congregate care facilities and to allow people with ID to live in supported apartments (up to four people). Committed to the UNCRPD, Bizchut pointed out that future policy should be driven by values such as self-determination, autonomy, and choices.

THE INTERNATIONAL PANEL OF EXPERTS' REPORT ON COMMUNITY-BASED RESIDENCES FOR PERSON'S WITH ID: SETTING AND PURPOSE

This committee of experts summarized the deliberations and recommendations regarding deinstitutionalization and community living of people with ID between June 12 and 16, 2011. The report was organized as responses to five core questions raised by MOLSA:

1. What were the common community residential policies and services in other Western countries? How did Israel stand in comparison to these countries?
2. Should Israel regulate or manage by law the location of integrated community residences (e.g., zoning)?
3. What community services would be needed?
4. What should Israel do with institutional care or large congregate care facilities?[9]
5. What should be Israel's community living policy in ten years?

Also, the CEO of MOLSA requested that the committee comment on the required care for persons with complex medical needs and challenging behaviors. Could they live in community settings? Who should be responsible for their support services?

COMMUNICATIONS AND DISCUSSIONS WITH STAKEHOLDERS

The committee held open discussions and was receptive to various comments, remarks and perspectives from numerous stakeholders.[10] The latter consisted, among others, of individuals with ID and family members of people with ID,

---

[9] The term "institutions" is considered to have negative connotations in Hebrew. Furthermore, the legislation that deals with "institutions" coins them *"me'onot,"* which can be literally translated as "dwelling places." Therefore, we will refrain from using the term "institution" throughout the report whenever possible. Instead, more neutral terms will be used such as big or large residences/facilities, etc.

[10] Government representatives consisted primarily of the commissioner for Equal Rights of People with Disabilities in Israel (Ministry of Justice), Mr. Ahiya Kamara, MOLSA's director general Mr. Nahum Itzkovich and various MOLSA employees, including: Dr. Chaia Aminadav, director, division for ID; Dr. Shlomo Elyashar, director of the division of Rehabilitation; Dr. Dalia Nisim, chief supervisor for information management, methods and training, division for ID; Dr. Joav Merrick, medical director, division for ID; Mr. Nahum Ido, head of the department of out-of-home placement, division for ID; Shoshana Lester, chief nurse, division for ID; Dr. Amanda Sinai, visiting scholar, National Institute of Child Health and Human Development, Office of the Medical Director, division for ID; Ms. Orna

representatives of the major service providers for people with ID, mainly AKIM,[11] and Elwin Israel,[12] the CEO of SHEKEL (Community Services for People with Special Needs),[13] representatives from ALUT (The Israeli Society for Autistic Children),[14] a large service provider for persons with autism and pervasive developmental disabilities (PDD), various advocacy groups, and a representative from Bizchut.[15] The members of the committee learned that there were various and at times, contradictory opinions and views on community living of people with ID. The CEO of AKIM, for example, stated that most people with ID could live in apartments of up to six residents. However, she believed that the government had to also offer other congregate living facilities. She thought that *me'onot* should be extensively downsized to thirty to forty people. Such facilities needed to provide extensive and protected outdoor spaces so that the residents would be able to enjoy freedom and not be confined to locked rooms. Small facilities could be more personalized, and provided privacy and the ability to choose.[16] Bizchut called for the closure of all large and segregated facilities in Israel, pointing out that future policy should be driven by values such as self-determination, choice, and autonomy.[17] Both stressed the primacy and importance of personal choice of where and with whom the person would like to live.

There was a debate in the open forum about desired community living policy. MOLSA's representatives as well as other private and public providers viewed group homes as valid community residences. However, the Bizchut representative rejected the idea primarily because group homes were inadequate in ensuring that people were treated as persons.[18]

Yogev, chief supervisor for out-of-home placement (large facilities), division for ID; Ms. Daniela Gov, director of assessment, placement, and promotion, division for ID; Ms. Vivian Azran, director of community services, division for ID; Ms. Lili Abiri, director of the service for persons with autism and pervasive developmental disabilities (PDD); Mr. Marselo Pontovitch, head psychologist, the service for persons with autism and pervasive developmental disabilities; Mr. Kuti Saba, director of research at MOLSA; and Mr. Mordechay Arbel, director of Ma'on Levzeler.

[11] Including the chairperson, retired admiral Ami Ayalon and CEO AKIM Ms. Sigal Yahalomi-Peretz. See AKIM's website at www.akim.org.il/.

[12] See Elwin Israel's website www.israelelwyn.org.il/heb/index.php.

[13] Deputy CEO Ms. Sara Sadovnik. See SHEKEL's website at www.shekel.org.il/?CategoryID=331.

[14] See ALUT's website at www.alut.org.il/.

[15] See Bizchut's website at http://bizchut.org.il/he/; Bizchut, the Israeli Human Rights Center for People with Disabilities, works to enable people with physical, intellectual, sensory, mental, and learning disabilities to participate as fully and independently as possible in the life of the mainstream community. The name "Bizchut" (by right) reflects the belief that all people are entitled to the same rights, and that the needs of people with disabilities must be met on the basis of entitlement rather than from a charity-based perspective.

[16] For the transcription in Hebrew of AKIM's stance, see Appendix 2.

[17] For the transcription in Hebrew of Bizchut's stance, see Appendix 3; see also N. Lerner and Y. Charumanchko, *The land of limited opportunities* (Jerusalem: Bizchut, 2008) (Hebrew).

[18] Association for Civil Rights in Israel (ACRI), *The state of human rights in Israel and in the occupied territories* 2012 (Jerusalem: Association for Civil Rights in Israel), pp. 59–62 covers Bizchut's report on rights of people with disabilities.

INSTITUTIONS AND COMMUNITY RESIDENCES
FOR PEOPLE WITH ID

The legislation supporting out-of-home placement is known as the Care for People with Mental Retardation Act of 1969. Historically, it defined care as living in a large institution (*ma'on*). However, the law was amended in 2000 to include any out-of-home placement facility, including community-based residences. In addition, MOLSA gave preference to community living over institutionaliza-tion. As part of its community-based preference policy, MOLSA since 2013 has encouraged all the large facilities to build twenty-two branches in the commu-nity. However, there is growing debate as to whether such facilities are real community-based residences, as they would be dependent on institutional care services and staff.[19]

According to Gorbatov, Ben Moshe, and Ben-Simchon, in 2009 MOLSA pro-vided services to 34,274 people ID.[20] It is noteworthy that the number of persons with ID in Israel is estimated to be larger than the aforementioned.[21] Nonetheless, according to these data, the prevalence of ID in the Israeli population is 4.6 in per thousand individuals. The majority (70.2 percent) of persons with ID in Israel in 2009 lived at home with their families;[22] about a fifth (21.3 percent) of individuals with ID resided in large facilities, and 8.4 percent were living in group homes or "satellite apartments."[23] According to MOLSA's data, there were about 2,906 people with ID living in 250 community-based residences. Most of them lived in sixty-four large group homes (1,428 people) and the rest in other modes of services.[24]

In terms of institutional care, in 2009 7,314 individuals lived in sixty-three facilities of institutional care.[25] The sixty-three large facilities varied in size, but also in location and ownership. Some were situated in city centers and were physically and functionally integrated into community life, while others were located in secluded areas; nine of the facilities were owned by the government, fourteen were run by NGOs, and the remaining forty were private facilities.[26]

---

[19] See a comprehensive article exploring the developing "right to live in the community" for people with disabilities under international law and the domestic laws of the United States and Israel by Arlene Kantor, "There's no place like home: The right to live in the community for people with disabilities under international law and the domestic laws of the United States and Israel," *Israel Law Review* 45 (2012), 181–233.

[20] Renta Gorbatov, Eliyahoo Ben Moshe, and Miri Ben Simchon, "Review of existing services: Jerusalem, Israel," The Ministry of Welfare and Social Services, 2009, 369.

[21] People with disabilities in Israel: Facts and figures. Jerusalem: Myers-JDC-Brookdale Institute, 2014, p. 10.

[22] Ibid., p. 370.   [23] Ibid., p. 462.   [24] Ibid., pp. 468–70.

[25] Among the sixty-three facilities, eleven had more than 200 residents, eleven housed 120–200, twenty-four facilities accommodated between fifty-seven and 119, and seventeen no more than fifty-six.

[26] Gorbatov, Ben Moshe and Ben Simchon, "Review of existing services," p. 477.

THE UNCRPD AS THE ROAD MAP

The committee used the UNCRPD to serve as a "moral compass," or a road map that might help guide the State of Israel in designing future community living policy for people with ID.[27] The purpose of the UNCRPD was not to create new rights or even a new species of "disability rights." Rather, as aptly put in Article 1, the purpose was to secure the full and equal enjoyment of all existing human rights by persons with disabilities. The paradigm shift in the UNCRPD was to view (and treat) persons with disabilities not as "objects" to be managed or simply cared for but as "subjects" capable of assuming control over their personal destinies and worth of equal respect. Principally, it meant a shift away from paternalism toward a policy posture of nurturing native capacities, empowering people to take charge of their own lives (with appropriate supports), and breaking down barriers into the lifeworld (society, economy, community, and political life). It greatly expanded the zone of dignity of risks to enable people make mistakes for themselves and struck a radically new (nonpaternalist) balance with the ongoing duty of the state to protect. The UNCRPD was built on the pioneering premises of US anti-discrimination law – but added a new social dimension in terms of the social supports that were needed to make this new freedom a reality.

There were four of fifty articles of the convention that exemplified this paradigm shift and were of utmost importance to the subject of this report: Article 12 (the right to make decisions for oneself), Article 19 (the right to live independently and being included in the community, Article 8 (raising awareness as a social precondition to create openness and tolerance for individual expression), and Article 16 (a new way of balancing the legitimate protective role of the state). The panel of international experts based the report primarily on Articles 12 and 19.

The committee was not asked to address the issues of guardianship and legal capacity. However, it was obvious that the subject matter of this report was closely tied to the debate about the reform of legal capacity law since the right to live independently assumed a legal capacity to make decisions about one's own personal destiny. The Israeli Legal Capacity and Guardianship Law was enacted in 1962 and had never since been amended.[28] Melamed, Doron, and Shnitt[29] explained: Israeli law stated that whenever "a person is unable, permanently or temporarily, to take care of his affairs, all or some" the court is authorized to nominate a guardian over her or his person and/or property (Legal Capacity and Guardianship Law, 1962, Section 22(a)(4)). The law enables this type of appointment in two situations: (a) the

27   See Chapter 3, "The Paradigm Shift of Articles 12 and 19 of the UN Convention on the Rights of Persons with Disabilities (UNCRPD)," with an in-depth review and analysis of Articles 12 and 19.
28   Israel Doron, "Elder guardianship kaleidoscope: A comparative legal perspective," *International Journal of Law, Policy and the Family* 16 (2002), 368–98; Yuval Melamed, Israel Doron, and Dan Shnitt, "Guardianship of people with mental disorders," *Social Science & Medicine* 65 (2007), 1118–23, especially pp. 1119–20.
29   Ibid.

status of diminished capacity results from a mental disorder or mental impairment (ID or dementia); (b) in other situations where the factors are not specified, but in practice the individual is unable to take care of his affairs, the process of appointment of a guardian requires cooperation between the attending physician, a social worker, and an attorney. The individual requesting the appointment is a relative of the patient or a representative of the attorney general.

It is of note that in both cases the person in question is heard by the court.[30] The first situation mentioned above, where a person is declared by the court "legally incompetent" (*pesul din*),[31] is a case of total and absolute guardianship (plenary guardianship), i.e., the loss of all of the person's legal rights in all life spheres. It should be noted that today the Israeli courts refrain from declaring a person as "legally incompetent."

In the second aforementioned situation, for the sheltered person (*hasuy*),[32] "the medical opinion ought to be related to the disorder or impairment of the individual for whom the request was made. The social worker's opinion should detail financial matters as well as the prospective guardian."[33] Of note that, "[t]he law does not determine the threshold beyond which a person cannot look after his own interests."[34] The current state of guardianship appointment in Israel resembles a "mental incompetence" regime whereby when a physician determined that an individual was incompetent, he or she was appointed a guardian – typically a family member – who was authorized to make all legal decisions concerning the person and his or her property.[35]

The common view expressed in the literature is that the appointment of a guardian is seen as a last resort as the law states that a guardian shall be appointed "only if there is no one authorized and willing to take care of the subject's affairs."[36] In 2016, the Ministry of Justice was planning on changing the law in April 2017 to comply with Article 12 of the UNCRPD.

The paradigm shift of Article 12 had significant implications on the right of choosing residency and living arrangements (among many other things). The committee report emphasized that, in keeping with the spirit of the convention, the right to make choices with respect to residency and living arrangements should not be arbitrarily limited or curtailed by outmoded thinking on legal capacity.

Article 19 was the center of the report, addressing the right to live independently and to be included in the community. It has been a logical outcrop of Article 12 (the

---

[30] "Legal aid clinic for the elderly and Holocaust survivors; clinical legal education program," Bar-Ilan University, Ramat Gan. Fact sheet on the subject of the legally incompetent and guardianship (Hebrew); available at law-clinics.biu.ac.il/files/lawclinique/shared/9.doc.

[31] Yuval Melamed, Lili Yaron-Melamed, and Jermina Heinik, "Guardianship appointment: Current status in Israel," *Israel Journal of Psychiatry and Related Sciences* 47 (2010), 260–68.

[32] See n. 566.   [33] Ibid.

[34] Melamed, Doron, and Shnitt, "Guardianship of people with mental disorders," 65; Doron, "Elder guardianship kaleidoscope," 381.

[35] Ibid.   [36] Ibid.

right to make one's own decisions). On the whole Article 19 reflected a positive philosophy of living independently and being included in the community. It did not mention the "institution," much less "deinstitutionalization." Instead, its focus was always on choice (and on individual and general supports to enable choice), as well as inclusion. What then of the argument that one should not foreclose the possibility that a free choice might be made to continue to live in an institution, and therefore state funding for institutions as such had to continue? It could certainly be contended that this argument, while superficially plausible, is not valid since the underlying purpose of Article 19 was to situate the person in a context that afforded maximum scope for flourishing and the development of one's personality. This was unlikely to happen if the residence's neighbors are apt to think of the individual more as part of a group and less as an individual. A smaller residential place of living is more appropriate when full participation in community living has been facilitated, including support by staff, from the perspective of individual choice-making and self-determination.

The report is very clear that if state funding were to continue for institutions then, in reality, precious little would be available to develop the kinds of integrated community resources necessary to make Article 19 a reality. At some stage a transition has to be made from directing resources into institutions to growing community supports. In sum, the totality of the UNCRPD makes it plain that individual choice is to be respected not merely as an end in itself but also as means to a higher end, which is individual self-realization in an expanded set of community relations and in contexts that provide tangible bridges into the community.

The committee noted the importance of Articles 8 and 16. Article 8 essentially addresses the dialectic that exists between individual rights and public responsiveness. It is considered essential since one of the main barriers to the equal enjoyment of rights for persons with disabilities is public or attitudinal barriers. Unless these misperceptions change then space would not be optimized for community engagement and full respect. One of the most important glues holding together these misperceptions was an ingrained unwillingness or inability on the part of many to look beyond the disability (or the label of disability) to see and appreciate the person. This has direct implications on the questions posed to the committee. For example, if Israeli institutions were allowed to continue – even on the basis of downsizing – then this would probably not be enough to dissolve the seemingly natural instinct of the public toward "group-think," toward thinking of the person primarily as part of a group (with a legacy of negative connotations) and not as an individual worthy of getting to know and being including in the life of the community.

It was noted above that the continued existence of institutions would probably undermine the capacity of a state to shift resources over time to community supports and would therefore probably not be in congruence with Article 19. It might be added that the continued existence of institutions – even mini-institutions – would seem to act as a barrier to the removal of attitudinal barriers in the community, contrary to Article 8.

Furthermore, Israeli legislation allowing residences for persons with disabilities to concentrate in certain areas might similarly have the same effect. It appears that the three articles that have been discussed (8, 12, and 19) seem to point to some optimum spreading of residences in order to erode attitudinal barriers and create the optimum conditions of community inclusion.

Finally, Article 16, which mandates freedom from exploitation, violence, and abuse, was relevant to institutions and deinstitutionalization. In the past, many states rationalized institutionalization with a concomitant lack of choice and community engagement on the basis that persons with ID needed "to be protected" against the exploitative intent of others and even from themselves, and that this was in their own "best interests." If that meant eliminating opportunities for them to exercise their "dignity of risk" to make their own choices (and suffer the consequences), then so be it. If that meant crafting restrictive or closed (or relatively closed) environments, then so be it. There existed a blurred line between this (natural) protective impulse that we all instinctively possess toward others (and which the state enforces on our behalf) and a gross form of paternalism. In most countries, including Israel, this had an overly broad, chilling effect on individual choice and freedom.

The implications for the committee were as follows: first, paternalist constraints on the individual had to be strongly questioned. To be sure, the state continued (even after the UNCRPD) to have a legitimate protective role, but this should not be allowed to act as a pretext to deny autonomy and liberty rights to persons with disabilities. Second, the newly rebalanced protective role of the states did not mean that the state has no role. On the contrary, in the shift toward independent living and being involved in the community, the state's role assumed a new form and shape. It was not expressed in terms of a block against living in the community; rather it took on a new role in protecting people in their new environment in the community. This was a more nuanced role for the state – one that was complementary to individual choice and community engagement and not a barrier to it.

COMMITTEE'S RESPONSE TO GOVERNMENT QUESTIONS: BENCHMARKING ISRAELI COMMUNITY LIVING WITH THE UNITED STATES AND EUROPE

The first question was a benchmarking assignment: comparing Israel's community living policy with other Western countries. The committee responded first by providing a brief overview of the major landmarks of legal rights legislation in Israel. The beginning of rights legislation in Israel was relatively new. In 1998, the Israeli Knesset (parliament) enacted the Equal Rights for People with

Disabilities Law.[37] The legislation was preceded by a well-known legal precedent dictated by the Israeli Supreme Court in 1996, in the case of Shahar Botser, a child who used a wheelchair. The Supreme Court ruled that Botser was entitled to access all areas in his school, thus tying the right to accessibility to principles of equality and human dignity.[38] The Equal Rights for People with Disabilities Law of 1998 was initiated by Bizchut in 1995 in form of an Equal Rights for Persons with Disabilities Bill, which was modeled after the ADA as well as legislation from Scandinavian countries. It therefore addressed a wide variety of disabilities as well as numerous social spheres, primarily, employment, accessibility to both public places and services, living in the community, personal assistance, education, culture and leisure activities, legal procedures, special needs, and social security.[39]

It was noteworthy that the Equal Rights for People with Disabilities Law of 1998 carried forward only five of the ten original chapters of Equal Rights for Persons with Disabilities Bill of 1995 (Basic Principles, General Principles, Employment, Public Transport Services, and Commission for Equal Rights for People with Disabilities). However, it was only in March 2005 that the law was profoundly amended and the chapter addressing accessibility of public places and services was enacted.[40] As of today, only part of the regulations concerning this chapter has been formulated.[41] As reported earlier in the book,[42] the first reference of the committee regarding the right to live independently in the community was the United States in the second title of the ADA, which views unnecessary and unjustified segregation by society as discrimination under the ADA.[43] In 1999, in *Olmstead v. Zimring*, the US Supreme Court decided that placement of persons with mental disabilities in institutions rather than in integrated community settings, under certain conditions may violate the ADA, particularly when placement was not justified by professional opinion and not necessary for cost or other reasons.[44]

In Europe, Article 19 of the UNCRPD did not simply reflect civil rights in isolation, as in the United States, but rather stressed the dynamic relationship between civil rights and social provision. This article weaved together two core

---

[37]   Arie Rimmerman and Shirley Avrami, "Israel's equal rights for persons with disabilities law: Legal base, process and impact," *International Journal of Disability, Community & Rehabilitation* 8 (2009). Retrieved March 21, 2016 from www.ijdcr.ca/VOL08_03/articles/rimmerman.shtml.

[38]   Ibid.

[39]   Michal Soffer et al., "Media and the Israeli disability rights legislation: Progress or mixed and contradictory images?" *Disability & Society* 25 (2010), 687–99.

[40]   Rimmerman and Avrami, "Israel's equal rights for persons with disabilities law."

[41]   All the regulations and amendments are available in Hebrew at www.justice.gov.il/Units/NetzivutShivyon/MercazHameidaLenegishut/HakikatNegishut/HukimTakanotUtkanim/Pages/HukTakUtkanMATOS.aspx.

[42]   For additional information about United States legislation, see Chapter 4.

[43]   For a comprehensive review of the legislation, see Peter Blanck et al., *Disability civil rights law and policy* (St. Paul, MN: West Publishers, 2009).

[44]   Kaiser Family Foundation, "Olmstead vs. L.C.: the Interaction of the Americans with Disabilities Act and Medicaid," 2004. Retrieved March 29, 2016 from www.kff.org/medicaid/upload/Olmstead-v-L-C-The-Interaction-of-the-Americans-with-Disabilities-Act-and-Medicaid.pdf.

principles: the right of people with disabilities to live independently and thus consequently to choose their place of residence, where and with whom they live, and the entitlement to be fully integrated in the community. The latter entailed that the placement in the community without the appropriate services to facilitate the involvement of individuals in community life and activities would fail to fulfill the principles of the article.

In contrast to the trends in Israel, Braddock and colleagues found that the majority (75 percent) of persons with ID in 2009 in the United States lived in various community-based residential settings that hosted six of fewer individuals. Additionally, 10 percent of all individuals served lived in residences that housed seven to fifteen individuals, and 15 percent of the population lived in various institutions, i.e., facilities with sixteen residents or more.[45]

In Europe, there was a determined movement toward community living and deinstitutionalization of persons with ID.[46] As was to be expected, the cultural context and policies related to this process varied from country to country and showed a heterogeneous picture.[47] In countries such as Sweden and Norway, residential institutions for people with ID have been completely closed and no one with ID lives in institutional settings anymore.[48] In the United Kingdom, the process of deinstitutionalization is well advanced[49] and the number of large institutions has constantly decreased in the 1990s and the beginning of the twenty-first century.

The committee learned from Prof. Gerard Quinn, who pointed out that Ireland and Israel were similar in population size, that Ireland was going through a fast-paced process of downsizing the larger institutions, the so-called congregate settings. A 2011 survey showed that far fewer people with ID resided in institutions in Ireland.[50] In a report of the Working Group on Congregated Settings in the Republic of Ireland, a new working model has been proposed:

[45] David Braddock et al., *The state of the states in developmental disabilities: 2011* (Washington, DC: American Association on Intellectual and Developmental Disabilities, 2011).

[46] For extensive review of Europe, see Chapter 5.

[47] European Coalition for Community Living, "Focus on Article 19 of the UN Convention on the Rights of Persons with Disabilities," 2009. Retrieved December 13, 2016 from www.community-living .info/documents/ECCL-Focus-Report-2009-final-WEB.pdf.

[48] Julie Beadle-Brown, Jim Mansell, and Agnes Kozma, "Deinstitutionalization in intellectual disabilities," *Current Opinion in Psychiatry* 20 (2007), 437–42.

[49] Jim Mansell and Julie Beadle-Brown, "Deinstitutionalisation and community living: Position statement of the Comparative Policy and Practice Special Interest Research Group of the International Association for the Scientific Study of Intellectual Disabilities," *Journal of Intellectual Disability Research* 54 (2010), 104–12.

[50] In Ireland, approximately 3,800 individuals with ID reside in seventy-two institutions ("congregated settings" with eight residents or more). See Report of the Working Group on Congregated Settings. *Time to move on from congregated settings: A strategy for community inclusion.* Health Service Executive, 2011, p. 21. Retrieved January 8, 2016 from www.slainte.ie/eng/services/Publications/ser vices/Disability/timetomoveonfromcongregatedsettings.pdf.

The Working Group is proposing a new model of support in the community. The model envisages that people living in congregated settings will move to dispersed forms of housing in ordinary communities, provided mainly by housing authorities. They will have the same entitlement to mainstream community health and social services as any other citizen, such as GP services, home help and public health nursing services, and access to primary care teams. They will also have access to specialized services and hospital services based on an individual assessment. People will get the supports they need to help them to live independently and to be part of their local community. A core value underpinning our proposal is that people should make their own life choices, neither the HSE [Health Service Executive – the body that manages community care as well as acute medical facilities] nor Service Providers own a client but have a responsibility to maximize their independence.[51]

Israel can learn from the Irish Working Group, which rejected the argument that choice was possible in institutional care: "[c]ongregated provision is in breach of Ireland's obligations under UN Conventions."[52] Living independently in the community was held by the Irish Working Group to equate to settings that house no more than four individuals, preferably mixed settings of nondisabled (not caregivers or personal assistants) and persons with disabilities. Home-sharing, whereby a person with a disability with security of tenure lives with a nondisabled person (e.g., a student) for reduced rent in exchange for some assistance, is fast becoming quite popular in Ireland. Of crucial importance is that the Working Group's report emphasized that the changes would require a transitional process stretching over seven years:

A seven year timeframe for the overall national closure program for congregated settings should be set. Within that timeframe, specific annual targets should be set at national and local level to guide the phasing and prioritizing process, in consultation with the HSE.[53]

In countries such as Belgium, the Netherlands, Germany, Spain, Greece, Italy, and Portugal, there was a varying pattern of institutional care,[54] even though the number of people in large residential institutions is also decreasing.[55] On the other hand, in countries such as France, Hungary, Poland, Romania, Czech Republic, and in general, Central and Eastern Europe, large institutional settings were the

---

[51]   Health Service Executive, *Time to move on from congregated settings*, p. 21. It is important to note that the Irish report suggested by Quinn, serves as a reference for the Israeli Panel of Experts, particularly the idea of using the UNCRPD as a road map.

[52]   Ibid., p. 27.   [53]   Ibid., p. 21.

[54]   Beadle-Brown, Mansell, and Kozma, "Deinstitutionalization in intellectual disabilities," p. 4.

[55]   Mansell et al., *Deinstitutionalization and community living*. An interesting project aimed to bring together the available information on the number of disabled people living in residential institutions in twenty-eight European countries and to identify successful strategies for replacing institutions with community-based services, paying particular attention to economic issues in the transition. It is the largest study of its kind ever undertaken.

predominant place for care. Although it has, in general, proved to produce poor outcomes for residents,[56] in some EU-member states institutional care still accounts for more than half of public expenditures in this area.[57]

There is resistance toward community living, and the resulting process of deinstitutionalization; policies, and practices have changed slowly.[58] The ratification of the UNCRPD by many of these countries between 2007 and 2012, however, would undoubtedly accelerate current trends in favor of independent living and bring about a new wave of deinstitutionalization with proper community supports and development of small-scale community housing in those European Union countries. An appropriate living environment has to be defined within the specific structural and cultural context of individual countries, for example, as compared to the living and residential conditions of nondisabled citizens of that country. But leaving cultural diversity to one side, the overall trend toward independent living and community engagement even for – and perhaps especially for – persons with ID is clearly recognizable.

ZONING OF COMMUNITY LIVING

The second question addressed in the Committee of Experts' report is zoning of community residences. Using Article 19 of the UNCRPD as a guideline, the committee stated that people with disabilities had the right to live wherever they choose. The report made clear that people with ID had the right to choose where and with whom they would like to live.

The Israeli Planning and Building Law of 1965 (section 63a, 1995 and 2002 amendment)[59] stated that persons with disabilities could live in a residential building, as long as the number of residents in each unit or apartment did not exceed six. The question of zoning discussed by the committee related primarily to a specific problem that has risen in Israel concerning condensed community services.[60] It is evident that people with ID have the right to live wherever they choose. Service

---

[56]　Freyhoff et al., *Included in society*, pp. 28–56; Mansell, Beadle-Brown, and Clegg, "The situation of large residential institutions in Europe," pp. 28–56.

[57]　Mansell et al., *Deinstitutionalization and community living*.

[58]　Barbara H. Vann and Jan Siska, "From 'cage beds' to inclusion: The long road for individuals with intellectual disability in the Czech Republic," *Disability and Society* 21 (2006), pp. 425–39. The article documented Czech human rights abuses taking place in institutions that purport to serve people with intellectual disabilities, the most prominent being the use of cage beds in psychiatric institutions. Czech laws pose barriers to the ability of NGOs to provide services specifically with regard to state funding that only recognizes community care for seniors.

[59]　See Meirav Sarig, "Not in my back yard (nimby)," *Haaretz*, December 24, 2002, on exclusion and marginalization in affluent neighborhoods in central Israel (Hebrew). Retrieved June 4, 2016 from www .haaretz.co.il/misc/1.849229;

[60]　See, for example, news reports on neighbors organizing support for "nimby" in affluent Herzliya in 2008: www.local.co.il/kfar-saba/36156/article.htm; and Haifa area in 2010 www.mynet.co.il/articles/ 1,7340,L-3890986,00.html.

providers (private or NGOs) use this right to offer community services where they choose to do so. It should be noted that service providers' interests are not always in accord with the individual's choice.

The committee could not obtain official data of residences and apartments for people with ID by region. Anecdotal evidence suggested that there were certain municipalities across the country that had concentrated or saturated residences. This might have a negative impact on the efforts to increase community awareness. Saturation and condensing people with ID into one neighborhood or location intensifies the resistance of the community to their integration and social participation.[61] Apart from the above problems, it constitutes a significant departure from the commitment to implement the right of people with ID to be integrated into the community (Article 19 of the UNCRPD). Therefore, excessive geographic clustering would also seem to defeat one of the purposes of the UNCRPD, grounded in Article 8, which is to nurture public receptiveness to the rights of persons with disabilities and inculcate positive community attitudes. This is most assuredly not the same as saying that there is a limit beyond which each community should not be expected to bear. It would only speak to an agenda of spreading "the burden." Such a negative philosophy only reinforces negative stereotypes of disability. Rather, it is to say that an equitable spread of such units (of limited size) stands a much better chance of connecting persons with disabilities with the community and of inculcating positive attitudes and practices.

The committee thought that it was important to prevent saturation, particularly of large residences, because it tended to obstruct successful community inclusion. One of the suggestions was to focus on apartments that better-fitted community climate and inclusion. It might well be the case that the barriers in question have less to do with the size of the apartment (and the quality of life within them) and more to do with attitudes toward people with ID. Nevertheless, these perceptual barriers were simply harder to dissolve when the very size of the unit or resident appeared to divert attention away from the person behind the disability to the disability itself.

---

[61]   See Michael Dear et al., "Seeing people differently: The sociospatial construction of disability," *Environment and Planning D: Society and Space* 15 (2007), 455–80. The article, which is based on meta-analysis of forty-four acceptance hierarchy studies since 1968, reveals both stability and change in community preference structures. The largest impetus for change derives from the appearance of new "disabilities" including most especially people with AIDS and homeless people. Evidence also suggests that significant attitudinal variations occur through space as well as time; when different facility types are considered; and that actual behavior may differ from expressed attitudinal preferences. The paper concludes with remarks directed toward a more adequate socio-spatial theory of disability. The implication for community living in Israel is that spatial consideration is crucial for developing favorable attitudes toward people with disabilities; The same applies to the article by Myra Piat, "The 'NIMBY' phenomenon: Community residents' concerns about housing for deinstitutionalized people," *Health and Social Work* 25 (2000), 127–38; and to the debate regarding whether to notify neighborhoods about incoming residents with mental illness; see Allison L. Zippay, "Psychiatric residents: Notification, NIMBY, and neighborhood relations," *Psychiatric Services* 58 (2007), 109–13.

The final suggestion was that an initial mapping study be conducted to identify the current geographic spread, to assess the impact of concentration of residences on community inclusion, and to prepare the ground for the phased transition to much smaller congregated settings (if needed). The state could also prevent saturation by providing funding for apartments or residences in nonsaturated areas.

COMMUNITY SERVICES FOR INDIVIDUALS AND FAMILIES

The experts committee referred to Article 19 of the UNCRPD, which supports the revolution of social services around the world that are moving from prepacked proxies of need to individualized services. In France, for example, a new terminology of "life plans" is being substituted for the old terms of "needs" and "services." Social services, according to this view, ought to promote individual goals, while formal support services are not always regarded in a positive light. Bryony Beresford related that parents frequently reported the need for a break from caring to provide time for themselves and their partners and time to spend with their other children. Children for whom provision is most inadequate include those with complex health needs or with challenging behavior or autistic spectrum disorders and children from minority ethnic families.[62]

The committee has introduced several projects in Australia and the United Kingdom that provide models for support coordination and direct family support services for aging caregivers of adults with ID. It recognizes that the increased life expectancy of people with ID highlights the dual issues of supporting aging parental caregivers so that they continue in their role and ensuring a smooth transition for middle-aged adults with intellectual disability to nonparental care. Unfortunately, there are few services in Australia that are specifically designed to respond to these issues and older caregivers. One, "Options for Older Families," funded by the Victorian Department of Human Services in 1995 to work with older caregivers on immediate needs and planning for the future, utilized intensive case management with access to discretionary funds, and demonstrated its merits to caregivers.[63]

The Sharing Caring Project (SCP) in the United Kingdom is an organization that supports family caregivers over fifty-five years of age. It has produced information packets for caregivers, "lifebooks" for people with ID, and partnered with the Sheffield National Health Service (NHS) Trust to provide direct preventative support for older caregivers, as well as with the Asian Disability Project to help ensure

---

[62] Bryony Beresford, *Positively parents — caring for a severely disabled child* (York: Social Policy Research Unit, 1994); idem, *Expert opinions — a national survey of parents caring for a severely disabled child* (Bristol: The Policy Press, 1995).

[63] See Christine Bigby, Elizabeth Ozanne, and Meg Gordon, "Facilitating transition: Elements of successful case management practice for older parents of adults with intellectual disability," *Journal of Gerontological Social Work* 37 (2002), 25–44; Carers FIRST: *Who we are*, 2008. Retrieved April 7, 2016 from www.carersfirst.org.uk.

culturally competent supports.[64] Carers FIRST in the United Kingdom is an organization dedicated to comprehensive help and support for caregivers of all types through information and resources, discussion, advocacy, one-to-one support, and groups where caregivers can meet others in similar situations.

The experts committee cited four studies conducting among 387 family caregivers in Northern Ireland concerning future residential arrangements for a family member with ID. McConkey, McConaghie, Barr, and Roberts[65] found that the majority of caregivers preferred that the individual remain to be cared for within the family, a finding which is in accord with the previous research. However, the most common out-of-home placement was a nursing home. In a study which was conducted among 180 people with ID in Northern Ireland concerning their present and future living arrangements, four overarching themes emerged: having one's own bedroom, taking part in household activities, having access to community activities, and staying in touch with family and friends. The researchers note that participants who lived on their own or in supported housing valued their independence and accessibility of staff support. Living with one's family was the most preferred option, followed by small group homes and supported living.[66]

Features of self-determination include having an individual budget, exercising control over services and decision-making, using person-centered planning, having independent support brokerage, and having a fiscal intermediary. Head and Conroy[67] found significant improvements in consumer choice and control, quality of life, satisfaction, and community participation following implementation of Consumer Directed Services (CDS) in Michigan. The largest changes in choice and control were in major service-related areas such as hire and fire of direct support staff, choice of agency support person, choice of people to live with, choice of house or apartment, and choice of case manager. In Michigan, a substantial transfer of control over services had taken place from staff and other professionals to individual consumers and their families after three years of CDS. Head and Conroy also reported that, from 1998 to 2001, average public costs (adjusted for inflation) for study participants decreased by 16 percent, although not uniformly across all participants. Those with the highest initial costs in 1998 under traditional funding and service delivery arrangements tended to have the largest decreases in expenditures following the introduction of individual budget and consumer-directed services, but

[64] Sharing Caring Project, *The sharing caring project*, 2008. Retrieved May 19, 2016 from www.sheffieldmencap.org.uk/sharing-caring-project.
[65] Roy McConkey et al., "Views of family carers to the future accommodation and support needs of their relatives with intellectual disabilities," *Irish Journal of Psychological Medicine* 23 (2006), 140–44.
[66] Roy McConkey et al., "Views of people with intellectual disabilities of their present and future living arrangements," *Journal of Policy and Practice in Intellectual Disabilities* 1 (2004), 115–25.
[67] Michael J. Head and Jim W. Conroy, "Outcomes of self-determination in Michigan." In *Costs and outcomes of community services for people with intellectual disabilities*. Edited by Roger J. Stancliffe and Charlie K. Lakin (Baltimore: Brookes, 2005), pp. 219–40.

a number of individuals, who tended to have lower pre-CDS expenditures, showed increases in expenditure during the three-year period.

In the process of planning responsive services to individual needs (Article 19, section 3) in Europe and North America,[68] there has been a shift to individualized or personal budgets ("direct payments"), whereby the money is given to the individual to purchase the services he or she chooses. It is of note that in the United States certain family members and friends might be regarded as service providers.[69] Two types of financial support are essential components of the family support system in the United States: cash subsidies and the Medicaid Home and Community-Based Support Waiver. Cash subsidies are direct payments to families that give them increased control over services and supports most suitable for their particular family member. Nationally, twenty-four states offer cash subsidies or vouchers to families and eighteen states have Supported Living waivers. There are forty-eight states and Washington DC that provide state or Medicaid-funded supported living or personal assistance (PAS) services for people with ID living on their own or in the family home.[70] In an evaluation of the Self Determination Initiative in Michigan, Head and Conroy found that individual budgets were distributed equitably, regardless of a recipient's personal characteristics such as gender, ethnic background, and levels of intellectual disability, adaptive behavior, and challenging behavior.[71]

Using case studies from Canada, the United States, and Australia, Lord and Hutchinson[72] support the finding that the allocation of individualized funds was designed to be equitable and accountable to both the funder and the individual. However, the size and type of an individual's residence affected whether they received an individual budget. People living in their own homes were more likely to have individual budgets than people living in group homes.[73] Head and Conroy hypothesized that the strong link between individual budgets and people living at

---

[68] For example, the United Kingdom; see www.barnet.gov.uk/personal-budgets; Janet Leece and Joanna Bornat, *Developments in direct payments* (Bristol: The Policy Press, 2006); Charlotte Pearson et al., "Personal assistance policy in the UK: What's the problem with direct payments?" *Disability Studies Quarterly* 25 (2005). Retrieved June 22, 2016 from www.dsq-sds.org /article/view/525/702. regarding Austria, Germany, Luxembourg, Sweden, the Netherlands, and Norway, see Jens Lundsgaard, "Consumer direction and choice in long-term care for older persons, including payments for informal care: How can it help improve care outcomes, employment and fiscal sustainability?" Paris, Organization for Economic Co-operation and Development, OECD health working paper no. 202005. Retrieved June 30, 2016 from www.oecd.org/dataoecd/53/62/ 34897775.pdf; information on New York State home and community-based services waiver (OPWDD); available at www.health.ny.gov/health_care/medicaid/program/longterm/omrdd.htm

[69] See, for example, www.cms.gov/MedicaidStWaivProgDemoPGI/05_HCBSWaivers-Section1915(c) .asp

[70] David Braddock, Richard Hemp, and Mary Kay Rizzolo, *The state of the states in developmental disabilities: 2008* (Boulder: University of Colorado, Coleman Institute for Cognitive Disabilities and Department of Psychiatry, 2008).

[71] Head and Conroy, "Outcomes of self-determination in Michigan," pp. 232–34.

[72] John Lord and Peggy Hutchinson, "Individualized support and funding: Building blocks for capacity building and inclusion," *Disability & Society* 18 (2003), 71–86.

[73] Head and Conroy, "Outcomes of self-determination in Michigan," p. 234.

home may be explained by people using their individual budgets to move out-of-home (showing how individual budgets allow for greater independence), by administrative convenience in accounting, or by a tendency to select individual budgeting to support a more individualized approach to services.

The committee thought that Individualized Budgets (IB) had to be monitored carefully for proper use of the money by caregivers and people with disabilities. Nicola Moran and her associates[74] examined these concerns in a cash-for-care initiative piloted in England in 2005–2007 and found that despite their primary aim of increasing choice and control for the service user, IBs had a positive impact on caregivers of IB holders. The findings are important in that they have implications for the widespread rollout of personal budgets in England and may also provide wider valuable lessons nationally and internationally about the tensions between policies to support caregivers and policies aimed at promoting choice and control by disabled and older people.

Slasberg, Beresford, and Schofield,[75] who studied the impact of personal budgets in the United Kingdom, believe that in order to achieve success with personalized budgets, there is a need to move away from a culture characterized by paternalism and institutionalization to one rooted in independent living and the social model of disability. This will also signal a shift away from the focus on seeking to achieve a culture based on consumerism that has underpinned the approach to personal budgets hitherto. In its place, there would need to be a new approach to working in partnership between the state and service users to ensure their authentic inclusion. Although the current strategy aims to achieve similar cultural change, there is no evidence that it has.

Should all forms of assistance or caring for person with a disability become a business transaction? In the Netherlands, for example, recipients of individualized budgets were at first people with severe disabilities. Loosening controlling procedures, however, and a programmatic shift included persons with less restrictive conditions, such as Asperger's syndrome, ADHD (Attention Deficit Hyperactivity Disorder), and mild learning disabilities for direct payments, resulted in a broad and expensive program which grew out of control with a yearly increase of 24 percent in the period 2003–2009, up to a total 2.8 billion euro. In principle, individualized budgets reflect first and foremost personal choice:

> [t]here is a movement towards allowing more individual choice for older persons receiving publicly funded long-term care at home. Having more flexibility in terms of how to receive care can increase the older person's self-determination and that of his/her informal care givers. Having a choice among alternative care providers can empower older persons as consumers and may help strengthen the role of

74 See Nicola Moran et al., "Personalisation and carers: Whose rights? Whose benefits?" *British Journal of Social Work* 42 (2012), 461–79.
75 Colin Slasberg, Peter Beresford, and Peter Schofield, "How self-directed support is failing to deliver personal budgets and personalization," *Research, Policy and Planning* 29 (2012), 161–77.

households in the care-management process. Choice can also help address quality aspects that are difficult to quantify but easy to experience for users, such as the personal interaction between the older person and the care giver.[76]

In addition to individualized budgets, more and more countries believe that social services in the community should be accessible to all. There remains no space for segregated or special services for people with disabilities. Instead, community services should be accommodated to enable all persons to use and enjoy them. Such notions and practices, which are spreading throughout the world, are reflected in the UNCRPD.

As was previously mentioned, individualized services and personal budgets are based on personal choice. An accessible and inclusive community creates the conditions necessary to be an equal member of the community.[77] It is evident that personal choice contradicts paternalistic notions and traditional guardianship laws and policies. Guardianship should be redesigned to assist persons in expressing and maximizing their choices.

In a similar manner, the state is still responsible for the safety of persons with disabilities; however, according to this paradigm shift safety, like guardianship, is not equivalent to paternalism. Many countries are now attempting to balance the tension between choice, risk, and safety, with regard to people with ID. The UNCRPD proposes to change our default choice, which has put risk before choice. In this sense, it reflects the notion of "the dignity of risk," or "the right to failure"[78] which is viewed to be a part and parcel of the right to err and learn as well as being a part of self-determination. Nonetheless, there remains a legitimacy in protecting people with ID from exploitation, violence, and abuse.

Many countries are in transition between traditional ideologies and practices and are faced with these issues. Each country needs to find its unique balance between choice and paternalism. The Irish government, for example, decided that there was no room in Ireland's future for large (or even mini) institutions, as the choice to reside in such an institution, which could be expressed by the individuals themselves, is argued to be inauthentic, or false. According to this view, if institutions remain in existence, the development of community services will fail or suffer.

DEINSTITUTIONALIZATION AND THE DEVELOPMENT OF HOUSING IN THE COMMUNITY

The fourth question addressed deinstitutionalization and the development of small-scale housing in the community. The committee thought that independent living and being included in the community was a core policy for the development of

---

[76] Lundsgaard, "Consumer direction and choice in long-term care for older persons," p. 4.

[77] For example, see Global Universal Design Commission at www.globaluniversaldesign.org/.

[78] Robert Perske, "The dignity of risk and the mentally retarded," *Mental Retardation* 10 (1972), 24–27.

services for people with ID in Western countries.[79] This policy is driven not only by principles of human rights but also by scientific research about the effectiveness and adequacy of small community-based residential facilities versus large congregate settings. There is no evidence at all to suggest that either a substantial or increasing proportion of people with ID would wish to live in "medium and high-density housing, villages and intentional communities."

As presented in Chapter 5, the committee presented the progress in Western Europe in implementing deinstitutionalization and development of appropriate community services. Institutions for people with ID have greatly and continuously diminished in England, the United States, Canada, and Norway, and have been completely abolished in Sweden.[80] The decrease in size of those large residential facilities occurred with an increase of places in small community residential settings. In the United States, for example, between 2006 and 2009 there was an increase of 9.4 percent in community-based residences. Between 1960 and 2009, 151 institutions (that is, residences for at least sixteen individuals) for persons with ID were closed in the United States.[81]

In Australia, the Republic of Ireland and Northern Ireland, there seems to be a decline in number and size of institutions. In other countries such as Belgium, the Netherlands, Germany, Spain and Greece, the downsizing and closure of institutions has just begun.[82] Israel is part of this third wave of deinstitutionalization.

The experts committee introduced updated research on deinstitutionalization demonstrating that community residences are often preferable to institutional care, albeit contemporary studies emphasize that there is more to the process than merely shutting down facilities. A review of thirty-seven studies on deinstitutionalization of people with developmental disabilities, which was conducted between 1999 and 2007, revealed that deinstitutionalization was positively linked to adaptive behaviors[83] and quality of life conditions and experiences. Additionally, a review of the literature by Lemay indicated that deinstitutionalization has to be evaluated also for cost benefit and cost effectiveness.[84]

In a 2007 systematic review of sixty-eight studies on effectiveness and adequacy of community services in the period 1997–2007, Kozma, Mansell, Beadle-Brown, and Emerson found that community-based services fared better than institutional care in

---

[79] Eric Emerson, "Deinstitutionalization in England," *Journal of Intellectual and Developmental Disability* 29 (2004), 79–84.
[80] Beadle-Brown, Mansell, and Kozma, "Deinstitutionalization in intellectual disabilities," 437–42.
[81] Braddock et al, *The state of the states in developmental disabilities*.
[82] Beadle-Brown, Mansell, and Kozma, "Deinstitutionalization in intellectual disabilities," 437–42.
[83] For a meta-analysis of the literature on deinstitutionalization and adaptive behaviors, see Jeffery P. Hamelin et al., "Meta-analysis of deinstitutionalization adaptive behavior outcomes: Research and clinical implications," *Journal of Intellectual and Developmental Disability* 36 (2011), 61–72.
[84] Raymond A. Lemay, "Deinstitutionalization of people with developmental disabilities: A review of the literature," *Canadian Journal of Community Mental Health* 28 (2009), 181–94; see also Mansell et al., *Deinstitutionalization and community living*.

the vast majority of tested outcomes.[85] The authors conclude that: "[r]esults have confirmed the picture that had emerged from previous research: People in small scale community-based residences or in semi-independent or supported living arrangements have a better objective quality of life than do people in large, congregate settings."[86] More specifically, community-based care was found in this meta-analysis to be superior to institutional residences in terms of the following seven outcomes: community presence and participation, social networks and friendships, family contact, self-determination and choice, quality of life, adaptive behaviors, and user and family views and satisfaction.

However, Kozma et al.[87] found much less evidence that small-scale community settings were better compared to institutional care in dealing with challenging behaviors, psychotropic medication, and health, risk factors and mortality. It is noteworthy that the lack of knowledge and training of general practitioners and other health services providers in the community concerning the treatment and needs of persons with ID and the emerging need to train and educate them since deinstitutionalization policies are spreading is documented in the literature.[88]

The review of the research supports the paradigm shift which is epitomized in the UNCRPD, as it clearly shows that community residences are preferable to institutional care. Notably, the former was found to promote choice and self-determination, values that align with the core principles of the UNCRPD. Self-determination and authentic choice, as the studies indicate, can be exercised in small living arrangements. Research on group dynamics show that self-determination and choice can be achieved in groups of six members or less. In addition, self-determination, autonomy, and opportunities for choice-making differed according to type of settings.[89]

The committee was asked questions regarding persons with challenging behavior and complex medical needs and whether they are able, with appropriate supports, to live anywhere they choose. The committee recognized the challenges of community living for persons with ID and challenging behaviors and thought that community living settings contributed to a person's adaptive behavior. Institutional care or

---

[85] Agnes Kozma, Jim Mansell, and Julie Beadle-Brown, "Outcomes in different residential settings for people with intellectual disability: A systematic review," *American Journal on Intellectual and Developmental Disabilities* 114 (2009), 193–222. Retrieved August 22, 2016 from www.community-living.info/documents/Kozma%202009%20AJMR%20Residential%20outcomes.pdf.

[86] Ibid., p. 210.

[87] Kozma, Mansell, and Beadle-Brown, "Outcomes in different residential settings," 193–222.

[88] Alex Phillips, James Morrison, and Ronald W. Davis, "General practitioners' educational needs in intellectual disability health," *Journal of Intellectual Disability Research* 48 (2004), 142–49.

[89] Jan Tossebro, "Impact of size revisited: Relation of number of residents to self-determination and deprivatization," *American Journal on Mental Retardation* 100 (1995), 59–67; Michael L. Wehmeyer, and Nancy Bolding, "Enhanced self-determination of adults with intellectual disability as an outcome of moving to community-based work or living environments," *Journal of Intellectual Disability Research* 45 (2001), 371–83; idem, "Self-determination across living and working environments: A matched samples study of adults with mental retardation," *Mental Retardation* 34 (1999), 353–63.

segregated settings that provide little stimulation and little opportunity for control and choice have been found to be a negative situation. There is no doubt that care has to be adjusted in terms of the ratio of caregiver to person and in terms of budgeting. The same applies to persons with ID and complex medical needs; they are in need of highly flexible individualized support teams with a key worker approach.

Kendrick, Jones, Bezanson, and Petty[90] reported on the transition of persons with disability and complex health needs from nursing homes to the community and argue that it is necessary to provide education for families and professionals who often hold erroneous beliefs that people with complex health needs cannot live safely in the community. Providing this education produces safe living arrangements and increased consumer satisfaction. The committee thought that effectiveness in achieving high quality outcomes and good quality of life was a critical factor when considering expenditures for services. Higher-cost services that deliver better outcomes ought to be supported strongly on cost-effectiveness grounds.[91] Two large-scale studies undertaken by Emerson,[92] which compared the nature of support provided to, and outcomes achieved by, residents of campuses, villages, and dispersed housing schemes, found stark differences between the different models of accommodation. Dispersed housing schemes in the Emerson study[93] included:

> all forms of long-term residential supports that provided 24 hour support in dispersed housing for no more than eight people. Supported living schemes (a subcategory of dispersed housing schemes) were defined as examples of residential supports in which no more than three people with intellectual disability were living in the same house as co-residents and the provider organisation defined the arrangements as examples of supported living.

Across a range of measures of resource inputs (e.g., staffing ratios, buildings), non-resource inputs (e.g., social environment) and process and service recipient outcomes (e.g., choice, activity, social networks, social integration, medical usage), residential campuses offered significantly poorer quality of life than dispersed housing schemes.[94] In relation to costs, the Emerson studies found that:[95]

---

[90] Michael J. Kendrick et al., *Promoting self-direction and consumer control in home- and community-based service systems. Third of three papers on unlocking the code of effective systems change* (Houston: Independent Living Research Utilization. 2006). Retrieved July 27, 2015 from www.communitylivingbc.ca/what_we_do/innovation/pdf/Key_Components_Of_Systems_Change.pdf.

[91] Head and Conroy, "Outcomes of self-determination in Michigan," pp. 232–34.

[92] Eric Emerson, "Cluster housing for adults with disabilities," *Journal of Intellectual and Developmental Disabilities* 23 (2004), 187–97; Eric Emerson, "Costs and outcomes of community residential supports in England." In Stancliffe and Lakin, *Costs and outcomes*, pp. 151–74.

[93] Emerson, "Cluster housing for adults with disabilities," p. 188.

[94] Emerson, "Costs and outcomes," p. 168.

[95] Emerson, "Cluster housing for adults with disabilities," pp. 187–97; Emerson, "Costs and outcomes," pp. 151–74.

- Village communities were cheapest, followed by residential campuses with dispersed housing schemes costing 15 percent more than residential campuses.
- There were no statistically significant differences in costs between supported living schemes, small group homes supporting 1–3 people and large group homes supporting four to six people.
- The additional costs of dispersed housing schemes were explained by significantly higher performance in relation to quality indicators of choice, variety of recreational activities, total size of social network, number of "others' in social network, number of days and hours of scheduled activities, and reduced perceived risk of exploitation.
- The additional costs of dispersed housing schemes may be justified in light of the substantial benefits noted.

In relation to costs and outcomes within dispersed housing schemes, the Emerson[96] studies found that:

- Larger group homes were consistently associated with poorer outcomes than either smaller group homes or supported living schemes.
- Smaller group homes and supported living schemes were associated with different patterns of benefits – consistent with other results suggesting that, for similar costs, supported living schemes may offer distinct benefits in the areas of resident choice and definitions provided community participation.

UK research demonstrates that across a range of measures of resource inputs (e.g., staffing ratios, buildings), nonresource inputs (e.g., social environment), and process and service recipient outcomes (e.g., choice, activity, social networks, social integration, medical usage), residential campuses offered significantly poorer quality of life than dispersed housing schemes. Whilst dispersed housing schemes were found to be 15 percent more costly than cluster housing, the preeminent UK researchers have concluded that the additional costs of dispersed housing schemes may be justified in light of the substantial benefits.

ENVISIONING THE FUTURE

In the last question, the committee experts were asked to envision Israel ten years from 2011. Basing their response on Rimmerman and Avrami's earlier paper,[97] the experts thought that the enactment of the Equal Rights for People with Disabilities Law of 1998 marked a significant change in Israeli legislation and the beginning of the rights era. However, they still recognized a realistic gap between the spirit of the law and current policies and practices. The latter were based on social-welfare/medical

---

[96] Ibid.   [97] Rimmerman and Avrami, "Israel's equal rights for persons with disabilities law."

legislation rather than rights and a functional model of disability.[98] The main difficulty is the lack of economic and social infrastructure in municipalities that makes it difficult to move from institutional care to community-based services. The gap between legislation and services that are in place calls for a long-term (ten years) transitional program. This fairly long but realistic transitioning period is needed to address both the gaps in legislation and in policy so that they match international standards and particularly Articles 12 and 19 of the UNCRPD. Specifically, Israel must finalize the transformation in ideology and policy concerning community residential options for persons with ID. The experts committee envisions future Israeli practices may be guided by the personal choice and preferences of the individual. Thus, future practices and services must facilitate authentic choice as well as reflect a variety of options to choose from. They should be person-centered and must be faithful to Israel's long-standing commitment to the dignity, personhood, and autonomy of the citizen.

SUMMING UP THE EXPERTS COMMITTEE'S CONCLUSIONS AND RECOMMENDATIONS

The recommendations are based on the committee's responses to Labor and Social Affairs Minister Herzog's questions. In responding to the benchmarking of Israel's policy regarding community living, the recommendations are as follow:

1. Israel should build on its positive track record to date in the disability field to set itself the goal of becoming a leader in the world with respect to the right to live independently and be included in the community.
2. There is a need to change in background legislation (i.e., laws and regulations), so that community-based housing and services become the clearly preferred and mainstream policy option.
3. There is a need to enact new legal capacity legislation to ensure that persons with ID are given an equal right to express their own preferences and to have others respect their choices. It is recommended that these broader law reform issues should be dealt with in depth by a separate committee or similarly open process.
4. A comprehensive and systematic ten-year transitional program needs to be designed in order to develop community infrastructure and services.
5. Parallel to these developments, the closing down of large residences ("institutions") needs to take place; that is, persons who reside in such housing arrangements need to be gradually transferred to community-based residences. Here it

---

[98] See, for example, Arie Rimmerman and Tal Araten-Bergman, "Disability legislation and its implementation: Trends and future directions," *Social Security* 68 (2005), 51–69 (Hebrew); Arie Rimmerman et al., "Israel's equal rights for persons with disabilities law: Current status and future directions," *Disability Studies Quarterly* 25 (2005). Retrieved February 7, 2016 from www.dsq-sds.org.

is most important to consider the elderly population in such facilities that have been living in such housing most of their lives and consequently view them as their homes.

6. It is essential to map all community-based services in Israel in order to design future quality services that would be provided to all Israeli citizens with ID, no matter where they choose to live.

In responding to the question about regulating zoning residences in the community to prevent saturation, the committee recommended the following:

1. That the State of Israel plan and promote integrated community residential services on the principles of equality and social equity. Such planning should seek to erode attitudinal barriers by ensuring that the community at large is primed to see the person behind the label.
2. Planning should be based on a systematic mapping of the existing services in Israel.
3. Planning of future residential services should be comprehensive, flexible, and should consider all types of housing for persons with ID.
4. Apartments, and other housing arrangements, should be close to the family and community of the person, and the buildings should allow aging in place.

As was stressed above, a core problem until now has been lack of planning. Since service providers are NGOs or private businesses, the members of the committee recommend that:

5. The Israeli government should consider granting certifications or authorization on the basis of statewide needs. As many of the individuals with ID in the large institutions do not live close to their families, and as the national distribution of service planning should be based on principles of equity and equality, macroplanning is needed rather than leaving matters to be decided by local municipalities and communities as is the current situation.
6. The government should provide incentives to service providers to open services in places where they are needed.

In regions that are saturated with such services, the government should not budget for service providers who wish to open new services. Mapping out the services and planning future services accordingly is of special importance in times of emergencies where large populations could be in need of relocation or evacuation. The members of the committee believe that if carefully planned on the basis of mapping, Israel can reach a unified, standardized, and just infrastructure of services in the community.

The committee responded to the question about needed community services with a clear recommendation, stating that service budgets should be individualized, that is, delivered services should be grounded in personal choice and the will and needs of the individual and family. Services for adults with ID should become person-centered and services for children, family-centered. This, of course, implies a new approach to the legal capacity of persons with ID.

The most serious and urgent question raised was about the status of institutionalization in Israel and whether Israel needed to initiate a policy change. The committee recommendations are aligned with Article 19 of the UNCRPD:

1. All large institutions should be phased down and eventually closed. It is of note that the members of the committee expressed two different, however similar, interpretations as to the number of residents that define such institutions. One view argues that large residences include *more than six individuals*, while the other stresses that large residences consist of *more than four individuals*. Nonetheless, all members of the committee have agreed that:

2. Community-based residential services should be quality services and should promote community inclusion and facilitate choice and self-determination. Residential settings should be located nearby public transportation, shops, and community public services.

3. Community-based services need to be small in order to also minimize attitudinal barriers in the community.

Finally, the committee outlined the next ten years encouraging government to use the UNCRPD as a road map and to follow in the footsteps of other Western countries, shifting the current policy toward community-based services with emphasis on inclusion and integration. It was the committee's belief, grounded in research and comparative values, evidence, and experience, that all persons with ID may live in the community with appropriate supports, including people who are defined as having challenging behaviors or medical needs. In extreme cases, shared cooperation and responsibilities can be sought with experienced medical, psychiatric, and forensic organizations. This can be done both in programmatically and economically effective ways as other countries have done.

The report called for carefully planning and preparation for the following:

a. Large facilities (as defined above) may be informed partners in the process and asked to deliver a plan for implementing the transition into the community; staff and managers should be trained and educated, and parents and consumers should be involved and prepared by information in the planning process. Persons with ID have to be active participants and prepared to move to the community.

b. Adult education programs of person-centered planning for adults with ID[99] with basic information on rights and training in decision-making in daily life

---

[99] Mindert J. Haveman, "Person-centered planning for later life: An evaluative study of a curriculum for adults with intellectual disability." Paper presented at the Beit Issie Shapiro Second International Conference on Developmental Disabilities in the Community: Policy, Practice and Research, 1998.

can be very helpful. Life skills needed for living independently in the community should be not only taught in educational settings but "in vivo," in realistic environments with support.

c. Programs to reduce negative behaviors that could cause problems in the general community should also be part of the transitional phase.

d. General and specific goals in the planning process should be operationalized in measurable objectives and with time limits that can be monitored and evaluated. As many partners, interests, and procedures are involved, it is suggested to form an independent Monitoring and Evaluation Team (MET) during this transitory stage of building a system of community-based living.

e. Standard assessment procedures and instruments to measure residential wishes of persons with ID as well as their support needs should be translated and adapted to Israel's cultural and social situation.

f. Incentives should be provided to service providers of segregated residential care to become community-based service providers, leaders, and social innovators instead. The more individuals that are successfully transferred into community housing, the larger the benefit a service provider should receive.

g. Budgets for large housing facilities should not be raised.

h. Additional community services need to be developed in order to facilitate the transition and changes to current services, which should be made with an emphasis on quality. Community services need to address leisure, employment, housing, and medical services. Education and preparedness of community medical service personnel should take place.[100]

All community services may be varied to support personal choice and individual preferences, as follows:

i. Support and assistance should be provided to individuals to exercise their choices. These should be designed and adjusted in partnership with consumers.

In-home supports are especially needed in Israel as few services and programs in the community support families that care for a child at home. Parents should determine their needs and services, which should be provided accordingly. For example, if parents are sleep deprived, night time services (a caregiver) may be a solution. An assessment scale measuring support needs of persons with ID and their family with regard to life cycle, use of supports, time demands, and subjective burden, which has been used in the Netherlands and the United States,[101] could be adapted for and applied to families in Israel.

---

[100] See, for example, training resources for GPs in the United Kingdom: www.rcgp.org.uk/clinical_and_re search/circ/innovation__evaluation/learning_disabilities_resource.aspx; Jenny Webb and Melanie Stanton, "Working with primary care practices to improve service delivery for people with learning disabilities—a pilot study," *British Journal of Learning Disabilities* 37 (2009), 221–27.

[101] See Meindert Haveman et al., "Differences in service needs among parents of persons with mental retardation across the lifecycle," *Family Relations* 46 (1997), 417–25.

j. Quality of services should be assured, monitored, and supervised.

The report ends with a recommended checklist of steps to be followed:

- Within ten years, all large residential facilities (segregated housing with more than four or six) should be closed permanently in Israel.
- During this decade, all residents will be transitioned to a small community-based living arrangement of their choice and with appropriate supports.
- Such residences, if not individual, will house no more than four or six, and primarily on a mixed basis of disabled and nondisabled residents (not including their caregivers).
- A planning committee with subcommittees, comprised of all relevant stakeholders (for instance, people with disabilities and their families and advocates, providers, experts, members of government agencies) should meet annually to assist in the transition and its planning.
- A Monitoring and Evaluation Team (MET) could assist the planning process and help abovementioned meetings with comprehensive and valid information.

IMPLEMENTATION OF COMMITTEE OF EXPERTS REPORT

While the report was discussed within MOLSA, it was not implemented or released to the public. The report was finally released by Meir Cohen, the new minister of MOLSA in September 2013. It appears that the main reason for not releasing the report was concern on the part of the administration that the report would demand major changes in policy, in particular closure of institutions and establishing new priorities in respect to community-based programs. The report was finally presented and discussed publicly on February 5, 2014.

However, the major change occurred after MOLSA's director general and the director of ID administration visited the European Union and Ireland to learn how deinstitutionalization policy had been implemented there. In fact, the visit to Ireland, which has initiated a new deinstitutionalization and community living policy, advanced the Israeli government's decision to adopt the Committee of Experts' Report and initiate a challenging program of transitioning 900 people from institutional to community-based care.

CONCLUSION

The Israeli situation regarding community living policy for people with ID is of particular interest. First, the Committee of Experts Report is one of the earliest reports of the twenty-first century that uses UNCRPD as a road map, particularly Articles 12 and 19, in transitioning from institutionalization to community living policy. International experts have noted that Israeli policy has been caught between institutional and community care, and had been using substantial resources to support congregate and institutional care. Articles 12 and 19, together with Articles 8 and 16, paved the desired policy direction toward the human rights model of services, focusing on personalization, choices, and supported decisions. Second, the Israeli case demonstrates the use of an interesting instrument – a panel of international experts to review current policy and practice and offer proposals for a desired transitional change from congregate and institutional care to community living policy. The merit of using a balanced and impartial panel of experts is evident in particular in a highly debatable area of community care. The experts provided a comprehensive report as well as detailed recommendations for policy changes to the Ministry of Labor and Social Affairs.

The panel recommended that Israel should ultimately and gradually close all the institutions for persons with ID and focus on creating community-based services and housing for this population. While the experts agreed on the fundamental issues, what was very evident in the deliberations of the International Panel of Experts on Community-Based Residences for Persons with ID was that what MOLSA referred to as "community-based living" differed greatly from what the experts, disability rights advocates, and the scientific literature defined as such. It is plausible that this somewhat unpleasant surprise for the ministry – which truly believed that it was actively implementing programs which aligned with community-based services – is partly why the committee's report was not made public until 2013. It is important to mention that this committee and its report supported fundamental changes in Israeli services both in terms of structure and conception. This could partially explain the reluctance to share the report as well as to implement it gradually over a period of ten years.

8

Closing Remarks

The twentieth century has seen a significant decrease in the number of people with psychiatric and intellectual disabilities in hospitals and institutions in the United States and Western Europe.[1] Another remarkable achievement is the prevention of the opening of new institutional care facilities and the expansion of community-based programs. However, there are exceptions; institutional care is still common in former eastern and central Communist countries. In the United States, there are a substantial number of people who have been placed in nursing homes instead of community care.[2] There is growing evidence and concern that significant numbers of people released from state hospitals in the first wave of deinstitutionalization became homeless. Some blame deinstitutionalization and lack of community care as being responsible for the dramatic increase in the number of people with psychiatric disabilities in jails and prisons.[3]

There is no doubt that deinstitutionalization and community living cannot be examined only in terms of the number of institutions or hospitals that have been

---

[1] See updated statistics: United States-ID/DD-The Coleman Institute for Cognitive Disabilities, University of Colorado – The state of the states in developmental disabilities' state profiles (through fiscal year 2013); United States-Psychiatric Disabilities; Joe Parks and Alan Q. Radke, *The vital role of state psychiatric hospitals* (Alexandria, VA: National Association of State Mental Health Directors, 2014), pp. 14–16; England ID/DD, http://ec.europa.eu/eurostat/statistics-explained/index.php/File: Hospital_beds_%E2%80%94_psychiatric_care_beds,_2008_and_2013_(per_100_000_inhabitants) _Health2015B.png; Psychiatric hospital beds in Europe 2008–2013 (http://ec.europa.eu/eurostat/statis tics-explained/index.php/File:Hospital_beds_%E2%80%94_psychiatric_care_beds,_2008_and_2013_ (per_100_000_inhabitants)_Health2015B.png).

[2] Dominic A. Sisti, Andrea G. Segal, and Ezekiel J. Emanuel, "Improving long-term psychiatric care: Bring back the asylum," *Journal of the American Medical Association* 313 (2015), 243–44.

[3] The United States has the highest rate of adult incarceration among developed countries, with 2.2 million people currently in jails and prisons. Those with mental disorders have been increasingly incarcerated during the past three decades, probably as a result of the deinstitutionalization of the state mental health system. Correctional institutions have become the de facto state hospitals, and there are more seriously and persistently mentally ill in prisons than in all state hospitals in the United States. See also S. Fazel and J. Danesh, "Serious mental disorder in 23,000 prisoners: A systematic review of 62 surveys," *Lancet* 359 (2002), 545–50; Daniel E. Anasseril, "Care of the mentally ill in prisons: Challenges and solutions," *Journal of American Academy of Psychiatry Law* 35 (2007), 406–10.

closed or the number of people who live in supported housing. The challenge is to effect a substantial change in values, legislation, and policies supporting personal choices and social participation.

SHIFT IN VALUES

It is almost impossible to understand the progress made in the human rights of people with disabilities without studying traditional and progressive theological aspects of disability.[4] Current Judeo-Christian approaches search for new interpretations of disability to bridge the dissonance between the original meanings of the texts and prevailing ideas of equality and inclusion of people with disabilities.[5] There is an ongoing debate as to whether people with severe disabilities have legal capacity or have to be released from responsibility to make decisions about themselves. Amita Dhanda believes that the capacity assessments instruments used in the past are typically overlaid with discriminatory attitudes and practices.[6] The UNCRPD is therefore a great opportunity to examine current practices in order to change them. Unfortunately, most of the guardianship laws and amendments assume that there are people with severe disabilities who are limited, fully or partially, in their ability to make decisions and personal choices, and to fulfill their personal desires. In fact, there is a tendency to adopt traditional medical approaches that have been influenced by eugenics. Most professionals still believe that severe or challenging behavior is a serious reason to deny the right of the person to live in the community.[7]

It appears that the threat of eugenics exists also today among utilitarian philosophers. Peter Singer, one of the new eugenics scholars, challenges the idea of "personhood" by claiming that not all humans are "persons" and therefore, some people with life-long cognitive disabilities never become "persons" at any time throughout their lives.[8] The path to infanticide and euthanasia and denial of human rights, or the right to live in the community is very close. Another example is the link between eugenics ideas, such as sterilization, in the Scandinavian welfare states.[9] Maciej Zaremba,

---

[4] Masala and Petretto, "From disablement to enablement," 1242–44.   [5] Eiesland, *The disabled god.*

[6] See, for example, Amita Dhanda, "Legal capacity in the Disability Rights Convention: Stranglehold of the past or lodestar for the future?" *Syracuse Journal of International Law & Commerce* 34 (2007), 429–62; Mary Keys, "Legal capacity reform in Europe: An urgent challenge." In *European Yearbook of Disability Law*, Vol. 1. Edited by Gerard Quinn and Lisa Waddington (Leiden: Martinus Nijhoff, 2009).

[7] See, for example, Sheryl A. Larson, Charlie K. Lakin, and Shannon L. Hill, "Behavioral outcomes of moving from institutional to community living for people with intellectual and developmental disabilities: U.S. studies from 1977 to 2010," *Research and practice for persons with severe disabilities* 37 (2013), 1–12.

[8] See Singer, *Practical ethics*, pp. 175–217.

[9] The history of sterilization in Scandinavia was placed on the agenda through Gunnar Broberg and Mattias Tydén's book, *Oönskade i folkhemmet. Rashygien och sterilizering i Sverige* [Unwanted in the welfare state. Eugenics and sterilization in Sweden] (Stockholm: Gidlunds Bokförlag, 1991) and Gunnar Broberg and Nils Roll-Hansen (eds.), *Eugenics and the welfare state: Sterilization policy in Denmark, Sweden, Norway, and Finland* (East Lansing, MI: Michigan State University Press, 1996).

a well-known Scandinavian journalist, thought that sterilization was related to the combination of strong social conformity, eugenics beliefs, and a concern for the inappropriate allocation of public funds.[10] Therefore, sterilization has been perceived as the acceptable response of a progressive government committed to society at large. These prevailing views in some countries raise doubts about the rights of people with intellectual and cognitive disabilities to express their personhood, and particularly their right to be parents. Article 23 (1) of the UNCRPD calls on states to take "effective and appropriate measures to eliminate discrimination against persons with disabilities in all matters relating to marriage, family, parenthood and relationships, on an equal basis with others."[11]

It is important to note that the primary motive of deinstitutionalization was to close institutions and hospitals because they violated human rights. Normalization was the leading principle in planning less restrictive environments in institutional care and then in the community.[12] It is clear that normalization was not based on personhood, self-determination, or personal choice but as a general rule to minimize restrictive alternatives or environments as soon as possible. Social role valorization, one of the interpretations of normalization, was not defined in personhood terms but as a theory of enablement, establishment, enhancement, maintenance, and/or defense of valued social roles for people.[13] The latter was primarily geared against inaccessible or deprived environments.

If the medical model focused on deficit, normalization, and the social model of unnecessary restrictions and societal barriers, the UNCRPD was the first call for personhood. At the heart of the UNCRPD is Article 12, the recognition that people with disability should enjoy legal capacity on an equal basis with others. This further includes the right to be recognized as a person before the law and the right to have one's decisions and choices legally validated and recognized.[14]

The right to live in the community (Article 19) is closely linked to fundamental rights such as personal liberty, private and family life, and freedom from ill-treatment or punishment, but is captured as a distinct right in the UNCRPD. The overarching objective of Article 19 of the UNCRPD is full inclusion and participation in society including three important key elements: choice, individualized supports, and making services for the general public accessible to people with

[10]   Maciej Zaremba, "Rasren i välferdsstaten [No mixing of races in the welfare state]," *Dagens Nyheter*, August 20, 1997.

[11]   UNCRPD Article 23(1), 2006 can be retrieved from www.ohchr.org/EN/HRBodies/CRPD/Pages/ConventionRightsPersonsWithDisabilities.aspx#23.

[12]   Bennet Nirje, "The normalization principle." In *Changing patterns in residential services for the mentally retarded.* Edited by Robert B. Kugel and Wolf Wolfensberger (Washington, DC: Department of Health, Education and Welfare, 1969).

[13]   Wolf Wolfensberger, "An 'if this, then that' formulation of decisions related to social role valorization as a better way of interpreting it to people," *Mental Retardation* 33 (1995), 163–69.

[14]   Kristin Booth Glen, "Changing paradigms: Mental capacity, legal capacity, guardianship, and beyond," *Columbia Human Rights and Law Review* 44 (2012), 115.

disabilities. This is the most difficult challenge of the twenty-first century, to promote personhood and facilitate changes in domestic legislation and policy.

CHANGES IN LEGISLATION AND POLICY

The second half of the twentieth century was the deinstitutionalization era in Europe and the United States; however, as demonstrated in Chapter 6, they used different perspectives and paths of implementation. The baseline of the US approach is civil rights legislation passed by Congress, particularly the seminal Civil Rights Act 1964, and particularly section 504 of the Rehab Act which prohibits exclusion and discrimination from participation in programs. However, the most important imprint is the ADA (Title II) and the *Olmstead* landmark Supreme Court decision that declared institutionalization to be discrimination. Critics claim that the decision is limited in its assessment of the statutory issue of the meaning of ADA Title II and declined to address Fourteenth Amendment claims.[15] The court recognized that for some people, community living was not an appropriate alternative.[16] In addition, the court just required states to provide working plans for placing qualified persons in the least restrictive environment at a reasonable pace. It is noteworthy that up to 2010, only half of the states had developed "Olmstead Plans," It appears that most of the states are still caught in the old guardianship system, which consigns such individuals to unwarranted and segregated institutional living that violates international human rights law.[17] There is no doubt that that it demonstrates the limitation of the anti-discrimination approach in ensuring community living implementation.[18]

It is impossible to discuss the merits of the ADA without recognizing litigation, the central spirit of US civil rights. For example, that the *Olmstead* litigation process was pivotal in quickening the pace of change flows from the fact that a judicial ruling can have an impact extending well beyond its strictly legal holding.

However, it is clear that while the *Olmstead* anti-discrimination decision allows states the freedom to determine the pace and cost of deinstitutionalization, the UNCRPD refers to the absolute right of persons with disabilities to choose where and with whom they prefer to live in the community. In this regard, the convention's

---

[15] *Olmstead v. LC ex rel. Zimring*, p. 588. [16] Ibid., pp. 604–05.

[17] See Terence Ng, Alice Wong, and Charlene Harrington, "Home and community-based services: Introduction to Olmstead lawsuits and Olmstead plans," UCSF National Center for Personal Assistance Services, May 2003. Retrieved January 23, 2016 from www.pascenter.org/olmstead/olmstead plans.php.

[18] See Flynn, "Olmstead plans revisited." See, for example, two cases: in *Bryson v. Shumway*, the First Circuit Court of Appeals held that qualified individuals with disabilities are not "entitled to reasonable promptness" for community-based services unless they are on a wait list (308 F.3d 79, 1st Cir. 2002); the Ninth Circuit Court of Appeals' decision in *Arc of Washington State, Inc. v. Braddock* allowed states to limit the size of their Medicaid waiver programs, permitting states to engage in practices that inhibit significant progress in integrating qualified individuals with disabilities into their communities (427 F.3d 615, 9th Cir. 2005).

human rights ideology champions the needs and desires of the individual over financial or political concern.

The European deinstitutionalization and community living approach is the product of the twentieth-century social welfare model, reflecting policies that cover the range of socialist, liberal, and conservative ideologies. Most of the deinstitutionalization reforms are based on ideological constructs and accordingly on the transformation of resources from institutional to community care. Most northern and western European countries were influenced by the normalization principle, placing people in the least restrictive environment, rather than from a human rights perspective.

In terms of progressive legislation, the Italian "Basaglia" legislation was not anti-institutional; it aimed to make the asylum a place fit for human habitation. Prior to Basaglia's interventions, asylums in Italy had imposed a system of punishment and control, in which the watchword was "custody" rather than "cure."[19] Its core mission aimed at prevention, care, and rehabilitation of psychiatric disorders through the integration of activities in different psychiatric services – mental health centers, day centers, residences in the community, day hospitals, general hospital psychiatric wards – and in other services such as substance abuse services and child psychiatry services. Although Italy has been successful in establishing a solid network of facilities to meet diverse care needs, there are efforts to improve quality of care and to develop a more effectively integrated system.[20] Efforts are being made to close the gaps between regions and to establish an evidence-based system that can track problems and challenges.

Deinstitutionalization policies in Nordic countries and the United Kingdom are similar but slightly different, according to domestic social welfare legislation. The emergence of anti-discrimination legislation in the United Kingdom is associated with the ADA of 1990 in the United States. The enactment of the Disability Discrimination Act of 1995[21] and the Equality Act of 2010 have been perceived as a parallel path to social welfare legislation.[22] The EU anti-discrimination resolution passed in the European Parliament on December 3, 1993, signaled the beginning of change in terms of disability policy.[23]

The challenge in the United States at the beginning of the twenty-first century was how to implement the *Olmstead* decision and ensure sufficient Medicaid funding at the state and local level. The European challenge is quite different; the European Union struggles with how to allocate the Structural Funds to narrow the disparities between Western and Eastern Europe, in particular with respect to institutionalization and the lack of community living programs. The European Court of Human Rights of

---

[19] John Foot, *The man who closed the asylums: Franco Basaglia and the revolution in mental health care* (London: Verso, 2015).

[20] De Girolamo et al., "The current state of mental health care in Italy," pp. 83–91.

[21] Disability Discrimination Act 1995, www.Legislation.gov.uk/ukpga/1995/50/contents.

[22] Equality Act 2010, www.Legislation.gov.uk/ukpga/ 2010/15/contents.

[23] "Report of the First European Disabled People's Parliament," Brussels, December 3, 1993.

the Council of Europe plays a pivotal role in protecting the human rights of people with disabilities in Eastern and Central Europe. Its important decision in *Mihailovs v. Latvia* in 2013 regarding violation of human rights in institutions set the norm for years to come.

The major effort of deinstitutionalization in the twentieth century was the transition of people with intellectual and psychiatric disabilities from institutions to community-based programs in Europe and the United States. Persons with disabilities were placed in the community according to their level of functioning and their support needs. The shift toward human rights and personhood is reflected in a growing recognition that services have to be personalized in terms of planning and budgeting.[24] This means that funding of services follows the person and not the service provider, and that users are free to choose their preferred degree of personal control over service delivery according to their needs, capabilities, current life circumstances, preferences, and aspirations. In recent years, the United States has offered HCBS opportunities for Medicaid beneficiaries to receive services in their own homes or community. Their range of options includes the right to custom design their own services, which requires that the user decides who is to work, with which tasks, at which times, where, and how.[25] In recent years, there has been growing recognition in England and Wales of the need to provide direct payments and the extension of the principle of "individualized budgets" for disabled people (merging funds from different sources including local authority social services, housing adaptations and equipment, and individual living funds).[26] A recent experiment in two municipalities in Finland during 2010–2013 demonstrates the merit of person-centered planning and personal budgeting in disability services. The research indicates that the lives of people with disabilities are

---

[24] See, for example, Simon Duffy, "Person-centered planning and system change," *Learning Disability Practice* 7 (2004), 15–19. Focusing on the tension between the kind of planning that professionals must do as part of their job and the planning that an individual might do for his or her own life, Simon Duffy and Helen Sanderson, "Person-centered planning and care management," *Learning Disability Practice* 7 (2004), 12–16. Discussing a model for case managers' role in person-centered planning and care, Jim Mansell and Julie Beadle-Brown, "Person-centred planning or person-centred action? Policy and practices in intellectual disability services," *Journal of Applied Research in Intellectual Disabilities* 17 (2004), 1–9. The article provides a critical review of the nature and importance of person-centered planning in the context of current British policy and service development in intellectual disability.

[25] HCBS provide opportunities for Medicaid beneficiaries to receive services in their own home or community. These programs serve a variety of targeted populations groups, such as people with mental illnesses, intellectual or developmental disabilities, and/or physical disabilities. The site introduces the final HCBS regulations which set forth new requirements for several Medicaid authorities under which states may provide home and community-based long-term services and supports. The regulations enhance the quality of HCBS and provide additional protections to individuals that receive services under these Medicaid authorities. Retrieved July 12, 2005 from www.medicaid.gov/Medicaid-CHIP-Program-Information/By-Topics/Long-Term-Services-and-Supports/Home-and-Community-Based-Services/Home-and-Community-Based-Services.html.

[26] See Department of Health, "Independence, well-being and choice: our vision for the future care for adults in England London," 2005. The consultation paper by the UK Health Department introduces the future direction of social care for all adults of all age groups in England.

controlled by institutional practices, regulations, and power relations. It has been a great opportunity for both professionals to release control and for people with disabilities to exercise their self-determination.[27] However, the concern is that professional power may remain influential, because self-determination is still dependent on their professional power and legal authority.

THE CHALLENGE OF IMPLEMENTING THE UNCRPD

The United States has not ratified the UNCRPD; the Obama administration has made it clear that US ratification of the UNCRPD is not necessary to protect and advance the rights of Americans with disabilities. President Barack Obama's letter of May 17, 2012, transmitting the UNCRPD to the Senate, stated that "Americans with disabilities already enjoy" the rights enumerated in the UNCRPD "at home" and that "the strong guarantees of nondiscrimination in existing US law are consistent with and sufficient to implement the requirements of the Convention."[28] Without getting into the political debate of ratification, the United States can benefit from two central articles that are critical to personhood.

In terms of legal capacity and people's autonomy, it is evident that guardianship laws are uneven among the states, so if America ratifies the UNCRPD, many states would need to amend their guardianship laws to bring them in line with Article 12. The same applies to living in community (Article 19). The UNCRPD offers a stronger commitment than the *Olmstead* Supreme Court decision regarding the right of people with disabilities to live independently and in the community. When determining whether conditions, pursuant to the ADA's limitations, cause a fundamental alteration in the provided services, US courts may take into account the economic impact on a state of moving individuals to community-based homes.

Although the European Union has ratified the UNCRPD, there are concerns regarding its implementation of Article 19, primarily because of the substantial high institutionalization rates among certain countries and the fact that they lack community-based alternatives. Part of the skepticism is related to the failure of the Structural Funds strategy in changing community living policies in Central and Eastern Europe.

The real challenge is the implementation of personal assistance schemes (Article 19b) which require states to ensure that people with disabilities have access to community support services. Only a few countries in Europe have initiated personal support services including personal budgets.

---

[27] Susan Eriksson, *Personal budgeting in municipal disability services: The first experiment in Finland* (Helsinki: The Finnish Association of Intellectual and Developmental Disabilities, Center of Research and Developments, 2014).

[28] President Barack Obama's message regarding the UNCRPD, in Treaty Doc. 112–7, 112th Cong., 2nd Session, May 17, 2012, www.gpo.gov/fdsys/pkg/CDOC-112tdoc7/pdf/CDOC-112tdoc7.pdf, p. iii.

Index

Aaron, 7, 8
Abdullah ibn Umm Maktum, 13
Abiri, Lili, 144n10
Abu Ubaidah Ibnul Jarrah, 13
Achish (king of Gath), 7
Act 150 (Pennsylvania), 133
Action for Mental Health, 56
Ad Hoc Committee, 34
ADA. *See* Americans with Disabilities Act (ADA)
adult incarceration, 170n3
AKIM (National Association for the Habilitation of Children and Adults with Intellectual Disabilities), 142, 144
Aktion T-4, 99
alcoholics, 21
ALUT (The Israeli Society for Autistic Children), 144
Amanda D. v. Hassan, 132
American Eugenics Movement, 151
American Journal of Mental Deficiency, 64
Americans with Disabilities Act (ADA), 69, 76n114, 123; Title I (employment), 47n53; Title II (public services), 2, 4, 47-8n53, 70, 71, 72, 73, 82, 138, 139, 173; Title III (public accommodations), 48n53; Title IV (telecommunications), 48n55; Title V (miscellaneous), 48n53
Americans with Disabilities Act Amendments Act (ADAAA), 47n53, 124
Aminadav, Chaia, 143n10
animal experimentation, 29n103
Appelbaum, Paul S., 80
Arbel, Mordechay, 144n10
Arc of Washington State, Inc. v. Braddock, 83n136, 173n18
Archives of Race-Theory and Social Biology, 20
Aristotle, 9, 18
Asperger's syndrome, 158

Association for the Help of Retarded Citizens (AHRC), 68
asylums, 23n81, 56, 58, 85, 85n4, 101n7, 101n8; charitable, 96; custodial, 62; in England, 96n50; in Europe, 87, 96, 97; in Germany, 94; in Italy, 86, 92, 93, 174; private philanthropic, 52; rehabilitation of, 80n124; Salpetriere, 97n51
Asylums and after: A revised history of the mental health services: From the early 18th century to the 1990s (book), 85n6
"Ataa" ibn Abi Rabah, 13
Atlanta Legal Aid Society, 71
Attention deficit hyperactivity disorder (ADHD), 158
Augustine, 11, 11n26
autopathography, 16n55
Avrami, Shirley, 163
Azran, Vivian, 144n10

Bachrach, Leona L., 84n2
Bagenstos, Samuel R., 80, 124n18
Baldini, Bill, 66n65
Balestrieri, Matteo, 93
Barr, Owen, 156
Bartimaeus, 10
Basaglia Law (Italy) (1978), 91, 92n35, 95, 174
Basaglia, Franco, 91n34
Battle of Mount Gilboa, 8
Bazelon Center for Mental Health Law, 65, 65n58
Bazelon, David L., 65n58
Beadle-Brown, Julie, 160–61
Bell, John Hendren, 22
Ben Moshe, Eliyahoo, 145
benefits for special living conditions (HbL), 107
Ben-Simchon, Miri, 145
Beresford, Bryony, 155